WORKING IN THE REALMS OF SPIRIT

MIKE WILLIAMSON

**A TRUE STORY ABOUT POLTERGIEST'S
AND HAUNTED HOUSES IN THE
20TH CENTURY**

ISBN 978-0-993021800

WITH THANKS FOR THEIR SUPPORT AND
ENCOURAGEMENT.

DANNY, TONY, PATRICIA, MARGARET ANNE

INDEX

Chapter 1

Back in the summer of 1981 my wife Jan noticed that our daughter Clair was limping and asked her what was wrong. Clair said her foot hurt and upon examination Jan discovered a swelling on her left ankle, about the size of a half tennis ball. Jan immediately telephoned the doctor and made an appointment for the next day. They went to see the doctor who referred them to a specialist at the hospital. When Clair saw the specialist he said an appointment would have to be made to cut out the swelling.

Jan and I discussed this and we were concerned as the specialist did not appear to know what the cause of the swelling was. Clair at the time was nine and went to ballet and gymnastics classes. During the next week Jan met up with an acquaintance called Francis and they got talking, Clair's foot came up in the conversation. Francis suggested that we take her for healing. Not knowing anything about healing Jan said we weren't religious and so didn't think faith healing would work. Francis said it wasn't faith healing it was spiritual healing and you didn't need faith or belief.

Jan and I talked about it and as we were reluctant to allow the hospital to cut the lump out without knowing what was causing it, we decided to try healing. So the next day she contacted Francis and asked how to go about taking Clair for healing. Francis said, come down

1

to my house and I will give Clair some healing, so they went.

When I got home from work I asked Clair how her foot was and she said the pain had gone. When I asked Jan, she said she had taken Clair for healing and after about five minutes the pain went. As the swelling was still there she said they were going again tomorrow. Not knowing anything about healing I asked what had happened, and she said Francis just held Clair's foot in her hand for about ten minutes and that was all.

Jan then told me that when talking to Francis she was told that Francis was a spiritualist and often did healing for people. I asked how much this cost and Jan said nothing, it was free. Over the next couple of weeks the swelling started to go down and we cancelled the appointment at the hospital.

Francis went to a spiritualist meeting once a week a couple of houses along from us and invited Jan to come to the meeting with her.

Jan asked if I wanted to come with her, I said no as she had been invited and I hadn't. I thought it would be a good idea for her to go so she could find out more about all this spiritual stuff. I had heard about mediums but thought they were either on the end of a pier or had something special that ordinary people didn't have.

Chapter 2

Jan went to the meeting one evening and when she came back she told me what went on.

She said a lady named Kay was in charge and after they had said a prayer everyone had a go at healing. They then got a small table out and sat one person on either side and started asking questions of the spirits that Kay said were there. Jan didn't have a go but she said some of the others did and when they asked questions the table tilted once for yes and twice for no. I didn't like the sound of this and said you shouldn't mess with things you don't know anything about. Jan said Kay had been doing it for years and seemed to know what was going on.

Over the next week I thought about this and come the Thursday evening
Jan said she was going to have another look at what was going on at Kay's house, and would I like to come along. Meanwhile Clair's swelling had gone down and she was fine, so I thought there couldn't be any harm in the meetings at Kay's house. I decided that it was Jan's thing, I wasn't much interested in religion as they said prayers and such, so said why didn't she go and get to know a bit more about it.

This time when Jan came back she said she had a go at the table tilting; she wasn't sure whether the other person was moving the table or whether the spirits were. They did the healing again and said more prayers and then had a general chat about spirits also called guides. Being a curious person I decided I should go the next week to see what Jan was getting in to. You never know, there are all sorts of weird people out there.

So the following week I went along. When we arrived we went up a wooden staircase at the side of a big old house, to a sort of loft room about twenty feet by twelve. There were about ten easy chairs around the sides and a couple of small tables in the middle and two stools. The floor was carpeted and at one end there was a window, the room had one light in the centre. At the end of the room sat an old lady about 60 with long grey hair (it wasn't looking good) who I was introduced to, whose name was Kay. We were asked to take a seat as there were some other people to come. I sat and looked at the people around the room, Francis was there whom I knew by sight and another couple who were the parents of Clair's friend from school there was no one else. I was feeling a bit edgy but decided I was there and I would stay and see what transpired. After about ten minutes three other people turned up and sat down, we were then introduced to everyone and a prayer was said and then Kay asked if anyone would like healing. One woman named Penny said yes please, so they sat her on a stool and three people went and stood one behind and one each side. They then closed their eyes and put their hands on her, nobody said anything they just stood there for about ten minutes and then one by one put their hands down. Penny said thank you and they all went back to their seats. Then a lady called Jane (Clair's friends mum) sat on the stool and again three people got up one of whom

4

was Penny and did the same again. Jane said thank you and they all sat down.

I was asked if I would like healing but I said there was nothing wrong with me, Kay said there didn't have to be. It was a healing of the mind as well as the body, even if it just made you feel peaceful that was fine. So I thought well I'm here I might as well try it out and see for myself, because I did have an ache in my back, but I wasn't telling them that. So I sat on the stool and was told to close my eyes and relax, bit difficult when you don't know what's going to happen. I guess you could say I was wary of them all. Anyway they put their hands on my shoulders and arms and I sat there and to me nothing happened. I don't know what I was expecting but I figured I would feel something. I felt nothing, and when they had finished I said thank you and went and sat in my chair. Kay said how do you feel, I said I was ok. Then after some of the others had healing she went on to explain for my benefit about table tilting.

She said they would ask the spirits to come and talk to us. We would sit at the table two at a time and see if they would answer our questions. So two people Arthur and Jane sat either side of the table, after a little while Arthur asked if the spirits were there and would one of them come and talk to us. The table tilted once for yes, as you can imagine, I was watching very closely, Arthur then said are you a man? Nothing happened, and then he asked are you a woman? The table tilted once for yes. He then asked different questions about the woman which required yes no answers and the table tilted accordingly.

After about 15 minutes the table stopped moving and Kay said the spirit had gone. So Arthur and Jane went back to their seats, and Bob and Penny went next with the same sort of results. Then Kay asked if Jan would like to have a go with Brian, she said yes, so they had a go. The table tilted a couple of times then stopped. Kay said that Brian and Jan who were new to it didn't have the energy yet and would have to keep practicing. I didn't want to have a go but then I wasn't asked so that was ok.

Kay then said would anyone like to try trance, Penny said ok as she had done it before. By now I was getting more interested but still feeling a bit edgy, I don't know why. Penny sat on the stool and closed her eyes, nothing happened for a while, and then she started to lean backwards. No one said anything as she went further back, so far, that I thought she would fall over backwards. But she didn't and then she sat upright and slowly she opened her eyes. Kay said that was good and Penny went back to her seat. Kay then said a prayer and that was the end of the evening.

We chatted for a while about who we were and where we came from, just getting to know each other. It turned out that Penny and Arthur were married, aged about fifty five and Brian was their son, one of three children, they had another son and a daughter, Arthur was a builder. Bob and Jane were married Bob was about thirty and Jane about forty five, Francis was married to a guy who ran the antique shop at the bottom of the road and her mother was a medium.

6

When we got home we sat and talked about what we had seen, we decided we were not sure whether the table was being moved by the people or the spirits. We couldn't see the point in spirits putting someone in a trance and then making them lean backwards. We thought we should go a few more times to see how things progressed.

We went the following week and because we had met everyone things seemed friendlier. We started off the same as the week before with healing, this time Jan got up and put her hands on Penny. She was told she would be a good healer as Penny had felt a lot of heat from her. I watched as the healing went on, then they tried the table tilting again with much the same results. Then Arthur said he had someone with him and he wanted to trance so we could speak to the spirit. Kay said that was ok so he did. He sat on a stool and closed his eyes after about five minutes he started to breathe heavily then cleared his throat a few times and started to speak. It was Arthur's voice so I thought he was pretending as when I had seen someone trance in films they talked in different voices. The spirit that was supposed to be with Arthur was talking in Pidgin English and was talking about how he was a Red Indian guide to Arthur and was there to protect him. I thought straight away what, was he protecting him from. Anyway he rambled on for a bit then said bless you and went away. After a while and a bit more funny breathing Arthur opened his eyes and drank some water, and then he was helped to his chair where he sat seemingly exhausted. I asked Kay what the guide was protecting Arthur from; she said you know the answer to that ask your higher self. I thought higher self is there a lower self as well. I thought there was only one of me, but decided I would wait and see if my higher self, made itself known to me. After all it was early days and I reckoned I had a lot to learn, if my higher self could give me answers, I needed to get in touch quick.

Jan and I went to the meetings for about three months and things carried on the same. I wasn't getting much in the way of answers and I couldn't find my higher self that they talked about to get answers. No one seemed to be able to tell me how to get in touch. Jan had taken over from Francis giving Clair healing and her foot was almost better now.

Then one night I was doing some table tilting, still wasn't sure who tilted the table but it wasn't me, with Arthur when a spirit came through Arthur while we were table tilting. He said he had done some bad things while on earth and wanted god's forgiveness so he could go to heaven. I said as I had been taught god forgives you bless you. To which I was told by the spirit, what right did I have to forgive him and who did I think I was, I didn't know what to say as this had never happened before, the spirit swore at me then went away. When I asked Kay why this had happened, she said I shouldn't have said god forgives you as I had no right to speak for god. I said that's how you have taught us. She said nothing so I left it but was pretty embarrassed. Later that same evening Penny sat on the stool and went into trance and the spirit that came through leaned her backwards and then started to wave her legs in the air. Well she had a dress on and

8

her modesty was not preserved, it was embarrassing for Arthur although Penny didn't know what happened.

I then sat on the stool for the first time and spirit tried to make me lean back. I tried to stay upright and I can tell you I struggled and by the time it was over I was drenched in sweat from my efforts. The spirit managed to lean me about half way and I was conscious all the time. I didn't like that and began to feel things were not as they at first seemed, or perhaps they were but I had gotten used to what was happening.

Arthur and Penny and their son Brian didn't like what had happened to Penny. Bob and Jane were disgusted too, so we discussed it and decided we weren't going to go any more as things seemed to be getting out of hand. We decided we were going to run our own circle at our house and Arthur who had most experience would be in charge.

Chapter 3

Our house was two farm workers cottages converted into one, built in the 1830s. It had three large double bedrooms and three receptions plus two toilets a bathroom and kitchen. I was busy renovating it but we had a decent lounge where it was decided to hold the circle. On the first evening we sat on armchairs and sofas and said a prayer to open the circle. We then had a meditation where everyone closed their eyes and meditated. (Wasn't sure what I should be doing) then after about fifteen minutes we opened our eyes and Arthur asked what had happened during the meditation. The others said they had seen things and heard short messages, which when they said what they had got seemed to me to be just the brain ticking over. All I saw was blackness and heard nothing other than the others fidgeting. Jan got nothing either. Arthur then said they were going to bring their guides through so that we could have some teachings. So then Bob, Arthur, Brian and Penny shut their eyes and started breathing heavy. All of a sudden Brian sat on the floor and crossed his legs and after a minute or two started chanting like the red Indians do. The others still appeared to be in trance and I didn't know what to do or say so I just sat and listened. Then he stopped and said greetings from beyond, then Arthur who I suppose was in trance but I didn't know, said greetings my friend it's good to speak again, to the Indian. They had quite a conversation about the old days when they were alive between them, but never said anything to us. Jane, Jan and I just sat with our eyes open watching while Bob and Penny just sat there with their eyes closed.

After about twenty minutes they stopped talking and went away and Arthur and Brian after some more heavy breathing opened their eyes. Then Penny started speaking, and said she was the lady in grey, whom the others seemed to have been expecting as they all said hello. She then went away and Penny opened her eyes. Bob started to cough and try to clear his throat and then he opened his eyes and said his guide had nearly come through. Arthur said they had done well and then said they were going to teach Jan and I how to heal. We said we would give it a try and Penny sat on a chair, we then all gathered round. Arthur put his hands on her shoulders and asked me to put my hands on her arm, and Jan to do the same on the other arm. Bob, Jane and Brian then put their hands on her head knees and back and we just stood there. Arthur said we should feel tingling in our hands or they should get hot. Well I felt nothing except the warmth from Penny's arm, but Jan said her hands were getting warmer.

After the healing Arthur asked Jan if she would like to try going into trance, she said ok and they sat her on the chair and apart from myself gave her healing energy to help her. After they had finished Jan sat back on the sofa and we asked her what had happened. She said she went all numb and couldn't hear any of us for a while, Arthur said that was good as her guides were getting to know her, and gradually as she got used to it they would come closer and maybe speak. We then said a closing prayer and they had a cup of tea and we chatted about leaving Kay's and what had happened in the circle.

It seemed that Kay was very annoyed that we had left her group and started our own circle. But we all agreed things did not seem right the last time we went. Francis was still going to Kay and said she did not want to join us. That was ok we were still friends.

That night after everyone had gone we heard a noise in the next room. We went to see what had caused it but could find nothing, so put it down to the age of the house and went to bed. Over the next week we heard other noises and the occasional word. We started to get a bit concerned as we thought the spirits had moved in ready for the next circle. When I phoned Arthur to tell him he said that was ok they were just getting used to the surroundings.

The next time we sat in the circle I felt edgy again and said so. Arthur said I just needed to get used to spirit being around. We practiced healing again but this time without touching, I then felt a tingling in my hands and was quite pleased that something was happening. Arthur said it was because spirit had opened me up over the past week and things should start happening for me. Jan said she could feel a lot more tingling when she wasn't touching and we agreed to carry on like that for a while. After the circle and everyone had gone we sat down and discussed what had happened. Jan was pleased, and she said women were more sensitive so she would feel more than me. She said I was used to not showing my feelings so it would be more difficult for me to let go. I asked her how she knew this and she said Penny had been talking to her, and Jan had asked why I wasn't feeling much.

Penny had told her that it would take time and I may not progress much further, we would just have to wait and see. Although I was disappointed I could see the point, I thought I would have to try and find this higher self that Kay was talking about, so that I could get in touch with it, maybe get some answers and find out more.

During the next week we talked about spirit and what it was all about and Jan practiced going into trance. One night while she was practicing she said she felt taller and not as numb as the first time, we thought this was progress and were encouraged to try again the next night.

The next night we sat and meditated and I gave her healing. She asked her guide to come and talk to us but nothing happened apart from her feeling taller again, we had a break for a while then we tried again and this time she made funny noises with her throat then said hello a couple of times, then she opened her eyes. I asked her if she knew what had happened and she said yes, somebody had said hello. This was great we had made a breakthrough, so feeling very pleased with ourselves we went to bed as it was late.

Chapter 4

During the night Clair who was nine woke up crying, so Jan went to sort her out and when she came back said it was just a nightmare. When I spoke to Clair the next day she said she couldn't remember anything, so I left it at that. While I was at work and the kids were at school, Jan said she had been hearing noises all day and in the end had gone out in the garden to get away from it. I asked her what sort of noises and she said just bangs and thumps coming from upstairs. It was then I noticed the ironing at the bottom of the stairs, and she said she didn't like to go upstairs until somebody was home. She also said she had seen a little girl looking out of our bedroom window, while she was out in the garden.

I didn't like the sound of this I had heard of haunted houses and ours was old, I wondered if someone who used to live there had died in the house and was haunting us, and maybe the circle had woken them up. I telephoned Arthur that night and asked him about it, he said it was ok they weren't trying to harm us they were just our guides looking round. I said would he talk to them and ask them not to make a noise as it was frightening Jan. He said we would talk to them tomorrow when we had our circle.

When everyone came the following night they said the house felt cold and they felt uneasy. I said it must be our guides getting closer. We then said a prayer and did some meditating and healing, then Arthur went into trance and a man said we were to get out of the house because we didn't belong there, it was his house. I said did he used to live here, he said mind your own business and get out. This bothered me and when Arthur opened his eyes I asked what was going on.

He told me that Kay was furious that we had left her group, and had sent someone from spirit to stop our circle, and they were haunting our house. I said, "How long have you known this?"

He said, he was speaking to Kay today and she had told him to stop the circle or there would be trouble as she had sent spirit to disrupt things. I was very concerned because of the children and said,

"Can't you get rid of it?"

"We will try" Arthur said,

He asked Penny to go into trance and the lady in grey came through. Arthur asked, if she could remove the spirit that was causing the problem.

She said, "Yes they would, and went away.

"There that's sorted; you shouldn't have any more trouble". Arthur said.

I told them about the little girl and asked who she was.

Arthur said, she was a rescue, and we would have to sort that out now. "What's a rescue?" I asked.

"The little girl is lost and needs sending to the light".

"Ok how do we do that?"

"Well we get someone to go into trance, Brian can do this one".

So Brian went into trance and brought his Indian guide through.

"There is a little girl in the house that needs sending to the light can you deal with her?" Arthur asked.

"Yes" said the guide.

Then Brian came back.

"Everything is ok now". Arthur said.

We finished the circle and discussed what had gone on and why Kay had done this. We decided that as she was only two houses away we would move the circle to Bob and Jane's house next week. Arthur said because it was further away she would not be able to send a spirit to their house as she didn't know where it was. I was relieved as I didn't want this sort of thing upsetting the children or Jan.

During the following week I started getting aches and pains, I thought perhaps I had done something at work. Maybe pulled a muscle or banged myself, I put it out of my mind as you do, thinking it will get better on its own. We also carried on practicing for Jan to trance in the evenings, as there were no bad spirits in the house anymore, Arthur said they were gone.

The way we went about it was that I would give Jan healing and she would meditate and see what happened. A couple of times she said that she could feel something but wasn't sure what, it was just a sort of feeling of being taller. During the next few weeks what with going down to Bob's house, and practicing meditating we began to settle down, we thought we understood what we were doing.

Down at Bob's house we carried on healing and the others were going into trance and giving little speeches. All the while we were hearing noises again in the house and things were going missing. Just little annoying things, like I would put a screwdriver down and when I went to pick it up it wasn't there. I was also still getting pains in my legs or arms and sudden headaches. We carried on practicing at home as well. After a couple of weeks of this Jan's guide managed to speak and I had a short conversation with him about who he was and where he came from.

Chapter 5

He said we should call him Richard after Richard the Lion Heart, he said it wasn't his real name. We wouldn't be able to pronounce his real name as he was a Minoan from Crete about 4 thousand years ago.

.The first thing I did the following evening was to ask if Jan wanted to try again, she said ok and I started to give her healing. I wasn't sure if it was working but tried anyway, as it seemed to help her to meditate. This time Richard came through much better without heavy breathing and throat clearing.

I asked if it was Richard and he said, yes.
"Is it difficult to talk to me?"
"Not now that I have got used to the body again and familiarized myself with how things work."
"What do you mean you had a body before didn't you?"
"Yes but you get used to your bodily functions and don't have to think about it because it becomes automatic, whereas I have to concentrate on making everything work normally. For instance sitting up and not falling over took a certain amount of practice as there were a number of different muscles to operate to achieve this."
It was then I noticed Jan hadn't taken a breath
and said,
"Richard you must breathe." he did.
"Sorry I had forgotten."

He then explained to me that after 4 thousand years these things have to be thought about. Because we had only just become aware of the spirit people we had to sort things out quickly, so that we could talk to each other. There is a lot that we had to cover now that we were aware.

"What about the noises we are hearing in the house could the spirits stop banging about?"
"You will have stop to them, it has to come from you."
"How do we do that?"
"You will have to learn to close your senses and impose your will on your territory to protect it."
"What are we protecting it from?"
"There are good spirits and bad spirits just like there are good and bad people."
"Were they sent by Kay and if so how could she do that?"
"Yes they were sent by her, all she has to do is ask and someone would come and disturb you."
"Why would they do that?"
"Because they enjoy it and since they died they had found they can do things to people without being found out."
"Are they making my arms and legs ache?"
"Yes." said Richard.
At this point I wondered what we had gotten into and how we were going to sort it out.
"How can I stop them from giving me pain?"
"They can only give you pain if you have had it before. They bring back the memory that is in your subconscious to your conscious mind, in that way you

become aware of the memory but think it is a current problem."

"How do I stop it?"

"You must first think whether you have caused that part of your body pain, maybe by banging it or straining it. If you can't remember having done either then the pain probably is not yours. You then use your mind and persuade yourself that you have no pain, gradually as you get more competent at doing this the pains will disappear. You can at the same time tell yourself that it is not your pain and tell it to go away, but you must continue to reinforce this thought until it has gone. Gradually as you become more proficient at this you will get less pain and be able to protect yourself more. It will then become automatic just like breathing and you will deal with these attacks almost before they start."

"What about the noises?"

"By protecting yourselves you will also be protecting your property."

As we had been talking for a while I thanked him for talking to us and said good night and Jan came back and opened her eyes. Jan wasn't best pleased about what had been said. She was concerned that the kids were getting attacked with nightmares, how could we stop that from happening? After all they shouldn't have to suffer because of what we had gotten into. I agreed and said maybe if we stopped then it would go away and the kids would be left alone. We decided to stop for a week and see what happened.

Chapter 6

That night Clair woke up screaming, she had another nightmare, I went down to sort her out and after she had stopped crying she told me what had happened.

"Something woke me up, when I looked round the room I saw a big horrible looking man standing at the end of the bed, He had this horrible smile on his face but didn't say anything just stood there looking at me."

I don't know how he had got in the house but she was frightened to death at what he might do.

"Where is he?"

"He disappeared when you came to the door of the bedroom."

"Where did he go?"

"I don't know he was there and then he wasn't."

"It's just a nightmare."

I settled her down and gave her a cuddle as she went back to sleep. I was very angry that the spirits were frightening my daughter and vowed they would have a fight on their hands if it happened again. I went back to bed and tried to ask my guides to protect Clair; she was only a child and was not involved in any of this. Anyway the rest of the night was quiet so I guessed my guides had looked after Clair for me. The next night we didn't try to do anything and when it was time for Clair to go to bed she was very frightened. We managed to calm her down and persuaded her that it had just been a dream, and when she was going to sleep she should think about something that she had done recently that she had

21

enjoyed. In other words think happy thoughts as she went to sleep. She seemed to settle ok and we heard no more for the rest of that week. Meanwhile I was still trying to sort out this mind over matter business and stop the pains I was getting.

I was busy renovating the house and I was now ready to do some major works. I had to lower the top floor by three feet and this meant all the ceilings on the first floor would have to be taken out. As the kids rooms were on the first floor and were about twelve feet high I had the space. I was also going to take out the chimney which ran up the wall between the kid's bedrooms, this meant taking the wall out as well and rebuilding it to the second floor. It was the summer so we decided that Jan and the kids, and the dogs, would go down to Lyme Regis with the caravan for a couple of weeks while I did the building work. I towed the caravan down and stayed the weekend then left them and came back to get on with it. I was so busy I never noticed my aches and pains; I slept in the lounge and was not disturbed for the whole time I was rebuilding. When I had done the wall and put the floor joists in for the top floor, I laid the floor and then went back for a weekend with Jan and the kids then brought them all home.

Now after three weeks we had not done anything with the spirits and things had been quiet. When everyone had settled back in and life was back to normal we started hearing noises again and I was getting different aches and pains. Jan and I sat down and discussed what we were going to do about this spiritual stuff. We agreed that if we were going to keep getting bothered by spirits and Arthur and the others didn't seem to know how to stop it we would have to sort it out ourselves. So we decided that I would continue going to Bob's house to the circle and learn as much as I could from them, and we would carry on practicing at home and find out as much as we could from Richard as to how to deal with the problem. We decided that there was no point in saying anything to the others as they did not seem to know much about the problems we were having. I wondered why they weren't having problems as they were as much a part of the circle as we had been. I supposed the spirits couldn't find them as Arthur had said. It was alright for them they didn't have to try and deal with the problem, basically it was in our house and so it was our problem. I did ask Arthur if he knew of anybody who knew about haunted houses, I didn't tell him why, I just said I wanted to know more of how it worked. He said there wasn't anyone that he knew of and I left it at that. I thought that if other people were having these problems then someone needed to learn how to stop it and help them, as there didn't seem to be anyone then it would be up to me to learn how.

We continued to do the same things in the circle until one night Penny said she had fallen down and hurt herself and could she have some healing. The others said yes and all jumped up and surrounded her and started giving her healing, they were pushing each other out of the way in their eagerness to heal. I just sat there I was very annoyed they weren't considering Penny only themselves, how could this be the way spirit would work. Soon after this I left and went home I was very angry but didn't know why, in fact on the way home, there is a single track road that goes over the Basingstoke Canal and I nearly hit the bridge I was so angry. This got me a little confused as I am not one to get angry without knowing why. When I got home I told Jan about what they had done but didn't say anything about the bridge although she could tell I was annoyed at what I had seen. The next day it was in the papers that an Indian 747 had crashed off the coast of Ireland and there were no survivors. I just thought how sad and left it at that, but later that day I saw Bob who said that he was very tired as he had been up all night rescuing the people on the plane who had died. He said they heard the report in a news flash while they were having a cup of tea and Arthur said they should try to rescue the people from the plane. They got someone through and after they had rescued him another then another until they had spoken to and rescued all the passengers.

Chapter 7

I didn't think any more of it until I was talking to Richard the next night when I asked him if it could be true that they all needed rescuing and that they had come to Bob's house for help.

"Be careful what you wish for as you may get it." Richard said.
"What do you mean?"
"They went looking for people to rescue and there are those in spirit who will give you what you want just to waste your time. They all had to go to work the next day, but were given all those people to rescue, when one would have been sufficient. They all passed the same way and would have gained the understanding of what had happened to them by listening to one of their number being rescued. Most of them would not have needed rescuing as very few get lost anyway. "

I began to understand how little Arthur and the others knew about the workings of spirit, although it seemed to me who knew nothing that they were very experienced at the time.
"You were upset last night, why was that?" Richard said.
"I was angry because of the way they pushed and shoved each other to give Penny healing and didn't think it was right. They gave her no consideration at all and I didn't think spirit would do that."
"No they wouldn't but if people were too eager they would not listen to their guide."

"Was it necessary for them all to give Penny healing?"

"No, it only requires one person, you drove a little fast coming home and nearly hit the bridge as you crossed it."

"Yes how did you know?" I hadn't told Jan.

"One of your guides was telling me."

Well this was a surprise I did have guides with me and they were passing on a message.

"The reason you were upset is because instinctively you knew what they were doing was not right, the same as when you went to Kay's house you felt uneasy."

I thought maybe there was hope for me yet.

"How does healing work?"

"When you give healing your guide stands with you and passes the healing energy through you to the person requiring healing. The energy is directed at the area causing discomfort and eases the pain, this is done by you allowing your guides to come close and letting them do their work. The guide who is working with you will have mastered a number of different healing rays and will use the one most appropriate for the problem."

"How many different healing rays are there?"

"There are thousands and each guide will have mastered a portion of them. This is why when giving healing you will start with one guide and they will sometimes change during the healing. That way a different energy can be used at the same sitting if it is required. Although your guides are able to heal a number of ailments one will not necessarily cover all energies that are needed. Your guide's abilities overlap so there are not too many changes during a session. If you can imagine all the colours of the spectrum, your guides will have mastered a portion of them and other guides will have mastered others. When you have a guide who specialises in healing they will have mastered many more than someone who specialises in something else. This means that although we can all assist with healing we don't all specialise in it. "

"So who was working with your medium when she was giving Clair healing?"

"You have not met yet"

"What was wrong with her foot?"

"The ligament was damaged and the body protected it by surrounding the damaged area with fluid, as the ligament healed so the fluid gradually drained off."

"I'm surprised the specialist didn't know."

"He had an idea but the fluid didn't show too well on the x-ray and the ligament appeared to be undamaged."

"I suppose he was erring on the side of caution."

"They have to be very careful."

"I suppose so, what other things do you specialise in?"

"That is for another time my medium is getting tired and wants a cup of tea."

"Okay good night."

"God bless."

Chapter 8

The following day I got a phone call from Arthur who asked if we would like to go and see a medium called Roy Squires at Bournemouth, as he was giving a demonstration. We had never seen anything like this, we said yes and so it was arranged for the following Saturday night when he would be giving the demonstration. We went and it was in a big old church building where there were rows of chairs, with a high platform at the front. This was the first time Jan and I had been to anything like this so didn't know what to expect. The medium said he worked with his mother and they worked very fast so please listen, and speak up if we should come to you. Well I could only see him on the platform and the woman who was in charge of the evening that had introduced him. I didn't know where his mother was but kept my eye out for her, as he was about 50, she was going to be really old. He spoke to a few people then spoke to me, when I didn't answer straight away, he said "You, I'm talking to you." I didn't get a chance to say much more than yes and he started telling me things which I have to admit, some of it I understood, and before you knew it he was talking to someone else. When he had finished they said a prayer and we left, I said to Arthur, who had said he was great, where was his mother who he said he worked with. Arthur said his mother was in spirit and was his guide.

I thought I would have to ask Richard about this as it didn't make sense to me, as Richard had said that you choose your guides from friends you know while you are

28

in spirit, who then stay with you all your life. If this is so did this Roy Squires have guides before his mum died? If so what happened to them, did his mother take over, or did he not have a guide until his mum died and then became his guide.

That night after the kids were in bed we asked Richard to come through.

"Can you tell us about guides?"

"What do you want to know?"

"How we get guides and how they work with us."

"When you are in spirit and you decide it is time for you to incarnate to another life. You will naturally ask your friends who have the right expertise to look after you whilst on the earth plane. It is an honour for us to be asked to be a guide, as you are placing the well- being of your soul in our hands. Once you have asked those whom you wish to help you. Then you sit down and discuss your aims and wishes. You then have to select your parents and you will do this based on the lessons both you and they wish to experience. You will approach a number of suitable candidates and by agreement sort out your collective aims. The reason you choose more than one couple is because for reasons of illness, accident or just simply that someone does not follow the path they intended, the two prospective parents may not meet. Although your guides help to guide you through the life you have chosen, it doesn't mean everything will go to plan. Sometimes you can be stubborn in what you want and don't listen to your guides or instincts. Your life's plan is a guide line, not set in stone and if you don't achieve all that you desired, then you can always come back another time if you want to. You may reverse some of the plans because you are not ready, or you haven't met those who will help you on the earth. When the time is right you will then wait until the prospective parents are born and grow up. Then you will monitor them to see who is on track, and whose circumstances fit your life's plan, and theirs, as agreed with them. It is every spirits intention to live a full life, but sometimes the circumstances change, and because of illness or accident, or you picked the wrong place and time your life may be cut short. For instance those who are born in places of troubles or famine have chosen them to gain that particular experience. It can be that they have misjudged the severity of the problem and things don't go as expected. You will still gain the experience but your life may be cut short. Like in a war where accidents can and do happen, or where there are people starving and food is more difficult to come by for longer than anticipated. When the circumstances are as right as they can be you will then prepare for your birth., To do this you will closely observe the chosen situation and when conception occurs you will inhabit the foetus for short periods, then gradually for longer and longer as the baby grows in the womb, until you will stay there once you have got used to the condition. The baby will grow in the womb and when the child is born you will then be on your journey. As you know there can be many complications to childbirth, but once you get past this stage you have really started your journey through life. You're chosen guides will be very close to you and in constant communication. This is why you will see a baby staring at a certain place in the room, they are still fully aware of us. During the initial stages of growing in the womb to birth it can be a difficult time for the spirit as there is a lot to get used to. Gradually as you get more used to your surroundings you will become less aware of us. The reason for this is the world around you fills all your senses. You become more and more used to touch and what you see with your eyes and hear with your ears, that the more subtle senses fade into the background. You do not lose these senses they just don't get used so much. Take a blind person their senses are more acute because they don't have the use of their eyes and the brain compensates. The conscious mind takes over from the subconscious, which is the physical brain taking over from the spiritual mind. As you progress through life you will have many conversations with your guides during your times of sleep. This is so that you know you are on track. If you elected to be aware of spirit during your life, when the time is right you will meet the right person and you will start to be aware of the spirits around you. You will if you are lucky get to know some of your friends again and be able to communicate."

"Depending on how you are taught will depend on your progress and to what degree you are aware. Your guides will work with you in the background but if you will not accept them working closely with you that's all they can do, until you allow them closer. You have free will and if you are misguided by some ones beliefs on the earth, then you are restricted in your development. The beliefs are many and varied, and because of this there are different degrees of understanding. If you believe you will have a parent or a certain person as a guide then we cannot stop you. We just have to stay back and try to do the job that you asked us to. The biggest problem for you is that man teaches man, and if someone believes there is only one way of doing something and it works, man will copy and say this is how it's done. Sometimes you must think outside the box and give spirit credit that they will work with you to make things easier to communicate. Most of the development is done naturally on tried and tested methods, but without experimenting you cannot change the way things are done or progress. Does this answer your question?"

"Yes and it has given us something to think about which I am sure will bring up other questions."

"You must take what sits right to you and question what does not and always, always question what is said."

"Thank you."

"God bless." Richard said and stepped back.

As you can see we had been given a lot of information. We discussed what we had heard and decided to sleep on it and see what we thought the next day.

Chapter 9

Well the next day I had plenty to think about what with the information we had been given, and trying to sort out the constant attacks of aches and pains. Clair seemed to have settled down, so I was no longer worried about her, but we kept a close eye on her anyway. After dinner that night I went into the lounge and sat down with an A4 pad and wrote down some questions that had come up during the discussion Jan and I had the night before. There were also many questions that had come to mind during the day so I put them down. When the kids were settled down for the night we sat and in the usual way that we had found to work, I gave Jan healing while she meditated. When she had gone off and her guide had come through I asked if it was Richard.

"Yes" he said.

I started to ask him the first question

"From what you told us last night, it would seem that when people die young it is not spirit ending their life it is just the way of things, like something has gone wrong with the body. Is that right?"

"Yes there are so many things that can go wrong that you don't know about."

"What about babies who are still born, or die whilst being born?"

"The reasons they pass are the same, something has gone wrong, every life is intended to be lived in full."

I asked about Roy using his mother as a guide he said.

"Sometimes a medium will not listen to us and we have to work as best we can with them. Their progress will be restricted because of this."

"So if someone insists on working with a particular individual you can't stop them?"

"We could but we would be taking away their free will."

"If our life's journey is roughly planned why are some people bad?"

"All spirit are born good the bad spirits don't get a chance at life until they have come to the spirit world. It is just the environment they are brought up in that makes them who they become, all are born good but life can treat different individuals to harsh lessons. Sometimes they have to fight the best way they can to survive, this can make people go bad or be very unpleasant to others. They don't listen to their instincts, as you know there are times when you do things or say things and afterwards you feel guilty for what you have done or said. This is your subconscious telling you that you have done wrong to someone. If you heed this, then you have learnt a lesson, and you will try not to do it again. Many people don't listen to their subconscious because they are too caught up in the moment."

"What about later on when the moment has passed?"

"People justify what they have done in all sorts of ways and are not caring enough about others, only themselves."

"How many guides do we have?"

"It depends on how aware and what sort of work you are going to do for spirit. Everyone has more than one guide as there is always work to do in the background for our mediums."

"So if you don't become aware does that mean you will have less guides?"

"Yes, but you will still have many to look after you."

"So if you are aware or going to be, you have more guides than others who are not?"

"You will have guides who specialise in the particular fields that you will be working in as well as guides who work in the background."

"How would we know which fields we will be working in?"

"As you become more aware you will find some things of more interest than others, this is how you will choose which things to do."

"What about healing and clairvoyance can you do both?"

"The first thing you need to do is open up to spirit and receiving healing can help with this. All can give healing, take a mother whose child has fallen and hurt themselves, when a mother gives comfort and rubs it better, that is healing, and yes you can do more than one thing."

"Oh, it's that easy."

"You have both been doing it all you lives, a kind word or a smile it doesn't have to be the laying on of hands."

"Why is it necessary to give healing to Jan when we want to talk to you?"

"It's not but in this case it is helping to open you both up."

"I don't feel anything."

"Don't you get a tingling on your shoulder sometimes?"

"Yes, but I just thought it was an itch or something." Richard just smiled.

"It's one of your guides letting you know he is there."
You can imagine my surprise as I thought I was not sensitive enough. I asked about this guide.
"You will find out more about him as time goes on and you must be patient. Your journey will be different from others as we will teach you.
You have much to learn and much to teach."
"From what you say how are we going to teach others when we don't know much ourselves?"
"It will happen when the time is right my medium was getting tired, I will step back now."
"Thank you for speaking
with us."
Richard said god bless
and stepped back.
Jan said.
"I have had a busy day and I'm tired."
"That's ok perhaps spirit used a lot of your energy and wore you out."

We talked a little about what we had been told and then called it a night.

Chapter 10

Later that night Clair woke up again with a nightmare and said she had seen that man again, it took a while to settle her, and she had also woken our son Darren who asked what was wrong with Clair. I told him she had a nightmare and said she was alright now and to go back to sleep.

The following night I went to the circle and we talked about what we thought of the medium we had seen. Arthur said he was very good and the others agreed with him. As he was the first I had seen I couldn't say, we then got on with the circle. We did the usual and then Arthur went into trance and brought a man through who the others said was his guide. Arthur was still doing the heavy breathing and the guide didn't say much, nobody asked him any questions, they said you weren't supposed to, they would say what they had to say and then leave. I asked how you could learn, and Arthur said they would give us teachings when they felt we were ready. I thought this a bit odd but didn't say what Jan and I had been doing, I didn't think they would accept that you could ask questions.

When I got home I told Jan that nothing new had happened, and I thought we could learn more from Richard than all their guides put together as they wouldn't ask questions. Jan said, "Are you going to go back to the circle?"
"I don't think so."

I reckoned we were on our own and would have to figure things out for ourselves.

When we sat down the next night I had another list of questions and so we started by giving Jan healing, while I was doing this a guide came through and said his name was Richard, we talked for a bit while I was still giving Jan some healing.

"Where does healing come from?" I asked.

"From your higher self."

Ah I thought now I was going to find out who this higher self was. I thought this an odd answer as Richard had already told us how it worked, but because I wanted to know what this higher self was I continued.

"Who is this higher self and where is it?"

"You don't need to know."

I thought that's odd Richard is usually more forthcoming than that.

"Do we choose our guides?"

"No they are chosen for you and change as you develop."

Now I was getting confused as this was not what Richard had said.

"Thank you for coming."

He just said bye and went. I said to Jan,

"Maybe it's a point of view in spirit just the same as here."

"It felt different I don't think it was Richard."

We decided to have another go and try to find out what had happened. So Jan started to meditate and I gave her healing. While I was doing the healing I found myself smiling for no reason but I carried on and Richard came through or so he said.

"How do I know you are Richard and if you are where were you just now?"

"Yes I am Richard, use your senses and try to sense me and tell me if it feels right. I have been here all the time my medium allowed the other spirit to come through."

"Why didn't you stop them from coming through?"

"It is up to my medium to stop the wrong one coming forward."

"I don't know how to sense when you are there."

"When you were healing what did you feel?"

"I felt happy and was smiling but I don't know why."

"One of your guides is close, try to use the same senses that you used then to tune in to me."

I tried but couldn't tell.

"What does your gut feeling say?"

"Run with it and see."

"Remember accept what you can and disregard that which doesn't feel right."

"What happened before and who was that?"

"Although we are here and ready to come through, if you accept someone else that pushes in then we can't stop you, remember you have the free will to choose even if it is wrong."

"If you don't come when we ask you to that's going to make it more difficult to work with you."

"With practice you will sort it out, be patient, how will you learn if you don't get it wrong sometimes."

I thought this is not as easy as I thought it was going to be but then why should this spirit stuff be any easier than anything else.

"Who was the guide that came to me and was he trying to put me into trance?"

"No he wasn't trying to trance you, just letting you know he was there."

"Can you tell me about him?"

"He comes from Egypt and his name is Elijah."

I asked for more information.

"All in good time, get to know him and you will get the information you seek."

Well I wasn't going to get anymore about Elijah so I decided to move on to some of the questions we needed answers to.

"Why is Clair getting nightmares?"

"She is sensitive and is seeing spirits"

"Why are you letting them upset her she is only a child?"

"We do not see her as a child but as the spirit that she is. Her guides choose what they are going to allow through it is not up to you."

"That isn't fair she has done nothing, why should she suffer because we've got involved?"

"It is not your right to control another spirits journey through life even if she is your child. Remember she chose you as her parents because she would gain the experiences she needs to learn her lessons. She will never be given more than she can handle and to stretch her is to help her to grow."

"Is that what you're doing with us?"

"It is part of your chosen pathway as it is for my medium."

"That isn't fair."

"It's not about being fair it's about your journey through life and you have chosen this one. You must try to remember that we are only doing as you have asked us. Even though we know you will suffer a bit, we know you will cope with it and look back on these experiences with a smile."

"It's a bit difficult to understand all this at the moment, I will need to talk to Jan and see if we can get our heads around it."

"We are here when you need us, god bless." and he stepped back.

Well as you can imagine we were quite upset that Clair was going to suffer because of us and decided to do everything we could to protect her. We knew that stopping wasn't going to put an end to it. We had to understand how things worked, so that we could protect ourselves and our children.

Clair was getting more and more frightened to go to bed, we thought if she was the spirit Richard said she was we ought to tell her what we had gotten into. We also realised that with all the healing she had had on her foot maybe it had opened her up. Maybe we should have had the hospital cut the lump out and not gone down this pathway. It was too late now we just had to learn as much as we could so that we could protect ourselves.

We tried to tell Clair about guardian angels and that she had one that was looking after her. She said she had heard of angels but didn't think they were real, so we decided to ask Richard to come through and help us to explain. We told Clair that mummy was going to close her eyes and in a minute one of her angels was going to come and talk to us. She said ok, so she sat on my lap and Jan went into meditation. We didn't know if it was going to work as I wasn't giving her healing, we thought we would think outside the box and see. After all if Arthur and the others could do it and they didn't do it as well as Jan, we would give it a go. Well after a minute Richard did come through and I said.

"Hello." I told Clair he had been alive about 4 thousand years ago and was one of mummy's angels who had come to talk to us and tell her about one of her angels. You can imagine our surprise when Clair said.

"Is he that big man sitting in the chair with mummy?"

"Can you see him?"

"Yes but he doesn't have any wings."

"Not all angels have wings." That seemed to satisfy her and Richard smiled.

"Hello Clair how are you?"

Clair was a bit shy but said,

"I'm alright."

I asked Richard if he could tell Clair about one of her angels.

"You have a Red Indian angel called Swift Deer who stands next to you. If you close your eyes you will see him in your head." Clair closed her eyes.

42

"There is a man with a feather in his hair and he is standing next to us. He's saying that he's here to protect me from the bad people. If I'm frightened by them I just need to think of him, and he will come and help."

I was surprised and a little envious that Clair could see and hear spirit without learning how.

"How can Clair see spirit?"

"She is still young enough to believe."

This made it easier, I was pleased for her as it would make things easier for her to understand.

"If the bad people come you should ask Swift Deer to come, and together you can make them go away."

This seemed to please Clair and after Richard had gone, we talked a little about what Swift Deer looked like so she would recognise him next time. She described him to us and asked.

"Why can't you see him?"

"It's probably because he is your angel and only showed himself to you."

"But I could see mummy's angel too."

"That's because he wanted you to so you wouldn't be frightened, and you would know who was talking to you."

"Do you see Richard?"

"No, what does he look like?"

"He is taller than you and about as old as you but he is wearing a long dress thing, like the Greek's did in the olden days."

"How do you know what Greek's wore?"

"We did some work at school about Greece."

"It was a toga."

"That's it, that's what they wore."

"Richard lived in Crete in the Mediterranean Sea, he was a Minoan. Lots of people from that part of the world used to wear togas, the Romans did too."

"Yes." she said,

Clair seemed to be quite happy now that she knew that she had an angel looking after her.

When she went to bed that night she called me and said.

"I was trying to go to sleep and I saw an old woman in here, so I asked Swift Deer to come and help and together we made the woman get smaller and smaller until she disappeared."

"That's good, so you'll be alright now?"

"Yes." She said. So I left her to go to sleep.

When I got downstairs, Jan and I discussed what had gone on and Jan said that while Richard had been with her she had seen Clair's guide as well. I asked her if we could talk to Richard again and she said ok. This time she just sat in the armchair and closed her eyes and after a minute he came through.

"Thank you for helping with Clair."

"That's what we are here for to help you understand."

"The other night someone came through that we thought was you and answered a couple of questions, but they didn't seem to answer them very well."

"What were your questions?"

"What or where is my higher self?"

"Your higher self is your soul or spirit and although this part of you knows all the answers to your questions it is blocked off from you."

"How can I ask it questions then?"

"You will instinctively know when something is right or wrong, this is you accessing your spiritual knowledge but you will not get answers in plain English, as you are from me. What happens is part of the preparation that you make before starting a new life's journey is to block off you spiritual knowledge, like giving yourself amnesia. If you brought this knowledge with you, you would not have the right perspective when you come to learn your lessons and it would interfere with your learning process. If you like imagine there is a bucket with all your experiences or knowledge in it and you put the lid on. That is locked away until you have completed your journey. As you learn, so the new lessons are placed in the bucket for your retrieval when you come back to spirit."

"How do we do that?"

"Do what?"

"Place the knowledge in the bucket."

"You have a brain which is for the physical thought processes, or your conscious mind, to keep your body functioning, and a mind which is your soul or subconscious which stores the knowledge as you gain it. When you pass, all your understanding is kept in your subconscious which you retain when you come home."

"What about guides, the other spirit said we don't choose our guides, they are chosen for us and change as we develop."

"I have told you this, you choose your guides, who stay with you through your life until you come back to us. They will come forward as you require their expertise and as you learn some will move into the background

45

and will not be as prominent. They are still there, as you progress you will be aware of other guides, who will work with you in that which is their expertise at the time you need them. Then when you come back to us, you discuss with your guides what you did in the physical. You will then see where your errors were, and whether you need to go back at some other time, to complete the tasks you set for yourself. The choice is always yours and yours alone, there is no one that judges you or makes you. Remember you have free will. Does that clarify things for you?"

"Yes it does."

"Remember accept what you can but always question, think about what I say and question me also. If you are not happy with the answer I give then explore the answer more until you are satisfied."

"Where does spirit come from?"

He never answered,

"Why don't you answer?"

"I cannot answer that."

"Why can't you answer?"

"It has been discussed between your guides and my mediums and it was decided not to answer at the moment."

"How are spirit born?"

"I cannot answer."

"How did spirit get to where you are now?"

"Your guides are here by invitation from you."

"I'm not asking the right question am I?"

"What do you want to know?"

"If you get here by invitation from us before we come here how do the bad spirits get here, after all we wouldn't invite them would we?" "The bad spirits are those that don't come back to heaven for whatever reason."

"Why don't they go back to heaven?"

"There are many reasons. It's not only bad spirits that don't go straight to heaven. For instance if someone pass's suddenly, in an accident and don't know they have died, they will wander around the earth plane until they come to the realisation that they have died, or their guides get through to them and explain what has happened."

"So when they die, why don't their guides just take them to heaven?"

"They will not know their guides are there, it can take a long time, in your time for us to get through to them."

"Why?"

"Because they are not using their senses and are not aware of us. You use the physical senses such as eyes and ears to communicate, whereas we use our mental senses. Just like you are learning to do now when you try to sense spirit, which is what they have to learn to do again. The difference is you are conscious of what you are trying to do they are not."

"How do their guides get through to them then?"

"By gentle and persistent thoughts and feelings."

"Why don't you just take them to heaven?"

"Because they may not want to go and we have to respect their free will." "If they don't know what's going on how are you taking away their free will?"

"That isn't the point; they must be given the chance to choose."

"Does everyone have the same problem when they die?"

"No, when most people die it is of old age or illness and it is a gradual decline, this gives the loved ones who have passed i.e. family and friends, a chance to come and greet them and get them acclimatised to their new environment. Your may have heard of people saying when they get near to the end that they could see their loved ones who had died. Well they can and this makes the transition and our job a lot easier. There are also those who no matter what the cause of death is, are aware enough or believe in spirit, know they will be met by a loved one. A few of those that pass in accidental circumstances get lost but not many; there are some exceptions, for instance there are those that believe that when you pass you go to sleep, which is exactly what they do. It comes back to their guides again trying to wake them and help them to understand that there is more. There are also those who believe when you're dead that's it, there is nothing else. Imagine their surprise when that get over here and find there is more. Some of these come to terms fairly easily and others take longer. Then there are those with strict religious beliefs, if it is not what is expected or as they have been led to believe, they will ignore those around them. Some religions teach that if you don't meet or are not met by whom you expect then you have gone to hell."

"How often do people have trouble when they pass over?"

"Not that often, but consider how many people pass from your world, and take maybe one per cent, which is a very large figure. When you consider that some of those that pass can be very stubborn and it can take us some time to persuade them. Sometimes we are dealing with a backlog especially during natural disasters, and your conflicts, when we get a rush of arrivals."

"So although it is fairly rare the chances of one of my loved ones having a problem are small?"

"Yes that is so."

I thanked Richard for explaining that to us and he said god bless and stepped back. Well, Jan and I had a lot to discuss, so Jan had a cup of tea and we talked about what we had been told. We both agreed that what had been said seemed plausible and we would wait and see if any more information was forthcoming at a later date. I found it interesting that he said they cannot answer the questions about where spirits come from. I wondered whether it was because they were not allowed or didn't know.

Chapter 11

The next few days I was busy with work and putting a new roof on the house so we didn't have much time in the evenings, as I was very tired. I found that I was not getting so many aches and pains so figured I was getting on top of the problem. We were still getting bangs and noises around the house but they didn't seem to bother us as much until we both heard someone dragging what sounded like chains along the hallway. This freaked us both out a bit. We both thought we needed to get more of an understanding as to how to deal with these spirits. Fortunately the kids were not in at the time, and we hoped it wouldn't happen when they were. I used to start work at 5am in the morning, and get home around lunch time, and it was normal for me to have a couple of hours sleep in the afternoon. This particular day I was lying on the sofa and Jan was out gardening. I was just nodding off when the end of the sofa was lifted about three feet in the air. I opened my eyes and looked round, I couldn't see anything, who was I kidding I didn't see anything anyway, but I looked just in case. I said very clever can you do it again so that I can watch. I don't know what I would have done if they had, but it didn't happen, so I went to sleep. Later I told Jan about it and she said she was glad it wasn't her, but it got her worried that next time it might be her or one of the kids. I said I didn't think so as Richard had said they will only let you experience what you could handle, that seemed to put her mind at rest a little bit. But we decided to talk to Richard next time and find out a bit more about the spirits in the house, and how we could stop that sort of thing happening. That night we were sitting talking just after the kids had gone to bed, when Clair came in a little upset. We asked what was wrong she said she had a stomach ache, so Jan sorted her out and put her back to bed. We then asked Richard to come through and after a couple of tries where we thought it wasn't him he came through.

"Were we right about the other two?"

"You were right about the first one but the second time it was me. Don't worry we would rather you err on the cautious side than accept anyone."

I thought we may be making some headway, I had listened carefully to what the impostor had said, and thought it wasn't the way Richard spoke and it didn't feel right. Jan said it didn't feel right as well, so between the two of us we were slowly learning to tell the difference. Richard then said.

"Would you like to give my medium some healing while I am here and I will answer any questions you have while you are doing it?"

"Ok,"

I put my hands close to Jan's head. As I was settling down I felt my stomach push forward, I couldn't stop it.

"What's happening my stomach is being pushed forward like I have a large tummy."

"You have another of your guides come close, he is interested in the type of problem my medium is having with her shoulder."

"Who is he?"

"He says call him Clive, he was one of the first to be deported to

Australia for stealing a loaf of bread to feed his children."

"Is he my height and quite tubby?"

"Yes."

"He's got a good sense of humour too."

"Yes he has."

I carried on healing but didn't get any more information, this was another first. I felt I had to move my hands to Jan's back.

"I feel I have to move my hand to your mediums back is that right?"

"Elijah is there now just allow yourself to go where you think you should it will be right."

Elijah felt smaller than Clive but they both felt ok.

"Can you tell me a bit more about Elijah?"

"Ask him yourself and trust your first
thoughts."

"What work did you do?" I said out
loud.

A thought came into my head, "I was an architect and designed and built pyramids."

I told Richard what I felt.

"Is that right?"

"Yes"

"How long ago were you alive?"

I couldn't hear an answer. I told Richard,

"Stop listening it will come in another way."

I thought how can I stop listening if I was hoping for an answer to my question.

"If I don't listen how will I get the answer?"

"You have other senses that you must learn to use."

"Like feelings?"

"Yes and thought, you don't have to speak out loud just think your question we can hear you."

I thought does he mean telepathic, some hope. Anyway I continued giving Jan healing.

"When you have finished you can put your hands down."

I never thought of that, how would I know when I had finished. In the past I had just stood there to give Jan healing until Richard came through.

"How will I know when I have finished?"

"Trust your instincts."

Well I stood there for what seemed the right length of time and then put my hands down.

"Why did you wait, Elijah had finished a few minutes ago."

"I couldn't tell."

"You will with practice."

Anyway I sat down.

"I seem to be getting on top of my aches and pains."

"Good, but don't get complacent there is still much to learn."

I was to remember that in the near future as I will tell you.

"How can we deal with the noises we are hearing as they are getting more frequent and more alarming?"

I also told him about the sofa lifting up and he smiled.

"It is all part of the same problem and as you became stronger you will stop these things from happening. What you have been doing to overcome the aches and pains is also making you stronger and helping you to deal with the other problems."

Just then Clair came in again saying her stomach still hurt.

"Richard's here" I said, I didn't want to startle her.

We couldn't give her anymore pain killers it was too soon.

Richard said he would step back and I said ok, but then he said Jan had asked him to stay as he might be able to help.

"Can you help?"

"Yes, Clair can you go and get a glass of water please and bring it to me?"

Which she did. I didn't want to leave Jan in trance and he must have realised that as he said while Clair was gone.

"You must never leave a person in trance and leave the room; you are protecting her while you are watching her."

Clair gave him the glass of water.

"I am going to put some healing in it so that it will make your tummy feel better. What flavour would you like?"

Clair looked at me and I said.

"What would you like it to taste of?"

"Chocolate please."

Richard held the glass for a few minutes then gave it to Clair.

"Sip it slowly."

She looked at me and I said.

"Try it."

So she did, and a big smile came on her face.

"It tastes of chocolate."

Clair sat with me and sipped her drink and Richard stepped back. I said to

Jan,

"How did you talk to Richard, and how did you know he could do something to help?"

"I could feel his thoughts and I just thought it would be good if he could help."

Clair said her stomach didn't hurt anymore so I took her back to bed and she went straight to sleep.

When I came down Jan said,

"Do you want to talk to Richard again?"

"Yes if that's ok."

So she closed her eyes and Richard was there straight away.

"How did you get there so quickly?"

"I was just in the background and my medium was already in the right state of mind."

"What did you do to the water?"

"I put healing in it."

"What about the taste"

"It is very easy to make someone believe what they want to believe, take your aches and pains for instance."

"You mean you just gave her the memory of chocolate?"

"Not me, her guides."

"How do you put healing in water?"

"Just imagine you are giving someone healing while you are holding the glass. If you have a stomach upset ask someone to put healing in a glass of water most of the time it will relieve the problem."

"Are there any other ways of giving healing besides putting your hands on or near someone?"

"Yes there is absent healing which can be done in two ways. One way is to think of someone who needs healing and ask your guides to send healing to that person. One of your guides will then go to that person and offer their guides help with the healing. It was then up to that persons guides to either accept the offer or not. Usually the guides will thank your guides for the offer and if they have got it covered decline otherwise they will accept with thanks. Your guide will then on your behalf attend to the healing. You must remember that ailments may take a while to come or you may have them for a while before you seek help. So it will usually take more than one session to alleviate the problem. Because of this your guides will stay until they are no longer needed and that is why you have many guides. As you can see everyone will send thoughts of healing to loved ones, and friends, when they know they are unwell. That's why everyone has many guides who do this work on their behalf; they do not have to be aware it is a natural process. You must of course, if you are aware, remember your guide is working on your behalf and continue to send your thoughts as this strengthens the process. It's like if you have someone who works for you and they are far away in another country, it is nice for them if you contact them to see that they are ok and not having any problems. It's just nice to be remembered. Another way is to place a clean handkerchief between your hands and ask for healing energies to be put into it. You then place it in a plastic bag and you can post it to the person requiring healing. When they receive it they should remove it from the bag and hold it to the affected area for about five minutes and then place it back in the bag. They will do this twice a day for a week when if required you will send another one. You can continue this until it is no longer needed. Of course hands on healing is the best but sometimes it is not possible."

"What happens to the bad spirits that don't go to heaven?"

"Some of them stay around the earth and try to contact people or pretend to be guides so that they can work with mediums. Others just try to disrupt people's lives by being a nuisance as you are experiencing, frightening people for the fun of it."

"Why don't their guides stop them, it's a bit unfair if they are not aware, and even if they are."

"Remember you all have free will and it may be part of your pathway. You have a saying god helps those who help themselves and this is what it means. You have to make the effort and then we know you mean it and we can assist, but we can't do it for you."

"Why is it that some people continue with the problem if you are helping them?"

"If you keep looking to see if the problem is still there, no matter what we do you will invite them back. By looking for them you give them credibility and thoughts are things, you give them the strength to continue. The less you take notice of them or think about them the less they can affect you."

"What about those that gave me aches and pains?"

"They were sent and are feeding off the sender as well as your thoughts, until you started to reject them. It is only by building up your strength that you have been able to reduce their effectiveness."

"How do they work then?"

"What you have been experiencing has taken more than one to do. Each will be taught how to do one aspect of what you feel. Put them all together at the same time and it can be quite distressing for you."

"Who teaches them?"

"There are those in spirit around your world who have studied and practiced so that they can do these things, and they are the ones who teach others. Remember what works in your world also works in ours. If they want to control someone over here they make them think they are in distress in all sorts of ways. Like giving pain or making them think they are having their worst nightmare, so that they can control them. With the children they may just be cruel to them."

"How can you let children suffer like that?"

"Remember they are children to you but spirits to us, with all their past history in their auras for all to see. They just don't have their spiritual memory back, as they have not come all the way back to spirit. You remember I told you about one per cent got lost or confused well some of them will be children."

"But there can't be that many."

"Not today or this year, but some of those around the earth have been there for hundreds of your years, time means nothing here it is always now."

"Well if you know they are there why don't you help them?"

"You have been told they have free will and if they don't ask, how do we know that is not what they want"

"Because they are suffering."

"They are in the now and one moment is all there is when they are suffering. When they are doing what they are told, then there is no suffering just fear of it."

"So that is how they control them?"

"Yes, but remember they are all ages not just children, although some will use children more than others."

"Where do they go or stay?"

"Those who control them lay claim to houses and buildings and make them their territory. There will be one or two that are in charge, and like any business they will have managers, managing different groups doing different things. They will also teach their charges to do things, and swap them with others of their kind, to get other abilities that they can use but are not able to do themselves."

"So if it is like a business how do they profit?"

"It's not profit they are after, as you know we don't use money but power, the more you own the more power you have and the more feared you are."

"Can we send them back to Kay's house?"

"You could but that's not how we do things, as you overcome them we then move them to a secure place and start trying to make them aware of where they are and what's happened to them."

"I see, it's getting late but I am sure I will have more questions on this."

"I have no doubt, god bless." Richard stepped back.

Jan came back and said,

"It must be horrible for all those people to be stuck in that kind of situation."

We talked a while about what we had heard and what had gone on and then went to bed. The next day I woke up with some new pains which I knew I hadn't caused and straight away I tried to make them go away, the way I had been taught, but it wasn't working.

The following evening as we were settling down to talk to Richard again, Clair came in and said her tummy hurt. We said we will give you a pain killer, but she said,
"Can I have some more of that water that tastes like chocolate instead?"
"Ok". Jan got her a glass of water and said,
"We will see if we can make it taste of chocolate again."
Sure enough it did, Jan tried it, and she said with surprise that it tasted just like a chocolate drink. I wondered what we had got ourselves into with Clair, but said nothing. Clair drank the water and went to bed quite happily.

Chapter 12

We decided that if I carried on giving Jan healing it
might help me to become more aware of my guides so
that's what we did. I was giving Jan healing and she
asked for her guide to come forward. When they came
through it wasn't Richard. We thought we had got it
wrong but I decided to run with it and see what
happened.

"Who are you?"

"My name is Sheena and I come
from India."

"Are you a guide?"

"Yes, we thought it was time our medium got to know
someone else."

"Who thought this?"

"My mediums guides discussed the way forward and we
all agreed it was time."

"How do I know you are a guide?"

"You must use your instincts, what are the telling you?"

"Not to trust what anyone says but run with it and see."

"That is a good way of checking, and don't forget
question what I say as you would Richard."

"If you know Richard where does he come from and how
old is he?"

"He is a Minoan who comes from Crete about 4 thousand
years ago."

"Do you know any of my guides?"

"You know of an Egyptian man who used to build
pyramids."

I was still suspicious but decided to let it go and see how things went. I told her about the pains I was getting, and how come they had come back when Richard had said once you overcome those who are attacking you they will not be able to affect you again.

"If you count on your fingers, there are different levels of ability, and you have overcome the first level. If you imagine there are ten levels to overcome, you will have gained the strength to deal with the first ten. There will be ten more levels and you will over time and with practice gain more and more strength to protect yourself and your territory. So multiply each level by ten and you will get some idea of what you have to do."

"What if someone from a higher level of ability than me, attacks me, how am I going to fight that?"

"You will only get what you are able to cope with, anything more will be dealt with by your guides. You may not think you can handle it but your guides will allow only enough to get through that will help you to learn and stretch you a little."

"Thanks, so I am going to have to work hard to stop all this aggravation."

"You will work together, this will show unity, which is very important. It gives those who are attacking you two people to defend against and to try to overcome."

"How long is that going to take, because we are being attacked now?"

"You are already gradually overcoming those who have been sent to disrupt your progress. It is not just learning to defend yourself but the more you understand the stronger you get."

"In that case the quicker we get our questions answered the better. Why are they attacking us, they weren't interested before we went to Kay, why now?"

"Before you went to Kay you were not opening up to spirit, you were still getting attacked you just thought it was your own aches. Now you understand what is yours and what isn't, that's the difference, plus you had some spirits sent to you."

"It seems to me we were better off before we knew about all this."

"Now that you have started on your journey of development you will be watched very carefully by those in spirit on both sides of the fence. You have much to do, and teach, and you will do things that will not be of the norm."

"What do you mean there is only trance and clairvoyance that I am aware of."

"There is much more but it will become clearer as you progress."

Well that gave me something to think about and I thanked her for coming to talk to us, and she said god bless and Jan opened her eyes.

I asked Jan how she felt about Sheena, she said,
"It felt ok, I think she was genuine. What do you think?"
"What she had said seemed ok and she did know about Richard and Elijah so maybe it was right. We will have to see how the information checks out next time we talk to Richard."
"I have noticed the difference between that one that wasn't right and both Sheena and Richard."

"What's that?" I asked.

"You can feel them thinking, how shall I answer that, as opposed to what shall I say, and they feel similar where the other one felt nothing like Richard or Sheena."

Well we had a lot to think about so we decided to give it a rest while we each thought about things, and then we would discuss it again before we talked to Richard or anyone else.

We spent about a week thinking things through and discussing what we had been told, and then we sat down and wrote out a list of questions to ask Richard next time we spoke to him.

We sorted the kids out and Clair seemed to be more settled and we sat down to talk to Richard again. We had decided to carry on with me giving Jan healing as it was helping to open me up, so I stood behind her and placed my hands on her shoulders. After a short while I was aware of someone with me, and then I thought Richard had come through with Jan.

He didn't speak. I said,

"Good evening."

"Good evening."

We were very polite.

"Is that Richard?" I asked.

"What do you think?"

"Yes it is."

"You are right."

"Why didn't you speak when you came through?"

"It is all part of your training; it is up to you to recognise when we are here and who is here. By greeting us we know you are tuning in to us and the more you practice the more it will become second nature. You will be expected to greet us with our name so that we know you know who you're talking to."

"What if I get it wrong?"

"You will not receive an answer. In this way you will learn to recognise us more quickly."

"If I can't see you how will I recognise you?"

"You must use your senses and watch for a slight change in the posture of my medium. We are making it obvious at the moment but it will get more subtle as you progress."

"What are you making obvious?"

"The change in posture and we are coming through stronger so that you may sense us more easily."

"Well it's not that obvious, I am not always sure you are there."

"If it was too obvious you would not try to sense and so you would not learn. As you become more proficient, we will become more subtle, you will sometimes make a mistake or be unsure. You must then err on the cautious side and start again by asking our medium to come back. You can then discuss between you your impressions and come to an agreement as to whether you were right or not. Yours is the harder task as my medium will be able to feel us and know whether it is right or not. You will only be able to work with your senses, and what you observe in our mediums posture but together you will enhance each other. When you start to recognise the subtle change in posture you must not tell anyone of it.

There are those in spirit who will use the information to try to come through and fool you. You will also have the way we talk and the type of phrases we use to double check that it is us and not an impostor."

I thought this is not getting any easier, and I still haven't asked any of the questions we had written down, it seemed a never ending task as the more you know the more you realise you don't know.

"What if I keep getting it wrong?"
"Don't worry if in doubt chuck them out, I think that is your terminology."
"Yes that will do."
Now I was worried about chucking them out all the time.
"If you have trouble and you doubt yourself too much then stop and try again another time."
"Going on from what we were told last time we spoke to Sheena we have written some questions down."
"That is a good idea then you won't be thrown off track and maybe you will get the answers you seek."
"Sheena was talking about the bad spirits claiming houses; I thought you didn't need houses in spirit?"
"We don't, but those around the earth plane use them so they can keep in touch with you, as they want to work through you or on you. They also use them as bases where they train those they have caught to do the things they want them to."
"What sort of things?"
"Well you are being given aches and pains, that's one aspect of what they do. They also play on emotions and

fears, for instance if there are more than one in a house they will try to depress one and lift the other this way you are always off balance and easier to get at. They will also make noises or sometimes show themselves."

"Why do they do that?"

"So that they can teach each other and show them how to do it, and to try and stop you from becoming a problem for them later on."

"Why do they do that to other people?"

"They use people to train on so that when the opportunity arrives for them to work on someone who is aware they are ready."

"How am I going to be a problem?"

"It is part of your journey, both of you."

"What do you mean?"

"All in good time."

"What other things do they do?"

"They will move things or remove items. They can't all do everything but some can do more than others. It usually takes a few of them to make themselves noticed. "

"So what's the purpose of all this then?"

"The more houses and people they own the more power they have, and the fewer problems they get from others of their kind."

"How do you mean?"

"They will try to take over each other's houses to become more powerful, and be able to control more territory and people. It is like a business only it's not profit they are after it is power."

"What are they going to do with all this power?"

"Whatever they like they think."

"Like what?"

"One of their aims is to control the communication between your world and ours"

"Will they achieve it?"

"No we monitor things and if they get too big we split them up or destroy their empire."

"What happens then?"

"They usually start again if they are stubborn, some will have had enough and come home."

"Why don't you stop them?"

"It is their choice and they still have free will."

"Are they nasty before they died?"

"Some are, there are others who have been down trodden through life and find they have the ability, to either affect people on the earth or control those who are lost. There are those, both men and women, who maybe were treated badly by the opposite sex, who want revenge, and will prey on men or women on the earth plane the gain satisfaction. Unfortunately they are never satisfied and they go on and on seeking revenge."

"How can you allow this to go on, preying on the innocent like that?"

"How do you know it is not part of those people's lessons?"

"They will stop when they finally get fed up or bored and then they will change their ways."

"What happens to them then?"

"They will finish their journey and return to heaven."

"Just like that?"

"Yes, we do not judge as we have not experienced what they have, and cannot then condemn them for something we might ourselves have done had we been in their place."

"Does that mean everyone eventually ends up in heaven?"

"Yes it is all part of the journey, it may not be planned but the experience is invaluable, how else can we empathise with those who are suffering if we have not had the same type of experience."

"So all of our houses are inhabited by bad spirits it just depends on whether we are aware as to whether they get through to us then?"

"No, there are many houses that we inhabit also."

"What do you use them for?"

"So that we can help lost souls to acclimatise themselves with the spirit world, we wean them away from the earth. There are those who have believed they are to be met by their god and when this doesn't happen it can lead to confusion and a feeling of being rejected. It can take us quite a while to convince them that religion is manmade and not the true nature of spirit. These are just some of the things we do, there are many more where the use of a house is beneficial to our work."

"So why don't you take over more houses?"

"We do, but when someone becomes very powerful they will sometimes try to take our houses away."

"Do they succeed?"

"Sometimes if we are feel that is going to be beneficial to our long term plans for that property we let them think we have been caught unawares."

"Do you take them back again?"

"Sometimes what they are doing in the house is beneficial to us so we just monitor them to make sure things don't get out of hand. Many of the houses we inhabit will be used as sanctuaries, so that we can keep people safe while they are coming to terms with what has happened to them."

"It seems like a war is going on, don't the good guys always win cause if they don't we are in deep trouble."

"We always win in the end but we must always consider free will. There is no time here so it doesn't matter how long it takes. We make use of the situation to teach each other and to learn, because then we also progress."

"It doesn't seem to be anything like the heaven we are taught about."

"We have not been talking about heaven that is totally different."

"How?"

"The bad spirits are not in heaven it is all around the earth plane where all that happens."

"Do they ever go to heaven and then leave?"

"Yes some find it less exciting than they would like and go in search of something else."

"If they leave and don't find what they are looking for can they go back to heaven?"

"Yes they are free to go where they want as long as they don't disrupt our work."

"Is it just those who first arrive and don't find what they are seeking in heaven?"

"No there are those who have been in heaven a long time who may choose to try another path, there is nothing to stop them as they have free will."

"Ok, we had better leave it there as it is getting late, thank you for coming and talking to us."

"God bless." Richard said and stepped back.

We chatted a bit about what had been said and we thought it was bad enough here, and now we find it is no better over there, at least not if you get lost. I had managed to ask one of our questions, but even so we were getting to understand a bit more about why we were being attacked and how to deal with it. We thought this business about sensing who was there and when, was a bit like catching smoke in your hand but we would try. We had nowhere else to go and ask, it seemed from what Arthur had said there either weren't any mediums dealing with problems in houses, or he didn't know of them. I reckoned there must be others with problems like ours since there was such a lot of houses with bad spirits in them, I couldn't see how it would be just us. I guess we were fortunate that we were able to communicate with our guides.

Chapter 13

For the next few days I was busy putting central heating in and didn't have time to sit and talk to Jan's guides. After I had installed all the radiators and pipes we got an electrician to come and wire it up and sort out the boiler. When we switched it on it was great, you can imagine, we hadn't had any central heating for two years and it was getting into winter now. We had two shelties and they had grown really thick coats the previous years to keep warm. The heating had been going fine for about a month when all of a sudden it stopped, I couldn't work out what was wrong so I called the electrician. He came and said what had I done with the heating controller, I said nothing, and he said some of the wires had fused together and we would need a new one. So we had a new one put in and after a month that one went as well. I was getting a bit annoyed at this and called another electrician who came and on checking said the same thing. I asked if it had been wired correctly and he said it wouldn't work if it wasn't. He said maybe we should try a different controller, so I said ok, and he put a different type in and it worked fine. During this time we continued to get to know our guides through chatting to Jan's guides and trying to sense them. What with Christmas and everything we didn't have a lot of time to think about our development we just practiced when we had a spare half hour.

The next time we wanted to talk to Richard I put down a question about the heating controller and when I asked the question this is what he said.

"Your heating controller works on energy and spirit is energy also, so it is easy for someone in spirit to interfere with your energy. When they tried they got it wrong as more than one was trying to disrupt it and they overdid it and caused it to fuse."

"That could have been dangerous we might have had a fire."

"No we were watching and would have prevented that from happening."

"Why didn't you stop them?"

"It is up to you we cannot interfere, you must protect your property."

"How come it was so easy for them?"

"It wasn't it took them a month of your time continually working on it. It was easier the second time but you have gained more strength and you slowed them down a lot. When you changed the controller to a different type they gave up, they thought you knew it was them and you were monitoring the situation. All's well that ends well."

"So they can interfere with electricity what else can they do?"

"They can do anything they can think of but they first need to learn how, and that is what stops them most of the time because they are lazy. They will not spend the time learning they just trade someone for the ability they are looking for. But what they wanted in this case they couldn't find."

I didn't know whether too believe Richard or not but there didn't appear to be any other explanation.

"How often does that sort of thing happen?"

"It is very rare."

"Can it happen to anyone?"

"We don't allow anything to happen without a purpose"

"What was the purpose here then?"

"You have to understand their capabilities so you can deal with situations when you are working."

"Are you saying you only allow things to happen if they are following your plan?"

"Most of the time, the other times when things happen that are not to plan it's when you exercise your free will."

"Ok we will have to call it a night now it's getting late, god bless."

Richard said. "God bless" and stepped back.

The following night Clair woke up screaming you would have thought her leg was being cut off. We both rushed up to her bedroom to see what the problem was. She was pointing at a glass of water she had taken to bed with her in case she got thirsty during the night. The water was red, we thought she had cut herself but could find nothing wrong. We asked what had happened when we calmed her down, and she said she went to have a drink and saw the water was red. Well because of the problems she had been having, we usually left her light on until we went to bed so we knew she would have seen or heard someone if they had come in. Darren was standing at her door; he had been woken by her scream and come to see what was wrong. The look on his face told us it wasn't him playing a joke which we thought at first. While Jan comforted Clair and I talked to Darren I threw the water away in the bathroom and got her some more. The water from the tap was fine so we couldn't explain it. We couldn't tell the kids what had happened, or even make something up to comfort them they were too old, and anyway we didn't want to lie to them; we just said we didn't know what had happened. Clair asked if maybe her guide had made her water red so that it would taste of strawberries, we both said they wouldn't do anything to scare you. We got them both back to bed and after a while went down stairs. We were puzzled as to what might have happened, there didn't seem to be any plausible explanation if neither of the kids had done it. We couldn't even work out how the water had been turned red like that. Although we were eager to talk to Jan's guides in case they had an answer, it was getting late and we decided to sleep on it and think about it in the light of day.

The next day passed and we were none the wiser Clair wouldn't play in her room she was too frightened. We told her that she would come to no harm it was just some coloured water, and was she sure she hadn't used paint or dipped one of her felt tips in her glass without thinking. I know we were clutching at straws but we couldn't think what could have caused the water to turn red. She said, no she hadn't been drawing, so I said well I've got some work to do in your room so why don't you come and play while I am working. I thought we needed to let her see that nothing was going to happen to her, if I could show her there was nothing to be afraid of she would settle down again. Clair said okay but only if you stay with me, I said okay. I didn't think anything was going to happen, well I hoped not. Richard had said I was getting stronger and was starting to protect my territory, I hoped I was strong enough. We went upstairs and nothing happened and Clair seemed to settle after a while, she got involved with her drawing. I went down stairs to get a tool that I needed and when I looked round she was right there following. I said I am only going to get a screwdriver I will be straight back, Clair said I'll come and help you, I said ok. This was going to be a bigger problem than I thought later on when it was time for her to go to bed. While the kids were watching television Jan and I discussed the best way to go about the potential problem of Clair being too frightened to go to bed. We didn't have any answers so decided to wait and see what happened. As it was a Friday night we figured we would let them both stay up later in the hopes they would be too tired to care about what had happened. This meant we couldn't talk to Jan's guides to see if we could get an answer from them. Well as it happened Darren asked Clair if she wanted to sleep in his room on his buddy bed, Clair said yes and they settled ok, problem averted for the time being. The next day being Saturday we went shopping and then took the dogs out for a run. We had decided to keep the kids occupied so that they wouldn't dwell on things. Later that day Clair asked if Jan would make some cakes and could she help. Jan said ok and they got on with it while Darren helped me. After a little while Jan came to me and said her red food dye had gone and then it all fell into place. Jan sat down with Clair and asked her if she had taken it, and if she had put it in her water. I sat down with Darren and asked him if he had. We told them they were not in trouble we just wanted the truth. They both said they hadn't done it and remembering how frightened they had been we were inclined to believe them.

That night we thought we might get an answer to our question about the red food dye. We had looked to the earthly possible reasons as to what had happened and couldn't get an answer, so we would ask one of Jan's guides if they could give us the answer.

I gave Jan healing after the kids had settled down Clair was in Darren's room again, while I was giving healing I noticed I was swaying a bit. It wasn't uncomfortable so I carried on and tried to sense who was there. I managed to recognise it was a lady but couldn't get any more information. Richard came through and I managed to recognise him and said hello, he greeted me and I then asked him.

"Is there a woman with me?"

"Yes what else have you picked up?"

"Nothing, except I could feel a swaying of my hips."

"Yes that's right, anything else?"

"Only that she is smaller than me."

I thought this was a guess.

"That's right how old is she?"

"Do you mean when she was here or how old is she showing herself?"

"How old is she showing herself?"

Well I didn't know but thought I would guess as it seemed to work before so.

 "About 30 I think she is a coloured lady."

"That's right."

Good I thought I am starting to get the hang of this until he said,

"What is she wearing?"

I didn't have a clue and said so, to which Richard replied.

"Just keep practicing you are doing well."

I thought great I am starting to move forward then Jan came back. I said "What's wrong?"

"Nothing Richard just disappeared."

"Why?"

"I don't know."

So we decided to try again and this time someone else was there, I worked out it was a man and he didn't feel wrong to me so I said.

"Hello"

"Good evening."

"Who are you?"

"I am a guide to my medium."

"Are you, well we will have to see." I said.

"What should we call you?"

"Samuel."

"Is that your real name?"

"No it is difficult to pronounce my name."

"Where do you come from?"

"Greece."

"What did you do when you were alive?"

"I was a philosopher and I used to teach."

"How long ago was that?"

"About 3 thousand of your years."

"How are you going to work with your medium?"

"I specialize in healing and have worked with my medium for many of your years and I will help with protection."

"Protection against what, as I understand it we have to learn to protect ourselves? "

"Yes, but when you get something you can't handle, we deal with the surplus. This of course will only be until you are both competent enough to deal with things yourselves."

"What about the food dye, did it have anything to do with spirit?"

"Yes they removed the colouring from the cupboard after your daughter had gone to sleep, and poured some into the water."

"Where is the bottle?"

"They discarded it elsewhere."

"What do you mean?"

"They removed it completely from your surroundings and left it somewhere else so that you would not be able to find it. This way they managed to cause more worry."

"How did they do that?"

"They dematerialised it and allowed it to appear elsewhere."

"Can they do that with anything?"

"Most of the time only small things."

"Oh like my screwdriver?"

"Yes. As you get stronger and are more able to protect yourselves it will become more difficult for them. It took quite a few of them to achieve it." It seemed a plausible answer so I left it there.

"How come Richard went away suddenly?"

"He didn't he just stepped back to allow me to come forward. We are giving you a few of us to recognise so that you get the practice. You are going to need to recognise us immediately as time goes on, so we thought we would start as we mean to go on."

"I have already got two now three of your medium's guides to recognise as well as three of my own; don't you think you're going a bit fast?"

"How many of your friends would you recognise if you walked into a room where they were gathered?"

"All of them."

"That's how it needs to be with us, remember we are also your friends it's just that you have forgotten us because we are not on the earth plane with you."

"It's not going to be easy, what you're saying is we need to sense you like we can see each other."

"Don't worry it will become second nature to you, you will just know when and who is there."

"Well if you say so."

I wasn't convinced. He was asking us to learn how to see again, but in a different way.

It was some time later when I finally realised what he meant by knowing as I will explain then. I thanked Samuel for coming, after I had got his reassurance that they would not be throwing any more guides at us for a while and he stepped back.

Jan and I talked about what we had heard and decided that short of a definitive answer about the red dye we would go along with it for now. We talked about this business of just knowing when and who was there. We came to the conclusion that Jan would get there first, as she had her guides coming through her and I only had them coming near me.

The following day we didn't say anything to the kids as we thought the less we made of what had happened, the sooner they would get over it. This proved to be the right thing to do as Clair said that night she was going to sleep in her room tonight.

Chapter 14

When the kids had settled down we talked about some of what we had been told and Jan said why don't I try to trance, then I would get to feel my guides better. I said ok I would give it a try and so she gave me healing and I meditated. After about five minutes I said,

"I can't feel anything."

"It isn't time yet."

I looked up and said.

"How do you know that?"

"All the guides have discussed it with each other and now is not the time your job is to oversee my medium for the time being."

This surprised me and I said, "Who is that?"

"It's Richard."

"Will you step back so that I can talk to Jan?" Which he did.

I asked her what had happened and she said,

"He came through quite strongly to tell us."

"But you were standing up."

"Well it was Richard and it wasn't a problem."

I asked her to sit down and sat opposite and then said,

"Can you ask Richard to come back?"

She got Richard back and I watched very carefully to see if I could see any difference in her posture or just anything. I saw a slight lifting of the shoulders and thought I will make a mental note of that and see if it happens next time.

"Why did you come through when I wasn't concentrating and watching, I thought I was to double check everything?"

"We wanted to show you that there are other times when we can trance our medium, like while she is standing as you have only seen it happen when someone is sitting."

"Ok so it appears I am to work on this side of the fence and learn how to look after Jan while she is in trance. Even if I am not concentrating I still need to know when you are there."

"Don't you think you have enough to learn at the moment without adding more? When the time is right you will bring your guides through. You already think there is too much to learn at the same time why would you make your task harder. Everything will happen at the right time you must trust us to teach you in the right way."

"Ok, you seem to have done a good job so far and by answering our questions we have got a greater understanding of things. Can you tell me about trance, I have heard that when mediums trance they speak in funny voices. When Arthur and Brian went into trance they spoke in Pidgin English, as if they didn't know the language very well.

"It depends on what people believe but let me ask you, how long does it take for you to learn a language."

"I don't know, when I was at school I started to learn French a couple of lessons a week and it took ages just to learn to say a sentence."

"Yes you spent a couple hours a week but as we don't require sleep and I have had 4 thousand years don't you think we have a better chance of learning your language?"

"Yes, but do you have to learn every language?"

"No think of it like this a bucket is a bucket it's just the word that is different in other languages. You will also know that at least a year, and sometimes more before you start on your earthly journey, we know which place you will be born. With 24 hours a day it doesn't take us guides long to learn the language you are going to be using."

"So when Brian and Arthur went into trance it wasn't their guides then?"

"That is correct."

"Who was it then some impostor?"

"Yes that's why you were feeling uneasy in their company."

"What about Penny she spoke in proper English?"

"Yes because that was her guide and she didn't have preconceived ideas about how guides spoke."

"Does that mean it could be your guide but they might still speak in Pidgin English if that's how you expected them to?"

"Yes."

"So now I see why it's important to tune in to who is there rather than just listening to what they are saying. What about when Arthur and Brian went into trance at the same time that was rubbish wasn't it?"

"There was no point in it, do you think if they were genuine they couldn't communicate with each other while in spirit, they were just wasting your time. You know the most precious thing you can give us is time; you only have so much, where we have eternity. When impostors take time up in your circle they are denying you the opportunity to develop and work with us. We communicate with each other, otherwise how could we discuss the next phase of your development."

"Do you discuss it with my guides as well?"

"We all discuss things together and if one does not agree then it doesn't happen."

"Why do you discuss things with my guides don't they know what my pathway is?"

"Of course they do but when you are working with others then we all work together also."

"So it's not a majority that decides then."

"No we all have to agree. Although you each have your own guides we work together for the benefit of both of you."

"Does that mean you can trance either of us?"

"If there is a need and you are competent then yes but not usually. Each person's guides will work with their medium and accede to their requests for healing and such when asked. But we work together when you are so that we can control your environment for the best results."

"Do you know what is going to happen then?"

"We know what is planned and providing you do as expected things will go to plan."

"It must be a little difficult then as we are all over the place; do you know what questions I am going to ask?"

"Your guides do but unless it is a question which is not going to get an answer we just decide who is going to be in the firing line."

"Am I that demanding?"

"No if you don't ask how will you learn it is good to be inquisitive."

"Can one of the other guides come and speak to us?"

"Are you getting fed up of me?"

"No it was just so I can practice recognising them."

"I know I was having a joke, we do still have a sense of humour you know it's not all serious. Although the way some interact with the spirit world you would think so."

"What do you mean?"

"Sometimes we are treated as gods and sometimes we are put on a pedestal metaphorically."

"Why would people do that you're no different than us except for being dead."

"We are not dead we are in our natural state."

"You know what I mean, from what we have been told we are the same as you only we have a body for the time being."

"Yes we are all good friends and have been for many of your years in the spirit world."

"Talking about the spirit world can you tell me where it is?"

"It is a faster vibration that is everywhere; it coexists with your world which vibrates at a slower rate so the two worlds can occupy the same space"

"Does that mean you only exist around the earth or do you mean all through the universe?"

"The spirit world is everywhere not just around the earth. The vibration you are on exists all through the universe the same as ours does."

"So does that mean you also have spirits in the physical on other planets?"

"Why not?"

"Are there?"

"We will not tell you something that cannot be proven by yourselves, as this could make you an object of ridicule by others, whose minds are not open to other possibilities."

"Well do you or not?"

"I have given you my answer, your credibility is important to us as well as you. If you lose it by saying things that cannot be proven then people will start to doubt you."

"What is spirit world like?"

"That will have to keep for another time my medium is getting tired so I will step back and bid you god bless and good night."

"Thank you god bless," Jan opened her eyes.

"Well that was interesting what did you think?"

"It would have been useful to know more about how the bad spirits do things so that we can stop them a bit quicker."

"Yes but I am getting the idea that I am not controlling the questions I am being led along."

"Yes I was getting that idea too."

"Maybe they have a certain way of teaching and if we ask questions out of turn we won't understand the answers."

"Maybe, you know I am starting to feel Richard's thoughts before he answers you."

"How do you mean?"

"Well, it's as though I know what he is going to say, well at least some of it."

"I wonder if he knows."

"He does now he is still listening."

"So what was he thinking when I asked about other planets?"

"Absolutely nothing, as far as I could tell."

"I reckon he knew you were picking up his thoughts."

"Probably."

Jan decided to have a cup of tea and then call it a night. It was then I realised we hadn't heard from Clair, which meant maybe she was ok now. We talked a little more about where the spirit world was and decided we wouldn't try to get too scientific about it. It would only make things more difficult and we had enough to sort out. We might learn more about it next time.

Chapter 15

Over the next few days we were busy what with work and me teaching gymnastics, and Jan running Clair backwards and forwards to ballet and gymnastics, and renovating the house. There was still a lot to do especially as Jan had decided while I was at work to strip the wallpaper in the lower hall. When I got home she had taken all the plaster off as well. I said,

"What happened, what have you done?"

"I thought I would get started on the wallpaper and as I pulled some off the plaster came with it. When I pulled the next bit off it was all crumbly so I decided to take it all off."

Well I had to laugh when I imagined her with a club hammer and a bolster chisel hacking away at the wall. What with one thing and another we never got round to speaking to our guides for the rest of that week, I was busy rendering the hallway ready to plaster it again.

I didn't know how to plaster so I had a chat with Arthur and he said you supply the materials and beer, and Brian and I will come over on Saturday and show you how to do it. He then told me what materials to get. I said ok you're on and that's what we did. They came round about eleven and Penny came too they all had a laugh when I told them what Jan had done and then we got stuck in, Brian mixed the plaster and Arthur flattened out my rendering by scraping off the high bits. I put a bonding all over the walls after he said he was satisfied with the surface, he also told me how to get it flat next time. Arthur did the plastering. It took about 4 hours and we then sat and had a few beers and a chat.

We talked about how we were getting on with spirit but Jan and I kept it low key we didn't want any arguments, we knew that Arthur had strong views on how things were. I asked,
"Do you know anything about things disappearing; you know being moved by spirit?"
"Yes they are called apports, I have heard about a physical circle that does it all the time."
Jan said, "What's a physical circle?"
"It's where you sit in a circle and spirit move things or talk to you out of thin air."
I said, "Do you have to be clairaudient to hear?"
"No some of the best physical mediums used to get ectoplasm which would build up into people who you could see and sometimes they talked. You don't need to be clairvoyant either everyone could see and hear them. The apports could be all sorts of things from drops of water and flowers to bits of furniture and other things like maybe a stone or a feather."
I said, "Where do they come from?"
"I don't know maybe someone's garden or house."
"Isn't that stealing or do they put it back?"
"No it stays there until you pick it up and move it."
"Oh great so now not only do we have to worry about being burgled but we could have spirit removing things as well." I said jokingly.
"It doesn't happen very often and most things you wouldn't miss anyway like a flower or a stone."

"Why do they do it?"

"To prove they are there."

"What's this about ectoplasm then how does that work?"

"Ectoplasm is spirit energy that comes out of the mediums mouth or nose, or even their ears when they are in deep trance. Spirit can sometimes mould it into a likeness of someone's relative."

Jan said, "What happens to it when they have finished?"

"It goes back into the mediums body before they come out of trance."

I said. "What is deep trance, is it what you do?"

"No I do light trance mostly. I go deep sometimes and when I do I can't hear what's being said. That's not all they do in physical circles they also levitate. You know when we did table tilting at Kay's well the way spirit make the table move is they make ectoplasmic rods which are put under each side of the table and when they answer they just move the rods. They get the energy from the sitters at the table but you can't see the rods because they are spirit energy. They are usually green."

I said, "How do you know if you can't see them?"

"Some people have, there was one man around 1869 D.D. Home who levitated and walked out of a second floor window and back in the next one"

"He had a lot of trust."

"He was in deep trance and didn't know till afterwards. Sometimes they tie two slates together and tie the mediums hands to the chair, where everyone can see them, then when the medium comes back they untie the slates and someone has written on the inside of them while they were tied together."

"What was the point in that?"

91

"Just experimenting to see what could be done. They also do transfiguring which is when some ones face appears on top of the mediums. For all of this they sit in what is called a cabinet."

"What's that?" I said.

"They have a chair which is put in a box basically standing on one end with the front open; this is so spirit can build up energy around the medium and it can't escape, it is also so the medium can't cheat."

"Why would they want to cheat and how could they?"

"They sit in a darkened room sometimes with a red light and sometimes in the dark. When it's dark it has been known for the medium to have an accomplice who is hidden behind them, who writes on the slate or swaps them for another pair that's already prepared beforehand. With the voices they have been caught using a pipe and talking down it. If you point a pipe in the air it can sound like the voice is coming from thin air. With the ectoplasm they have used muslin cloth to pretend they have produced it from their body. You have to remember that with a small red light you can't see too well."

I said, "Why do they cheat?"

"If they get famous people pay a lot of money to sit with them. There are some genuine mediums though."

We discussed other things for a while and then they went home, we looked at each other, Jan said,

"How do you know the difference between a physical circle and one that isn't or are they all the same?"

"I don't know we will have to ask."

92

The next day being Sunday we went out for the day and took the dogs for a long walk, when we got back I looked up at the window to our bedroom on the top floor and saw a face looking out. When I told Jan she looked but couldn't see anything. We didn't say much because we didn't want to frighten the kids but I went upstairs to see if everything was alright. I have no idea what I expected to find but there was no-one there and everything seemed ok.

We sorted the kids out and when we were all fed and watered, settled down for the evening, when the kids went to bed we decided to have a chat with one of Jan's guides

I thought I would try sitting opposite Jan and not do healing this time. I wanted to check whether I had been right last time about the lifting of the shoulders. When her guide came through it wasn't Richard, the shoulders never moved so I asked.

"Who is that?"

"Who do you think?"

"I don't know."

I asked Jan to come back.

"Who was that?"

"I don't know but it wasn't Samuel or Sheena."

"How do you know?"

"Well although they feel different they also feel similar, I suppose it's like right and wrong. When I got that last man through who wasn't right he felt kind of different like this one we just chucked out."

"So you are beginning to tell the difference at least you can chuck them out then if it's not right."

"Yes but if I throw them out straight away how will you learn?"

"Good point maybe if I try and sense who it is, if I get it wrong and they aren't a guide then you chuck them out. If it is a guide then stay in trance and I will try to figure out who it is."

"Ok let's give it a try."

So we tried again and this time it still wasn't Richard but I knew it was a man.

"Hello Samuel."

"Good evening."

"How are you?"

"I'm fine and how are you?"

"I'm ok, getting rid of the aches and pains again but it's taken longer this time."

"Well we have allowed the next two levels in so you have done well."

"We were talking to Arthur last night and he was talking about deep trance mediums and physical circles".

"Yes we heard."

"Why do mediums sit in a circle?"

"Because there is no break in a circle and it is easier to protect you, and so that you can see each other and learn from each other's lessons."

"So the idea is each person who sits will get a different lesson from all the others and we are to learn from their mistakes?"

"They are not mistakes just the next lesson."

94

"How do we know when we have learnt a lesson?"

"When you don't get it again. One of the things about a circle is that the circle leader can if they are good at their job, understand the lessons and explain it to the sitter to make sure they realise what has happened. In this way it is highlighted for all to understand. We will however throw an old lesson in now and again just to make sure you haven't forgotten."

"What is the difference between a physical circle and any other kind or are they all the same?"

"No they are not the same, a physical circle takes a long time to produce anything, and up until now they have used what you call deep trance mediums. It is for physical phenomena as opposed to a normal circle which is for mental mediumship. The physical circle needs dedicated sitters who will sit and give their time to develop one person."

"Why do people want physical phenomena?"

"Because there can be no doubt about what has happened when it is done properly and it is proof of something more than the earthly. You must remember when all this became popular most of the people were not as educated as they are today. They didn't have the schooling you have now.

Your mind is trained better and you are more able to think for yourselves. So the more obvious it was the more people didn't have to think for themselves."

"Isn't that taking away their free will?"

"Yes it is "

"Considering how important you say free will is why do you do it?"

"We don't but we allowed it to happen to try and wake people up to other possibilities."

"So it wasn't the good guys then?"

"Not then but later we worked with those who were dedicated to try and teach you about spirit."

"Why did you start doing it if it takes away free will?"

"We only work with mediums that have been mental mediums and have had all the proof they need. They are then looking to try other things and they have to be dedicated and sit with others of like mind."

"Why?"

"It takes a long time for anything to happen."

"Why is that?"

"We want to make sure there is a good balance of dedicated people sitting and they all want the same thing. It can also take a long time for the mediums guides to get close enough to work and the medium to allow them to."

"What is the difference between what your medium is doing, and deep trance and will we be doing deep trance?"

"What my medium is doing is what we call light trance, this is when we come and sit with you, and although we take over the workings of the body you are still aware of what's going on and what is said. My medium also has complete control over how long I stay and can remove me anytime she wants to. With a deep trance medium they relinquish everything to those who come through them. They are not aware of what is going on and can only come back when the spirit allows them to."

"What happens to them?"

"Some just step aside mentally and they are taken somewhere. They are not conscious of the time that

96

passes and what goes on. When they come back they are told what happened."

"Why don't they want to be aware of what's going on?"

"Because if they don't know, then they know it wasn't them, they don't have to argue with themselves about what was said."

"So what is the purpose of light trance then apart from being able to talk directly with our guides and knowing what is being said?"

"There are many reasons for light trance apart from the teaching aspect and you will become aware of other uses in good time."

"Can anyone sit in a deep trance circle?"

"No because once a circle of that type has settled, by others sitting it can unbalance the circle."

"What's the point in it then if no-one outside the circle can experience what they do?"

"They do invite people in to see what is going on but only after they have been sitting for a while and have bonded. Sometimes they will invite maybe one or two people at a time, they have to be trusted and of the right mind."

"So why do spirit do physical circles then, you don't usually do things that cannot be denied, you've said in the past that there has to be free will. If you showed us something that can't be denied you are taking away our free will."

"As I said the mediums we work with already used their free will to decide to sit in a physical circle. If they are going to sit then we will sit with them to control what is happening."

"So you are stopping the bad spirits from misleading people?"

"Yes."

"How will the mediums know when it's not their guide, if they don't know what's happening?"

"That's why we are working with experienced mediums; there is less chance of it going wrong."

"Does it go wrong very often?"

"It depends on the medium and their beliefs. A lot of them study the old mediums and try to work in the same way. They are stuck with the old ways."

"Like you said then we have to think outside the box, it doesn't have to be done like they used to do, we can do it in other ways?"

"Yes but we still have to be careful, there are others that will try to disrupt things, these circles can be an easier target for them."

"You watch these physical circles closely then?"

"We monitor these circles very closely and allow the things that go on to happen; it is a way of awakening your minds to spirit. Over the last hundred years we have been working more towards mental mediumship, but people needed a kick start and physical phenomena was a way of showing there was something else other than the physical. There have been many mediums over the years but your institutions have either burnt them or in more recent years imprisoned them. Not surprisingly they hide their abilities so they are not persecuted, but now things are changing and things are a little more open. In fact they are still putting some in prison; it is believed that if you talk or work with us you are working with the devil."

"You mean the church don't you?"

"Yes."

"Who is the little girl that we keep seeing upstairs?"

"She is one of many who have been put in the house to cause problems for you."

"Is she one of the ones who are causing me pains?"

"Yes"

"She is only young why would she do that?"

"She is being made to do it, you remember you have been told about people being forced to do things to people well she is one of them."

"So if you know where she is why don't you rescue her and the others?"

"Remember all the while she does as she is told she will come to no harm and you are learning."

"So you are making use of the situation to teach us?"

"Yes, we will not cause you discomfort, but we can allow others to help teach you, in this way you will learn how to help these lost spirits."

"How can we do that when you don't?"

"One of the uses of light trance is to bring these people through and help them to understand what has happened to them."

"Why do you need us to do that? Why can't you talk to them?"

"Because it can take us nine or so of your months to gently persuade them to accept what has happened, even though they are able to affect you they don't understand much else. But when you bring them through the first thing they feel is the weight of your body and subconsciously they realise something is different.

Because of this it is easier for you to take them on as you have that small but very important advantage over us. They are also using their eyes to see and because they can see you they are more able to associate with you. If they aren't using their senses they will not see us."

"So that's another use of light trance then?"

"Yes."

"So why don't we help them?"

"You are not ready yet all in good time."

"How long is it going to take before we can help them and stop things going on in the house?"

"You will know when you are ready, don't be impatient it will happen soon enough. Then you will be on a different journey."

"Ok, but it is frustrating knowing they are there and the kids are being bothered and not being able to do anything."

"When you help them you want to do it right don't you?"

"Of course we do."

"Then be patient and learn."

"Can't we just get rid of the bad spirits?"

"You are not ready yet."

"We could do it with your help couldn't we? Then the children wouldn't be in fear."

"Yes you could but you have a saying better the devil you know than the devil you don't. In this sort of situation it is always good to be aware of the enemy, and then you know their limitations and can deal with them when it suits you."

"Thank you for talking to us we have to go now goodnight and god bless."

"God bless."

Jan and I discussed what had been said and Jan said.
"There must be lots of people in the same situation as
that little girl; I can see what Samuel was saying. If we
don't get it right we could cause them more upset.
Imagine being told you are in the wrong place and
sending them to the light only for them to be caught
again because we did it wrong."
"Yes we really must try to learn more so that we can
help, not only those in spirit but also people who live in
the properties that are being used for that sort of thing.
What did you think of what he said about deep trance?"

"Well it seems a bit limited to me as only the few can
experience physical phenomena, I don't think I would
want to disappear and not know what's going on. You
would never remember everything that is said, so I would
not learn so much. It seems to me these people that do
deep trance haven't the confidence to know when it's
them or when it's someone else. They must get mundane
information, but then again if they think they can't ask
questions they wouldn't. The guides would only give
them teachings like Arthur's guides do, and we can see
where that has got them."
"Yes, I suppose if you expect certain things that's what
you'll get, remember what Richard said be careful what
you wish for cause that's all you will get."
"Yes I know what you mean, it's like restricting yourself
to what you already know, how can you learn like that."

We talked a bit longer and decided that was enough for tonight, there was a lot of information to absorb, and we both knew there were going to be many more questions.

Chapter 16

The next few days were spent pottering about the house getting odd jobs done and thinking about things. I was getting the aches and pains sorted again, but it finally struck me, I was getting them but Jan didn't seem to be, why was that?. I asked Jan if she was getting any unusual aches and she said.

"No it never occurred to me that I would."

"That's interesting, why not? I've been getting them and we are in the same house, and Clair has had aggravation but Darren doesn't seem to be."

"No, we will have to ask about that."

"I would have said if it was just Darren then it's because he's not sensitive, but as you don't either it can't be that. You must be protecting yourselves somehow, we'll have to ask."

We carried on with the chores and when something came to mind we would talk it through. We were storing up lots of questions for the next time we spoke to Jan's guides. I was writing them all down but I knew it was going to take a few sessions to get through them, that's without any other questions coming up as a result of the ones we were going to ask.

We finally had a free evening so I thought I would have a little meditation on my own just to settle myself down ready for later. While I was meditating I heard voices for the first time as clear as anything. There were two people or spirits having a conversation. The only problem was it was in French so I couldn't understand a word. I asked them to speak in English but they took no notice of me. After a minute or two it either stopped, or I just couldn't hear them anymore. I thought maybe if I was going to hear voices that would make things easier. This sensing lark was difficult, anyway I carried on meditating for about 20 minutes and during that time it went very dark. I was sitting in a room by myself and the light was on, so when my eyes were closed I could see a sort of orange through my eyelids where the brightness of the light shone through. Then it went completely black, I couldn't see the light through my eyelids, that's when I first heard the voices. When they went I suppose I disturbed myself because I could see the orange from the light again. When I carried on meditating it went black again and I started getting flashes of a mauve colour drifting in front of my eyes. It was coming from the bottom towards the top of my head before disappearing, then another would come and it was like a succession of mauve shapes just drifting past. I then started seeing pictures of unrelated things which stopped after a while, so I opened my eyes. Now I had more questions it seemed to be never ending.

After tea we sorted the kids out and then sat down to try and get some answers. This time, Jan sat without me giving her healing and asked one of her guides to come through. It was Richard I was certain. I didn't sense him I was relying on the change in posture the shoulders had lifted slightly.

"Good evening Richard."
Nothing was said. I thought maybe I had got it wrong.

"Good evening Samuel."

Nothing again, I thought I am sure it's a man, and then Jan came back. "That isn't one of my guides, it felt wrong but I thought I would give you a chance to see if you could figure it out."

"Well I was so sure it was Richard, because of the change in your posture."

"What do you mean?"

"Well Richard did say there would be a subtle change in the way you sat, which was distinctive to each of your guides and to take notice of the change as backup."

"Did you sense him then?"

"No, I didn't seem to be able to sense anything."

"I wonder why, maybe you were concentrating on what you could see rather than your senses."

"Could be, but it's like I have to turn on a switch but forget to because I don't know where it is."

"Let's try again."

"Ok."

I tried to find a way of tuning in to my senses so that I would know who was there when they came through. Again I noticed the posture change only it was very slight this time, I decided to wait a moment to see if I could sense anything then said.

"Good evening."

"Good evening"

"Is that Richard?"

"Yes."

"Well forgive me if I'm not sure but I will check you out."

"How will you do that?"

"Where do spirits come from?"

Richard smiled. "I cannot answer that."

"Ok then how are spirit born?"

"Very good have you made up your mind yet?"

"Yes good evening Richard."

"Good evening."

"Why couldn't I sense you?"

"You were relying too much on what you could see, and not enough on your senses."

"How do I stop that then?"

"You must try not to concentrate too much on what is in your mind and allow us to influence you and assist you. It's not so easy for us to get through to you if your mind is set."

"So what you are saying is go with the flow?"

"Yes you will get it wrong sometimes but you will be more often right."

"What about the posture of your medium when you come through I saw a change?"

"We are not going to be so obvious anymore as there are those who are trying to copy as you have just found out."

"Why is it so important for them to work with us?"

"They know where you are going and are trying to neutralise you before you become a threat."

"How can they know, I don't, and you said our pathway is kept secret by our guides so how do they know?"

"They have an idea by what type and how many guides you have, but it's only an idea. Enough for them to try and stop you."

"I can't see how we can be a threat to anyone! I can't even tell who's here."

"You are looking at now; they are looking more long term. It is easier to try to stop you now than when you are more able."

"Are they trying to stop us communicating with you?"

"They are trying to stop you working altogether unless it is with them. They can then control what you do."

"How else are they trying to stop us?"

"Well a little while ago you stopped communicating with us to see if it quietened down in the house didn't you?"

"Yes but although it was quite for a while they were still here."

"Yes just to remind you they were around."

"So when we decided to carry on as there was no-one else to deal with the problem they started up again?"

"Yes, really they shot themselves in the foot, if they had left you alone maybe you wouldn't have carried on. They are not very clever really, although some of them think ahead there are those who work for them who don't."

"Ok, so now we are involved we have to get on with it. Can you tell me what happened in my meditation?"

"What do you want to know?"

"Well I heard voices for the first time but they were speaking in French.

It's the first time I have heard voices and when I asked them to speak English they faded away."

"You overheard two of your guides having a conversation."

"But I thought you communicated by thought? "

"Yes we do but we can make ourselves heard if we want to."

"Then what was the point in my overhearing their conversation?"

"You weren't supposed to, what happened was you were trying to tune in and got a frequency that was unexpected they were testing your ability."

"What do you mean unexpected?"

"Imagine your radio it has a tuner so that you can tune to different frequencies, well you were tuning your radio and got a frequency that we didn't think you would get, at least not yet."

"So I am learning to tune in then?"

"Yes but you are in such a hurry."

"Wouldn't you be in my situation? What with all this going on in the house and all the work you say we are going to be doing. I just feel the sooner we get on with it the sooner we will be in control again."

"You are determined but try and be a little patient."

"When it went all dark while I was meditating what happened then?"

"You had managed to still your mind and allow us to communicate with you."

"Is that what the mauve shapes were?"

"No, that was just your mind coasting, had you stayed there a little longer you may have got an impression of something."

"I did, I got some pictures of things but they were unrelated to each other."

"Well there you are then you are moving forward."

"Why is it that you're medium and Darren, don't get the aggravation that Clair and I do?"

"They do get interference but in a different way, Darren doesn't believe in us so like you before you became aware he is not noticing when he gets attacked. While my medium hasn't considered that they will attack her so that in itself is a kind of protection."

"So if I don't believe they can get through to me they can't?"

"It will certainly make it much harder for them."

"I suppose that means if I can convince myself that they can't do anything to me then they won't be able to?"

"Yes that's right."

"Oh great another angle to work out, does that mean instead of trying to defend myself I just concentrate on my belief?"

"No for the time being you will need to do both."

"Why?"

"So that you can build up your strength to protect your property, don't worry it will become automatic after a while."

"Ok I guess. Going back to the little girl in the house, how do you send them to the light?"

"We don't send them to the light we take them."

"Why do you have to take them?"

"There are many false lights in the darkness surrounding the earth; we take them so that we know they have arrived safely."

"Why are there false lights?"

"There are many circles around your world who sit to help these people that are lost, in fact you both sat in one and experienced the results."

"How do you mean?"

"You sat with your friends and asked them to rescue the very girl you have talked about."

"You mean when Arthur asked Brian's guide to send her to the light?"

"Yes, and you can see how that turned out."

"Yes not only is she still here but that means his guide didn't do it properly."

"That wasn't his guide I thought we had discussed that and you understood."

"Well you didn't say he wasn't his guide."

"I gave you enough clues to work it out for yourself."

"I think for the time being you need to spell it out so we don't misunderstand."

"We will bear that in mind."

"Ok so now that we know it wasn't Brian's guide we can assume it wasn't Arthur's guide who was talking to him that time?"

"We told you that."

"Well you told us so much its getting easier but we can't get it right all the time. We are still human and can forget things, especially when it is all new to us."

"Alright when we rescue someone, first they have to understand what has happened to them. You remember we spoke about how it takes a long time for us to gently persuade them we are here, and how it is much quicker for you."

"Yes you said because we can give them the feeling of weight they subconsciously feel a difference."

"Yes but to give them that feeling you must bring them through in light trance. Then you have the opportunity to talk to them, as you draw them nearer to you they will see you and when they come through they are more able to relate to you as they have seen you. Then by talking to them you are able to help them understand what has happened to them. You must never tell them they have died but get them to realise it for themselves."

"Why is that?"

"It can be quite traumatic for them, just think if you were asleep and passed away and someone said you had died how would you feel, thinking you had lost those that you love and maybe would not see them again."

"Yes I see what you mean, so once we have got them to realise what has happened what do we do next?"

"It's a good idea to make sure they aren't in pain or suffering in any way."

"If they are how can we change that?"

"Don't forget the pain belongs to the body, it is only the memory that they are experiencing. The spirit does not feel pain."

"How do we take the pain away and make them believe they don't feel it?"

"Just by saying we will take the pain away, we will then remove any memory of the discomfort they are feeling."

"So that is going to help convince them they have come to the right place for help."

"Once they are comfortable with the idea you can then ask them if they want to go to heaven."

"But why wouldn't they?"

111

"Well they generally do but you have to give them the choice."

"Ok so if they say yes then what?"

"Well then you need to make them aware of the spirit world where they are."

"How do we do that, if we tell them it is going to be difficult to persuade them that what we say is true? After all where have they just been?"

"They have been in the dark, by telling them to open their eyes they will automatically open their senses and be aware of spirit. Because they were looking with their sight rather than their senses they were in effect blind."

"So does that mean once they open their eyes they can see everything?"

"No but then you will show them the light and explain that it is the light from heaven."

"Won't they be in heaven once they can see spirit?"

"No they will see the light at a distance like at the end of a tunnel."

"Oh you mean like when people sometimes die and come back they say they went down a tunnel?"

"Yes once they see the light you can then take them down the tunnel to heaven where they will be met by their loved ones."

"Well if there are false lights how will I know we have got the right one?"

"Because you will feel it and by the time you do this work you will be more sensitive and have less doubt in yourself. When you have taken them to the light and they are happy to stay, you will come back and come out of trance."

"Sounds ok but if we can only trance one at a time how can we both take them to the light?"

"My medium will be in trance and you will follow what is going on with your senses."

"I see why you said we aren't ready yet."

"It will come just be patient."

"Are there many rescue circles that do it that way?"

"No but even those that don't, manage to get people to the right place most of the time, providing they are working with their guides and not impostors. When it goes wrong they don't know about it but the poor souls who were sent certainly do. You will come across some of them when you start working, you will know because they won't believe you at first until you tell them you will take them."

"How will we know when we have got there and that they are safe?"

"You will sense who is waiting for them, by describing those who are waiting before you get there. You will know whether it is right by what they say and what you sense."

"What if they don't want to go to the light?"

"Then you will have to let them go their own way. You will have to explain where they will be going and some of the dangers, but many of them will go to the light."

"What about the bad spirits they won't want to go, will they."

"Some will and some won't those that do will be glad to get away from the persecution they have been suffering. You see many of those who are termed bad are being forced to work as they are. Its only when they see a chance to get away that they will take the plunge to be free. They have often heard others talking of heaven but it's like a rumour, they don't know whether to believe it or not. As it is dark and cold where they are they can't always accept there is something like heaven where it is warm and bright. They often think they must have done something bad, and although they are not in what they expect hell to be like perhaps that is where they belong. They don't realise that everyone is welcome in heaven no matter what they have done."

"What about those people who have committed murder can they go to heaven?"

"Yes of course it's not for anyone to judge them, they are their own judge. If they feel they have done wrong they will want to make amends."

"Do you mean everyone judges themselves?"

"Yes when they get to heaven part of the process of getting acclimatised is to look back over your life with your guides. Partly to see if you achieved your goals and partly to see where you could have done better. No-one can say whether you did something right or wrong apart from yourself. They weren't in your shoes at the time. It's easy to judge when you look on something from a distance but when you're involved you get a totally different perspective."

"So we decide whether we feel we have hurt someone and need to make amends then. How do we make amends?"

"You will decide what you are making amends for, and find an appropriate job to do here in spirit until you feel you have achieved a balance."

"Like what for instance?"

"Well you may decide you will help people to come to terms with their new situation, or you may use some of the experience you have gained to help those who are going through the same situation as you did. Remember if you have not suffered it, how can you empathise with someone who is."

"So just because you have got to heaven it doesn't mean everything is ok then?"

"You will still have to work out any problems you had when you were on the earth, they don't just go away because you have passed over. You still have your mind and your feelings. You will also be dealing with the loss of your loved ones and friends that have been left behind. Much the same as you do when you lose someone you love when they pass."

"So they miss us as much as we miss them even though they can see us and come and visit?"

"Yes of course, they are not able to touch you or interact with you as they did while they were with you. Although they can talk to you, you don't hear them as easily and they can't have a two way conversation with most of you like they did. They also worry about you, and because they have a different view about what is going on around you, they can see what's likely to happen. That's why they try to help you by talking to you whilst you're asleep, when you come to visit the world of spirit. Some get the opportunity to help by giving you a message through a medium but that is not always possible as most of you don't visit mediums. Once they have settled down they then start looking at how they can progress. They may try something they always wanted to do, but didn't have time when they were with you on the earth."

115

"Like what?"

"Travel maybe, learn to play music or study something that interests them. Remember we have a lot of people here that are well known on your world, to speak to them first hand is an opportunity many would not want to pass up if they get the chance."

"Does that mean those that are well known are bothered all the time?"

"No it means if both see an advantage in a conversation which will benefit the other then they will make arrangements to meet."

"I suppose travel is not a problem either, how do you move around?"

"By thought, we just think of where we want to be and we are there."

"What do you do when you're not working?"

"We have our leisure times when we may get involved in a hobby or just sit and chat. We can do anything providing it doesn't interfere or hurt anyone else."

"What about when you want to specialise in something? Like maybe healing or trance. Do you work with someone who can do that? Who will teach you?"

"Yes we all have our goals and we are happy to help someone to learn if we have the ability they seek. We may be apprenticed to a guide or work with healing those who come over who are sick in their minds or body."

"How can you heal a body when you don't have one?"

"It is the perception that some come over with that we are healing; this can be with healing rays or talking to them and helping them to understand. There are those who pass with an overdose of drugs, they are still in the drug influenced state when they arrive, so there is a lot to

116

do to sort them out. Much of the time they think they are hallucinating and we are not real, they think it is the drugs. Then there are the suicides they have the same problem that caused them to commit suicide to deal with. There are many different problems to sort out, these are some of the ways people make amends for their misdemeanours."

"It sounds to me like there is more work to do there than here?"

"No not really there are many of us, not all have problems when they come over."

"So when you talk about being an apprentice to a guide is that what we call helpers?"

"Yes but not all apprentices are with guides it just depends on what they want to learn."

"Ok, well I think that's enough for now time is getting on, thank you and god bless."

"God bless."

Well we certainly found out a bit more about spirit and what happens in the world of spirit. We had a chat about what had been said and then went to bed.

Chapter 17

The next day on my way to work about 5.30 I had an accident. A woman ran out from behind some railings from the other side of a dual carriageway and appeared about ten feet in front of me. She kept running and I thought she had gone past my nearside wing and swerved towards the railing in the hopes that I had missed her. Although I jumped on the brake I had no chance of slowing down much in ten feet. Anyway I tried and I heard a bang on the wing, I thought I had caught her shopping bag which was in her hand behind her. When I looked in the mirror after I had swerved back from the railings I couldn't see her. I pulled across to the inside lane and stopped, I ran back to see where she was and a woman was running the other way towards me. I later found out she had been standing at the bus stop, anyway she crouched down over a bundle of what appeared to be rags in the gutter and did something then stood up. She looked at me but said nothing, as I came closer I saw it was the woman. The woman who had run from the bus stop crouched down again and put her jacket under the woman's head. The car that was following me had stopped and two security guards got out, one was a woman. They came over to me and asked if I was alright, I just looked at them I must have been in a state of shock. The woman security guard took my hand and led me up the road a bit. She said you never stood a chance she came out of nowhere. I said is she going to be alright I thought I had caught her bag. She said we don't know we have called an ambulance which just then arrived along with a police car. The police asked what had happened and the male security guard was telling them. A woman came running up, she was about 50 and shouted who did this. She looked around and then came running up to me and started to hit me in the chest and face shouting what have you done to my sister. I just stood there. The woman security guard pulled her off and the police came and took me to their car and sat me in the back. They left me there with the security guard while they talked to the ambulance men. When they came back the said the lady was dead, well I couldn't speak I just sat there thinking what have I done. The lady security guard kept saying it wasn't your fault you didn't stand a chance. Then the police came back after talking to everyone and measuring the skid marks on the road. They said they would have to take my car to the police station to test it and I would go with them to make a statement. Then I heard them talking to each other and they said I don't know why these people don't use the subway it was only twenty metres from where she crossed.

Later the police took a statement while they had a police mechanic check my car. They said the brakes were fine and there was nothing wrong with it, they said I could go but I would be hearing from them as there was to be an inquest. When I was ready and the police were satisfied I was ok, I left. I carried on to work; there was nothing else to do. (Jan was at work all day and I had another two jobs to do.) I felt I needed to keep occupied otherwise I would just break down. On my way back from London I was feeling pretty miserable when I pulled up at some traffic lights. In front of me was a car with a sticker in the back window. It said preserve wildlife pickle a squirrel. Now I know that's not very funny but it's relevant because it cheered me up a bit.

When I got home Jan was still at work so I just sat around wondering how I was going to tell her. When she came in and got a cup of tea, she asked me what was wrong so I told her. She was very supportive and said after tea we would talk to one of her guides and see what they thought.

When we sat down Jan asked one of her guides to come through I was a bit numb and when the guide came through he said.
"If it's any comfort to you I was there and you did everything you could."
"Who are you?" I said
"I am Elijah." That made me sit up.
"You were there?"
"Yes and if you had swerved anymore you would have hit the railing."
I hadn't told Jan about swerving so it proved my guides were with me all the time.
"Is the lady alright now she is over there?"
"Yes she is fine she knows what happened and does not blame you; she says she was in too much of a hurry to catch the bus, that's why she ran across the road instead of taking the subway."
I hadn't told Jan about the subway either. Elijah said.
"Is there anything you want to ask me?"
"Yes why have you come through Jan, I thought you only came through your own medium?"

"This was a special occasion and we wanted to help you. You may remember we said on rare occasions this could happen."

"Yes I remember and thank you for being so concerned."

"Did you like the squirrel joke?"

"How do you know about that?"

"You were feeling pretty awful so we thought we would cheer you up a bit."

"Well it did thank you."

"I will step back now god bless."

Well that was totally unexpected but I appreciated the support and concern, at least I now knew there was nothing I could have done to avoid what happened, and the lady was ok. It made it a bit easier to come to terms with what had happened but I still had the inquest to deal with.

The next few weeks were worrying as I didn't know what was going to happen at the inquest. It appears that I could be sent to prison if a verdict of manslaughter was returned. This would mean I would lose my business as I was the only one doing the work.

The day finally arrived and when I got there the two security guards were there to give evidence for me. I said they were very kind to give their spare time for me and they said that's ok we wanted to help. The ladies name was Mrs. White and the magistrate returned a verdict of accidental death and said I was free to go. Well you can imagine the relief I felt I telephoned Jan to let her know and then went home.

That night we sorted the kids out and then asked one of Jan's guides to come through.

"Good evening Samuel." I wasn't sure but thought I would give it a try, it turned out I was right, lucky guess I thought.

"Good evening, how are you feeling now?"

"A lot better than I was this morning. I have some questions for you."

"Yes I thought you might."

"Is it just you or Richard that comes through when I have questions?"

"For the time being yes."

"Can all our guides answer our questions?"

"Yes, but it's easier if we stick to a few of us, as we are used to it."

"Does that mean you have answered questions like this before? You know while being in trance."

"Yes but that was a long time ago."

"So you have been a guide before then?"

"Yes I have had that privilege, but we have never had such an inquisitive pair as you."

"So how many times have you been a guide?"

"This is the second time; I have been studying for many years."

"What have you been studying?"

"I had an interest in how the bad spirits work and why, so I have studied them and learnt how to deal with them."

"Has Richard also studied them?"

"Yes and also many of your guides, there are quite a few who are able to deal with them here."

"Well if that's the case why have we had all the problems we have had?"

"Because you also need to learn."

"It seems to me you have an advantage over us. It's like walking around blind, will we ever get it sorted?"

"Yes of course you will, you have already worked very hard when you were here, now you are relearning."

"What do you mean relearning, if we could do it there why can't we still do it here?"

"You can but because you are on the earth plane you have to overcome your lack of sensitivity and allow yourself to blend with your surroundings. This way you will sense everything that is going on around you. It will be difficult, but in time your understanding will come back." "Does that mean that if I can't do it in spirit then I can't do it here?"

"All that you are able to do when you are here you are capable of now. You have just forgotten how, it is by going through the experiences that you remember."

"Does that mean everything we do when we are working spiritually we had to learn to do first when we were in spirit?"

"Yes of course, it is your spirit that has the ability not your body that is just a vehicle to house your spirit while you are there."

"So can we do what our guides can then?"

"You can both do all of what you need for the journey you have undertaken."

"Does that mean clairvoyance and healing as well?"

"Yes healing is where you allow us to pass the healing energy through you and clairvoyance is an awakening of your senses to that which is not obvious to you in your world. You will find that as you both progress it will become second nature to you, as it is when you are here. Of course you will still have the restrictions of the body but you will manage adequately."

"So how do we learn when in spirit, do we have to have been guides to others before we came here?"

"No you can learn here in preparation for your journey, or you may have had an interest anyway. It is just one of the many skills you need for your own progression."

"What are we progressing towards?"

"You are working your way back to the source where you came from."

"Now that's interesting. Where did I come from then?"

"For the purpose of this conversation we will call it the source, it is sometimes referred to as the godhead by some mediums."

"What is the source and where is it?"

"The source is not a place but rather a vibration that we attune our minds to. You see we as you know are not burdened with a body, we are energy and we are able to exist in a communal conscious state together. This may be a little difficult for you but it is the closest I can get to describing it to you. This is where we come from and where we return when we have achieved the necessary enlightenment."

"So you go back to where you started, can you leave again?"

"Yes but it will then be a different journey as we retain the knowledge from our other journey's."

"How do you get there in the first place?"

"I thought that would come up, we are eternal there is no first place. It will be hard for you to conceive but think of it as a circle no beginning and no end."

"Yes it is a bit difficult to get my head round, I suppose it is no different than trying to imagine the size of the universe."

"Good analogy, when we decide we are going to leave the source, we alter our consciousness to become aware of our surroundings on the lower vibration that is the spirit world. This encompasses heaven and earth and all that is in between. Our spirit becomes tainted with the feelings of deceit and mistrust that are in these realms. We then have to work our way through all of this until we have learnt to be unaffected by these feelings. This means we will experience all of the deceit and lies by travelling through an existence where we interact with all that is going on. We will take many journeys through the earth plane so that we can learn, and spend many of your years in the spirit world, both in heaven and surrounding the earth. We have to overcome personal feelings and understand how to allow thoughts and feelings to wash over us and drift away, without it affecting our spirit. During this time we will work for the benefit of all that we come in contact with, and ourselves that we may progress back to the source. We will in the process, learn one or more of the many skills required to assist those we meet on their journey."

"Does that mean you have to learn everything before you can go back to pure spirit?"

"No the most important part of the journey is to become unaffected by negative influences, the only way to

125

overcome these feelings is to experience them and deal with them. Much like you when you need to put aside your feelings about someone so that you can help them. From your own experience you will know that it is not always easy. When we have come to that situation we can then go back to the source but it is a long journey. If you consider the different problems you face then multiply that by humanity then you will get some idea of the task."

"So are you saying you have to get to a stage of not caring about anything before you can go back?"

"No, we will always care, but we will gain the wisdom of knowing when to allow others the opportunity to learn from their experiences, rather than interfere with their journey."

"What about the things you have to learn, what sort of things?"

"We may take an interest in say healing and become an expert in all the different healing rays. During the pursuit of our goals we will gain the wisdom of non-interference, when we have come to the position of master of our soul we can then enter the source."

"Once you have done that what happens then?"

"All the experience we have gained is shared with those already there, which is what encourages us to leave in the first place. To know how to do it is one thing but to experience it first hand is another. Much like being a man, you know what experiences are like to be a man, but how can you know what a women experiences until you have tried it. This is why we have many lives on the earth, to gain the understanding that comes with each circumstance that we experience."

"That makes sense, so as there is no time for you it doesn't matter how many lives you have, or how long it takes?"

"That's right we are there for the experience as are you."

"How important are we to spirit?"

"You are very important, you are our friends."

"No I mean how important is this one life that I have now?"

"It is but one of many, but we still want you to complete your journey, we also learn from your participation. "

"So if our life is cut short through disease or accident it's not that important?"

"All life is important, if that should occur you can always come back again if you want to."

"So we decide whether we come back or not then?"

"Yes of course that is your free will."

"What sort of things have we done while we were in spirit?"

"You have worked in the realms around the earth and are very familiar with what goes on. Otherwise you would not be getting the problems you are experiencing now."

"Is that true of all of our family?"

"Do you mean immediate family or your siblings and parents?"

"I mean your medium, myself and the children."

"You have all been very busy in those realms. Not so much your extended family which is why you never became aware until you had set up your own family unit."

"So what for instance did I do?"

"You were for a long while a policeman."

"A policeman? Why would you need police in spirit?"

"Imagine your world, in your cities you have areas that it is not safe to be in, if you don't come from the area. We also have areas where the bad spirits congregate around your world. They are doing what they do, looking for likely candidates for their houses. It is not safe for spirits who have just come over to be in these areas. So we need spirits to patrol these areas and pick up strays that are lost and make sure they get to a safe place. We then start the process of helping them to understand what has happened to them and where they are. It was your job among others to collect them."

"So although people get lost you have spirits who deliver them to a place of safety?"

"Yes if we can, some will resist because of beliefs or stubbornness, these we have to monitor and when they realise where they are and ask for help, then we go and get them."

"Did I do this on my own?"

"No you will always work with others it is too dangerous for you to work alone. There are cases where they have ganged up on you and sometimes it can be like a war. It is the same when your loved ones communicate through a medium, they are always escorted to the mediums vicinity otherwise they may get caught by the bad spirits."

"So is that why sometimes it takes a while for our loved ones to communicate?"

128

"Partly, but mostly they need to come to terms with their new surroundings and situation. There are those who quickly adapt, they are the more enlightened souls and understand the rules. They are more able to protect themselves when visiting loved ones. You will have noticed when someone communicates through a medium; they often say they have met other members of the family. Sometimes the medium will say there are a lot of your family here. Well that's because they all travel together for safety so that some can pass on advice or just get in touch and give a message. "

"What about them being around us at home to give us comfort or encouragement?"

"They will still travel together until they have arranged a safe passage to and from heaven and you. Remember some houses that you occupy have bad spirits in them. Your guides will arrange safe passage to you and keep your loved ones safe while they are visiting. That's another reason why you have many guides."

"Were pretty high maintenance aren't we."

"All are the same; it gives us the opportunity to progress, everyone has a different set of circumstances that we can learn from. That is why it is a privilege to be asked to be a guide. We get the opportunity to learn under circumstances we otherwise wouldn't get the chance to experience."

"What about people who have been caught do you rescue them or do you have to wait for them to ask?"

"Some will become aware that things aren't right, they may not know what is wrong, just get a sense of things. They will send out a thought and we will collect them when we are working with our mediums for the benefit of people who are experiencing problems with the bad spirits. We are able to move those they have caught to a safer place, where we can look after them, and help them to come to terms with their new reality."

"Is that part of what I did?"

"If you were in the vicinity then you would have helped those who were working in that way."

"Ok well that's given us a lot to think about, it's getting late so we had better stop now god bless."

"God bless and good night." Jan came back and said.

"All of a sudden I am really tired, I was fine while Samuel was here but now I feel completely worn out."

"We have been talking for quite a while, we better get some sleep."

Chapter 18

The following day I was working in a large empty office, no furniture or anything. I was cleaning carpets when I noticed, out of the corner of my eye people walking about at the far end. When I looked up they were gone, so I carried on working and started to see them again. I looked again but they were gone. The next time I saw them I didn't look up I just stayed where I was and took notes on what they were wearing. I did this because I could see some odd outfits and strange hairstyles. One person whom I had realised by now was a spirit was wearing a long off white sort of cloak which came down to the floor. Something like they wore in Greece a long time ago. Another was wearing armour like a roman soldier. There were quite a few spirits standing around but when I walked towards them they disappeared again. So I went to the end of the office where I had seen them which was about 50 yards away and I could sense something around me but wasn't sure what. I knew it was the spirits but couldn't pick out any individuals. I got on with my work while I was thinking about it. I wasn't bothered by them and didn't feel anyone was attacking me so I just ignored them. When I got home I told Jan about it and she said,

"I've been seeing small dark shapes flying through the air out of the corner of my eye and when I turned to look they were gone."

"Have you seen any people?" I asked.

"No just these dark shadows flying through the air."

"I wonder what they are."

"I don't know it looks like we have some more questions to ask, as if you don't have enough" she said and laughed.

I was settling down now after the accident and life was getting back to normal for me. I had overcome my aches and pains and wasn't getting any more, at least at the moment. I had taken on board what Richard had said about not trying to defend myself but to ignore them. As I wasn't responding they don't know whether they are getting through to me or not. It seems to work ok I just have a twinge now and then and if I ignore it, it goes away. We were quite busy for a while what with renovating and work but finally things eased off a bit and we arranged to sit and have another chat with Jan's guides.

This time I thought I would give Jan healing and try to sense when they had come through. I placed my hands on her shoulders and asked my guides to help and protect me. I felt a prickling at the back of my neck and cold all around me. I thought this doesn't feel right so I tried to tune in as I had been told to, to who was with me. I couldn't pick up anything except an uncomfortable feeling so I stopped healing and stepped back.

Jan said,

"What happened there it was like I was in a freezer it didn't feel right?"

"No it didn't, I couldn't tell who was with me but I got a prickly feeling all down the back of my neck."

"That reminds me when that spirit came through and pretended to be one of my guides I got that feeling too."

"Why didn't you tell me? When I go in the dining room I get it too." We weren't using the dining room at the time it was full of building materials and I was using it as a workshop. Jan didn't go in there so she had not felt anything from there.

"Well anyway let's try again," I said.

"Ok are you going to try giving healing again?"

"Yes I want to see if I can sense your guides when they come through."

I started by asking for protection and waiting a moment to see how I felt before I put my hands on Jan's shoulders again. I felt ok so I carried on and tried to sense who was with her. I felt something, it is difficult to describe, suffice to say something was different.

"Good evening Richard."

"Good evening you are getting better."

"Well I knew someone was there but I must admit I guessed it was you."

"Was it a guess or were you using your instincts?"

"Well I suppose I was anyway it worked."

"Yes you will find that when you don't think you will more often be right. You tend to know who it is, but then you allow reason to come in and that is when you get it wrong."

"I see so I just allow myself to believe in my instincts?"

"Just go with the flow it will usually be right."

"Ok, the other day I was working on my own and I saw some spirits at the other end of the office out of the corner of my eye. When I looked at them directly they weren't there, what was that all about?"

"Well because you were concentrating on what you were doing your mind was just ticking over, there were no solid thoughts so it was easy for us to open you up."

"So I wasn't sensing them then?"

"No you were seeing them."

"Oh and what about your medium she has been seeing dark shadows flying across the room."

"Yes they are birds that she sees here in spirit."

"So we are both starting to see things?"

"Yes it is a beginning, you will progress away from seeing to impressions and thought and finally to sensing. You are both doing a combination of all of them at the moment but it will end up as sensing or just knowing."

"What were the spirits doing in the office?"

"Well, they may be passing through or they may be staying there for a time. They may even be some of your guides who had gone along with you."

"But I was on the seventh floor."

"Height isn't a problem for us you know."

"No I suppose not, just didn't think of it like that."

"So all the animals go to heaven as well then?"

"Yes why not, we also have plants, the colours of which are much brighter here."

"Why is that?

"Because there is nothing to taint them, they are affected by the bad vibrations too you know."

"So do all the animals and insects go to heaven?"

"Yes of course we like the beauty of the flowers and the company of animals as well you know."

"How come the animals show themselves to us, if they are in heaven and it's dangerous to leave? "

"The animals roam where they will; your pets are in tune with you so it's no problem for them to come to you."

"What about wild animals like a lion or something? "

"What about them they are here as well?"

"Isn't that a bit dangerous, them roaming around?"

"They all get along together with each other and us, you have to think in a different way when you are thinking of the spirit world."

"How do you mean?"

"They are spirits and have no need for food so they don't attack each other they all live peacefully here."

"Oh yes I see what you mean. Can animals come back as people and vica versa?"

"No, animals although they are spirit's they are not human spirits they have a different level of intelligence. We don't inter mix just live in the same worlds."

"Do animal spirits progress then?"

"Yes in their own way, you will notice with some pets that they are more sensitive to both you and their surroundings. These are usually old spirits."

"There must be a lot of different kinds of spirits then."

"No take a dog for instance they will only ever come back as part of the dog family."

"You mean any of the different breeds?"

"All dogs come from one so they are all the same type of spirit; it is only man that has interbred them with mutations to get different looking dogs. The wolf, fox and coyote are all of the dog family. Similarly cats will only inhabit felines like lions, tigers and the like."

"So horses only come back as donkeys, horses, zebras that sort of animal?"

"Yes fish are fish and insects are insects, birds can be any type of bird marsuples like squirrels, rats, mice and the like are all inhabited by the same type of spirit."

135

"Well I'm not telling the Buddhists."

"Like all religions there isn't a lot of truth in their beliefs of the hereafter."

"On a different note I am starting to overcome the aggravation I have been getting it seems if I ignore them they give up fairly quickly."

"Yes you are beginning to understand how it works but don't get complacent there are other things to learn."

"Ok what about when we hear about people being possessed how does that work?"

"Possession is when a bad spirit takes over the body of a person. They still want a life here or just want to disrupt someone else's."

"How do they get in?"

"They force their way in."

"What about the persons guides?"

"If the person accepts them their guides can do nothing but stand aside and wait."

"Why would anyone accept that type of spirit?"

"As we have said they will pretend to be friendly by giving you what you want until they have got you hooked, and then they move in and take over. There are many circumstances where this can happen. People are sometimes very lonely and anyone that shows any kind of notice will be welcomed. Many of the people are not right in their mind, so they are easier to control."

"What about when you read about people being molested?"

"It's just another type of attention. Take your battered wives they keep going back in the hopes things will get better but they don't. It's the same sort of thing they just want attention no matter how they get it."

"What about these films about true stories like the exorcist? "

"When they make those films they put many different kinds of attacks together for dramatisation. A film with a lot of things going on is more dramatic than if maybe you just get noises or things moved. Usually only one or maybe two things will happen at any one place at one time. As we have said it takes the bad spirit's a lot of time and many of them to make things happen, so it's not as common as people may think."

"But individually, do those things happen?"

"Yes, but most are not talked about, it's not so long ago that people who spoke of these things happening to them were regarded as insane or mentally unstable. There were a lot of mediums who were put in mental institutions because they were hearing voices. It's no wonder people keep quiet about it nowadays, although it is becoming more acceptable."

"Well it's time to call it a day but just one last question before you go, how come your medium feels tired all of a sudden when she comes back?"

"It's because we are using our energy not hers, her body is still two or three hours more tired than when we started, it comes on her as soon as we leave. You are not aware of it because you are feeling it in a gradual way."

"Ok thank you god bless"

"God bless and good night."

Jan came back and said,

"That makes sense we were on the right track about feeling tired then."

"Yes maybe you will get used to it after a while, I see why these deep trance mediums make such a fuss now. I

137

never asked if you would go into deep trance, better ask next time we don't want you going off and I can't get you back when its time."

"No I don't think I want to deep trance I like to know what is going on, especially with all the questions you ask, you would never remember all the answers. It was interesting what Richard was saying about animals progressing I swear I see the dogs looking at something. Maybe they are old souls as they say."

"Yes I've noticed that but didn't think of it that way, maybe they are."

We called it a night and went to bed, a lot more to think about as usual. That night I had a dream about being on a raft on a river drifting with the current, I was in a bad way, I had been beaten up and was badly injured, it was so vivid, and it seemed as if it was real. The next day when I thought about it I seemed to have a faint memory of shooting energy beams from my hands at someone. I just put it down to a nasty dream and thought no more about it. It was a few days before we spoke to spirit again although we had a go at meditating to see what we could get. I felt someone around me but didn't know who it was they were talking to me and telling me about something I can't remember what it was now. Anyway when I had finished my meditation which lasted for about ten minutes I opened my eyes. I asked Jan how she got on, she said,

"I was talking to Richard about why he is with me and how we were going to work together."

"What did he say?"

"He said apart from answering questions and teaching us about spirit, when I am asleep we are helping people who are lost and ask for help. He said we will be doing that in a circle when we are ready, and there will be others who we are teaching working with us."

"That's interesting did you ask him where these other people were going to come from. I don't think Arthur and the others would be happy with us trying to teach them."

"No he said we hadn't met them yet and to be patient, our guides are working to arrange for us to meet the right people when it is time."

"So they can make things happen then?"

"It appears so, at least he said things were being sorted out."

"While I was meditating someone came and started talking to me I could hear them as clear as I can hear you."

"What did they say? "

So I told her, it took me about fifteen minutes to tell her what they said.

"But you only meditated for about ten minutes," Jan said.

"Yes and I had to settle down first I don't see how they could tell me all that in less time than it takes for me to tell it. They talked at a normal pace not all that fast."

"Let's see if one of my guides will come and talk to us."

Jan closed her eyes and this time I didn't give her healing, I just closed my eyes and tried to sense when they came through and who it was.

When I opened my eyes again I said, "Good evening Samuel." There was no reply.

Good evening Richard" Again nothing.

"Jan have you got someone with you,
and is it right?" She nodded.
There was only one guide left and that
was Sheena.
"Good evening Sheena"
Nothing, I thought about it, I knew it wasn't someone
new so I said, "That's a man isn't it."
"Yes."
"Well if you are not Richard or Samuel and I know
you're not somebody new you must be one of my
guides."
"No."
"Ok then I know its Richard."
"Yes it is."
"Well why didn't you answer me when I greeted you?"
"Because the note in your voice was unsure, you must be
confident about who is here even if you are wrong."
"So if I'm not sure I have to sound as though I am?"
"Only if you are sure."
"This isn't making sense, I either am sure or I'm not."
"If you doubt then you must send us away."
"Oh, I see what you mean now, it's like you said when in
doubt chuck them out."
"Yes only in this way will you be confident when we
come forward."
"Maybe I shouldn't close my eyes when you are coming
through."
"You should always work with your eyes open, that way
you are aware of everything going on."
"What do you mean everything?"

140

"If you just use your senses you will direct your thoughts in a particular direction whilst you are learning. You need to use all your senses at the moment so that you can pick up everything that is going on."

"I'm still not quite sure what you mean."

"You need to watch my medium when she is going into trance as well as sensing who is coming through. If it is wrong they may cause my medium some distress. If you are watching then you can deal with any problems immediately."

"I see that's why you said I was responsible for the welfare of your medium I have to be aware of what's happening to her at all times."

"Yes and you can't do that if your eyes are closed. Much the same when you start running circle's it is your responsibility to look after the wellbeing of your sitters."

"So that means when we do a meditation I will always keep my eyes open?"

"You should keep your eyes open at all times unless you are meditating alone."

"Ok I will try. I was sure you were a man."

"Yes but you didn't sound it, remember there are many listening to our conversations and some that would try to pull the wool over your eyes."

"Right, why would they all be listening to us?"

"Because they learn as well, and we teach those on our side through these conversations."

"You make use of every opportunity don't you."

"Of course, why not?"

"So it's not a problem to let the bad spirits know what you are telling us."

"They will only hear what we want them to, we are able to close off our conversation when we need to, otherwise they will know how much of a threat you are. It is not for them to know too much we just feed them enough to keep them docile. We want you to be a mystery when you start working, that way you will catch more of them by surprise."

"How many are listening?"

"There are many who will go and tell others."

"Why are they so interested, we don't know much and can't be a threat to them?"

"It's what they see in your aura that tells them what you are capable of. Remember to them you are spirit not people and all that you have learnt is there for them to see."

"Everything?"

"Yes but they don't know your journey so they don't know how much of what you can do you are going to use."

"So what did your medium do when she was in spirit, I imagine much the same as me as we are here together?"

"Yes much the same although there is another side to her."

"What's that?"

"My medium has upset a lot of people around the earth and they have a vendetta against her."

"What do you mean a vendetta?"

"They are out for revenge because she interfered with their plans, she is more vulnerable while in the earthly body so they think they are going to disrupt her journey."

"Well great, so not only have we got to get our heads round what we have got to learn we have to deal with them as well?"

"We are dealing with them they aren't interfering with your progress."

"What happened in my meditation just now, someone was telling me something but they gave me more information than there was time to say it."

"There is no time in spirit so we can pass information faster than you can perceive it."

"But I heard every word of what was said."

"Yes but it wasn't said out loud you were getting it directly into your mind, which as you have now learnt is much more efficient. When you start communicating with peoples loved ones, that's how you will get the information you will know what you are going to say. You won't need to stop and wait for more. "

"That means I am going to be doing clairvoyance then."

"Yes, it is how people measure your ability, they won't take you seriously if you can't communicate. How will you be able to teach if you're not taken seriously?"

"Does that go for your medium as well?"

"Yes of course, you will be working together."

"Will your medium be doing deep trance at a later stage?"

"No."

"Why is that?"

"She doesn't want to, she said so when you were discussing things."

"Well I know we were talking the other day but what if she changes her mind?"

"A medium will do one or the other they will not do both."

"Why not it seems to me deep trance is just an extension of light trance?"

"It's not whether she can do it or not, it is the reason why that is important and the work you are both going to do. Take light trance for instance, how would it be if you didn't know whether my medium was going into light trance or deep trance."

"Well we would decide before she went."

"A medium will only do deep trance or light trance they will not do both. The reason is we need to know what's happening because the mechanics are different. A light trance medium stays in control and deep trance medium hands over control to us."

"Well if she decides to go deep can't you take over control?"

"There are many other reasons why not, one is, once a medium goes into deep trance they will not want to work in light trance again. The work you are to do requires light trance. Another reason is it will be difficult for a medium to hand over control one time and not another. It's all about confidence, when a medium goes into deep trance they don't have to do anything except step aside mentally. It also takes longer to acquire the deep trace state. You can't go into deep trance and come out at the drop of a hat. You certainly can't do it in the presence of strangers who don't understand what's going on, it would be too dangerous."

"Why is it dangerous?"

"Because a deep trance medium's body changes vibrations slightly so that we can control it better, and

144

they are not conscious of their surroundings. If someone were to touch them or startle them out of trance, then it can cause great harm to the nervous system. Another reason is when you start working you will be required to go and collect spirits good and bad and hold them under control whilst they are with you."

"Wouldn't we be forcing them against their will if we did that?"

"To an extent but how are you going to rescue these poor souls if they are too afraid to come to you, or don't know how to find you?"

"How are we going to find them?"

"We will bring them to your vicinity and you will home in on their distress and like a dog follows a scent you will find them through their feelings of unrest. You will also be required to control bad spirits, when they try interfering with your work and deal with them accordingly, which you can't do if the medium is in deep trance. The medium will not know what is going on, so won't be able to follow the instructions that you give."

"But if you are in deep trance can't the guides do that?"

"They can but it is more efficient if it comes from you, and your medium can come and go quickly if you need to change tactics or stop to discuss anything."

"I see I didn't realise it was going to be so complicated."

"If it were easy there would be more mediums working in that way, it is a specialist subject and you don't want too many ways of working to confuse you. It is also dangerous for the medium which is why it will be your responsibility to control the proceedings and look after the medium that is in trance."

"So that's why I have to be sure of who's there and what's happening?"

"Yes but don't concern yourself, you won't start working until we are sure you can do what is required of you. The safety of the trance medium is paramount."

"Ok so when do we start learning to do all this?"

"You are already well on the road, you have been learning to recognise us and my medium is getting more comfortable with the trance state. She is now able to converse with us while we are here and ask her own questions."

"When does she ask you questions?"

"Usually while we are coming in and while you are giving healing."

"Can she stop you from coming through once you have started?"

"Yes she has complete control. We would never force ourselves on our medium or make her feel uncomfortable."

"So you don't make things uncomfortable for us but you allow others to?"

"How else will you learn if you don't have the experience, we as you are aware, make use of the opportunities that are available to us to teach you."

"So it's not our guides that make us feel cold then?"

"It is not us we would never cause discomfort either by making you too hot or too cold, you will find when that happens it is a distraction."

"What about Arthur he said when you feel cold around your legs that was spirit coming close?"

"Well he was right, he just didn't say which spirits it was did he?"

"No he thought it was guides or loved ones. Richard time is getting on and we have to get some sleep so thank you for talking to us."

"God bless and good night."

"God bless."

Jan opened her eyes and I could see she was a bit concerned so I said, "What's up?"

"I was wondering what we had got ourselves into, from what Richard said we are going to be doing clairvoyance, teaching, visiting people's houses and getting rid of bad spirits. When are we going to have time for all that?"

"Well I don't think it's going to happen tomorrow, we've got to learn how to do it first. If it's taken us two and a half years so far it could be as long again or longer before we are working."

"Yes I suppose so, I just thought when are we going to have time for the children and our own lives that's all."

"Well we can give it a break for a while if you want."

"Let's see how things go and decide then, I'm as interested as you to know more about all this."

"What sort of questions do you ask your guides when they are coming through?"

"Just about their lives like where and how they lived."

"What have you found out about Richard?"

"Well he said he was a Minoan king and they used to make and export big pillars for buildings, like they have on those Greek buildings. It was one of their main industries, and they went all over the Mediterranean on big barges to deliver them."

"Why would you have a king as a guide, I thought they were worried about our credibility and having a king is a bit special isn't it?"

"That's what I said, but he said kings are two a penny and I don't have to tell anyone. It was just that he had some kind of crown on and I asked him what it was. He said he wasn't that famous, like everything it was a job although there were privileges, it wasn't as easy as it appeared. He was only a king for about ten years."

"Was he married and did he have any children?"

"Yes but that life has nothing to do with now it was a long time ago he said."

"You know Richard was talking about getting bad spirits and hanging on to them, you got any idea of how to do that?"

"Not really when my guides come through I just let them. I suppose I could push them out if I wanted, so it must be the opposite of that but I haven't tried it."

"What about when the wrong one came through you didn't have any trouble getting rid of them."

"No I just opened my eyes and they were gone."

"So once you opened your eyes you couldn't feel them anymore?"

"That's right they were just gone."

"What do you think of what he said about deep trance?"

"Well as I have only done light trance I don't know what it would feel like. I wouldn't want to do deep trance in case the wrong one came in at the last moment. I wouldn't get the chance to throw them out. No I don't think I would want to deep trance."

"Well that's just as well as he said you can't do both."

148

"Good I don't have to worry about the wrong one coming in and taking me off then."

"No and it will make it easier for me to control what is going on if you can hear me."

"Yes but although he said you had to control things if you don't recognise the bad spirit at least I can throw them out."

"Yes it's a good safety net."

"I'm not getting that feeling of being tired all of a sudden so much when they go now, perhaps I am getting used to it."

"Good it will make things easier if we have to do a long session when we start going round people's houses."

We went to bed feeling quite pleased with our progress but a bit daunted by what we still had to learn. One thing was becoming clear, when we have learnt things in the past, we have known what we have been getting into. But this was like being drip fed, when they thought the time was right and we didn't know what was coming next.

Chapter 19

During the next day I remembered my dream about the raft and realised I hadn't asked about it. I knew it wasn't an ordinary dream so I wrote a reminder to ask about it next time we spoke.

That night when the kids were settled we sat down and I asked Jan if she had any questions for her guides. She said not at the moment so I decided to give her healing, so I could practice sensing my guides and learn a bit more about how to heal. I placed my hands on her shoulders, after a few moments I felt one of my guides come close. I knew who it was straight away by the way he made me stand. It was Clive the Australian. I tried to talk to him and all I got was a picture in my head of a big rock in Australia. I didn't know what it was but I remembered it from when I was a child. I used to have bad dreams about trying to climb out of a sort of basin of rock. Every time I got so far up the side I would slide down again. After I had got over the surprise I found my hands wanted to go to Jan's lower back, I just let it happen.

"How did you know my back was hurting?" Jan said.
"I didn't I just felt that my hands should be there."
"So your relaxing a bit more and letting your guides direct you."
"Yes, you know if I wave my hand sideways a little, it's like when you push two magnets together it kind of bounces, it's all round my hands. I've never had

that before maybe they are right I am becoming more sensitive."

"That's good do you know who's with you?"

"Yes its Clive, I feel I want to move my hands to your right arm near your shoulder does it hurt there?"

"Yes I think it's that new shoulder bag I got. I carry a lot of things"

"I would never be able to carry all that in my pockets."

"When you're a mother you do."

"Have you got a guide with you yet?"

"Yes but he is standing back until you finish healing."

"Why do I get the feeling they are testing me again?"

"What do you mean?"

"I think they want to see if I can tell when Clive has finished."

"Well you better concentrate then hadn't you?"

"Ok."

After a few minutes I felt I needed to go back to Jan's shoulders, and then I felt I had finished so I put my hands down and went and sat down. I watched Jan and tried to sense who was there, it felt like Sheena.

"Good evening Sheena."

"Good evening you're getting better."

"Not really I knew you were a woman so it was easy."

"In that case we had better introduce you to another of my mediums guides who is female."

"Isn't that a bit soon I am just getting used to the three of you?"

"I was kidding, but it will happen soon so be careful."

"Ok, I have some questions for you."

"Very well what is your first question?"

"While I was healing I felt Clive was there so I asked him a question. What I got was a picture in my head of a rock formation. It reminded me of when I was about ten. I used to have dreams about trying to get out of what seemed like a basin of rock like a wave where it curls over at the top. Every time I tried to get out I just kept sliding back down again. Why is that?"

"Why is what?"

"Why did I get that picture?"

"It was a reminder for you that your guide has been with you all your life."

"The dreams were like a nightmare, my guides wouldn't do that would they?"

"The dream was you trying to work out your frustrations, you always managed to get out didn't you."

"Well yes eventually."

"That's because your guide was helping you."

"How do you know all this you weren't there were you?"

"No but your guide is explaining as we go along."

"Oh, why didn't he show himself?"

"You were not ready. Your guide has lived your life with you and he understood how you were feeling and tried to help you overcome your frustrations."

"I thought all our guides were always around us?"

"Yes but there is at least one who grows with you so they can understand how you are feeling. That way the rest of your guides can best help you when the need arises."

"Do you mean Clive has been my age so that he could tell the rest of my guides how I was feeling?"

"Yes how else are we going to understand your feelings at any given time, it is also his pathway to understanding you. If he experiences what you do and with the knowledge you have we can guide you better."

"Does that mean Clive is my age now?"

"Yes although he has grown with you he still retains his memory of who he is and what he is doing. He just lock's away his historical memory, so he is working with the limited knowledge you have. That way we can see why you do what you do in any given situation."

"I see so why did he show me that picture?"

"To remind you of your dreams when you were a child."

"Did he make it up?"

"No there is a formation of rock in Australia just like it, check it out."

"I will the other thing I wanted to ask is have our guides helped us before we were aware of them?"

"Yes there have been times when we have had to step in and influence you to keep you on the right pathway. You remember you were going to move away from London into the country once, and everything was arranged but then it fell through?"

"Yes we were going to move north of London."

"Well if you had, you would not have met my medium."

"So you messed up my dad's dreams so that I could meet my wife?"

"No the people you were going to exchange with changed their minds your parents stopped looking after that."

"Did you or my guides have anything to do with that?"

"No their guides just didn't encourage them to try again."

"What if they had gone ahead and found somewhere else?"

"Then you would have moved. We would then have had to arrange for one of your alternative arrangements to be available. This was your first choice and when you discussed it with us, we agreed that it was the best way for you both to achieve the goals you had set for yourselves before you came to the earth."

"What about my parents and brothers and sisters goals?"

"As none of them were going to be aware it didn't matter to them where they were."

"Still sounds like manipulation to me."

"To some degree yes, but it happens all the time to manoeuvre everybody into the right pathway. As long as everyone achieves their goals to the best of their ability no-one loses out."

"I see, another question, about a week ago I had a dream about floating down a river on a raft. I had been hurt badly and was alone. What was all that about?"

"It wasn't a dream you have been building up your anger at the way your children have been attacked and you decided you wanted to stop them. When you went to sleep that night you went off to challenge them. You took on more than you could handle and you were beaten."

"I thought my guides were protecting me, didn't they help me?"

"You have always been stubborn, when you said what you were going to do your guides advised you against it, but you went off anyway."

"Why didn't they help me?"

154

"Because you issued a challenge, when you do that we can't help."

"Why not?"

"Because you acted on your own you will remember us telling you about what you did in spirit? Do you remember us saying that you always worked with others never alone?"

"Yes."

"Well you broke the rules so your guides had to let you go on your own."

"How come I was bleeding and badly injured then. If I'm in spirit I don't have a body to get injured?"

"You still think in earthly terms and remember those you challenged are able to make you think whatever they want. Although you are strong you can't take on a dozen or so spirits and expect to come out ahead."

"Bit kamikaze then was I?"

"Reckless anyway."

"What about the beams from my hands?"

"Yes we can do that but then we can do anything you can imagine, don't forget we are energy so it's not difficult to send out energy beams. It wasn't quite like that, but your mind thinks in earthly terms and that's as near as you could get with the knowledge you have."

"So basically what your saying is don't challenge anyone or accept a challenge?"

"That's right we are a team and always work as a team."

"I guess sometimes we have to learn the hard way."

"You don't have to if you listen to your guides."

"Ok, consider me well and truly told off."

"We are not telling you off we don't have that right, you just exercised your free will at the wrong time that's all. If we didn't explain things to you who could imagine what you might do next. Now you understand that there are rules over here as well as in your world."
"I think we will have to stop there I can see your medium is getting fidgety,"
"Yes good night."
"God bless."

Jan and I talked about how our guides had set everything up and we both came to the same conclusion. We talked about the rock that Clive had shown me and when I looked it up it was sure enough in Australia and it was called Wave Rock. Jan said.
"You were a little head strong fancy getting in to trouble like that."
"I didn't know what I was getting into."
"Your guides told you."
"Yes so it seems but I don't remember."
"Ah well, put it down to experience maybe next time you will listen. Why didn't you ask about what was happening when you were giving me healing?"
"I got led in another direction."
"Do you want to ask now?"
"Yes ok if you are up to it."
Next thing I knew she had gone.
"Good evening Richard."
"Good evening, you're getting there."

"Yes I thought you were there before your medium closed her eyes, you said be confident so I was. When I was giving healing I wasn't touching your medium but I felt I had to move my hands, am I now starting to feel my guides influence."

"Yes your guide came through quite strongly so that you would take notice."

"What about the magnetic feeling I had around my hands?"

"You were feeling you guides energy, it was a way of confirming that you were in the right place."

"Do I have to put my hands on the place that needs healing?"

"No it can all be done from one place."

"Then why was I influenced to move my hands?"

"If you place your hands where the pain is it gives the person you are giving healing to confidence that you know what you are doing."

"Why, when I had finished did I place my hands on the shoulders instead of just holding them above?"

"It is a way of letting the person know you have finished."

"So why did I start by touching, then when I moved my hands I didn't touch then when I had finished I touched again?"

"So that you could feel your guide's energy and know you were in the right place."

"But your medium had her eyes closed, how would she know if I went to the place that hurt?"

"Because she could feel the energy, once you are confident that you know what you are doing you will place your hands on the affected area. Until then you will work in this way."

"So it's just while I am learning then?"

"Yes when you become more proficient you will work both ways. Some people don't like to be touched, and there are times when it would be inappropriate to put your hands on the affected part of the body."

"Oh I see like if I was healing a woman?"

"Yes, and sometimes men don't like to be touched in certain areas."

"Of course that makes sense. Does healing always work?"

"Yes but you must remember if you have had a condition for a while then it will take a while to heal."

"Can you heal anything?"

"No there are times when your drugs or an operation will be needed."

"When you are with your medium can you give her healing?"

"Yes after all she is surrounded by my energy and she also has another of her guides standing behind her."

"Why does she have a guide behind her, can't you do it by yourself?"

"Yes of course but they are my backup."

"Why do you need backup?"

"Whilst I am with my medium I am more vulnerable to those who would wish to disrupt us, they are my protection."

"I see that's what you mean by working as a team?"

"Yes we never work alone even when we are talking to you."

"On another subject, I have seen a car but the place was closed, it's a good price and it looks ok, but it's a long way to go if it's got problems. Is there anything wrong with it?"

"It's ok for its age but check the oil when you get it, and one tyre is a bit bald."

"Ok thanks, we had better stop now it's getting late again, by the way why do you always say god bless when you go?"

"Well you believe in god don't you?"

"I'm not sure what god is, it just seems to be a name people use for something they're not sure of. I just wondered if because of where you are you would know. If you use the expression then I suppose there is one."

"Yes well good night then."

"Good night."

"God bless," And he was gone.

Jan was smiling when she opened her eyes I said,

"What are you smiling at?"

"Well you asked him about god and then he just added it on as he was leaving, he said to me, this will give him something to think about."

"So what do you think about the car then?"

"I think we should go and have a look at it, Richard said it was ok I think we should check it out."

"Ok well go tomorrow."

Chapter 20

In the morning we went to have a look at the car. It was on the other side of London which is why I asked if it was ok. I didn't want to go all that way for nothing. We looked over the car and sure enough the tread on one tyre was low so we thought Richard was talking about the same car, we couldn't find anything really wrong with it so we bought it. The car needed oil and this confirmed for us what Richard had said.

Now we felt we had a reliable car, the other one was on its last legs we were more confident when we took the kids out. There seemed to be some perks with talking to spirit.

That night Clair woke up after being in bed for about an hour. We asked what was wrong and she said,
"I found myself up in the corner of the room, I could see myself asleep in bed and it frightened me when I woke up my whole body jumped."
"Were you asleep?" I said.
"I think so."
"Well don't worry it was probably a dream go back to sleep I will stay with you until your asleep."
I had heard about out of body experiences and wondered if that was what had happened. I spoke to Jan about it and we decided we would ask her guides what had happened. After what Clair had been through we were taking no chances we wanted to know if it was

interference. There was no time like the present so Jan got comfortable and closed her eyes.

"Good evening Samuel"

"Good evening how's your car?"

"It going fine thank you, and thanks for your help."

"Good we try to help when we can."

"What happened with Clair earlier she seemed to have an out of body experience?"

"Yes she is very sensitive."

"How does that happen?"

"Clair was in that state of half asleep and half- awake as her mind drifted from consciousness to sleep. As you know when you go to sleep your spirit leaves your body. Clair left her body while she was still partly conscious that's why she was able to remember what had happened. It frightened her and she woke herself up."

"So it wasn't interference?"

"No she is protecting herself a lot more now, it was just one of those things, it has happened to her before but she thought she was dreaming."

"So she is becoming more aware of things?"

"Yes she will be fine, she talks to her guide and seems to take comfort from the knowledge that he is looking after her."

"Good at least we have got someone she can turn to when she needs to apart from us. I have heard of people doing that when they have operations or are very ill. They say they could see everything that was going on in the room, sometimes they talk about seeing a tunnel with a light at the end is that the same sort of thing."

"Similar but not the same Clair was not ill just in between sleep and wakefulness, there are those who have practiced that are able to astral travel. This is when they meditate to a state of almost trance, and are able to leave their bodies and travel on the astral."

"What's the astral?"

"It is the realms around the earth."

"They can do that at will, why would they do that?"

"No, it takes a lot of practice, they do it to learn more about themselves and the spirit world."

"Clair isn't going to have problems with it like not being able to come back?"

"No she is attached to the body by a cord or energy, like you when you leave your body during your sleep (which is perfectly natural) and her spirit is aware of all that happens around her body. You know when you feel a bump sometimes when you are waking up? That's your spirit hurrying back to the body."

"It doesn't happen very often but I know what you mean why is that?"

"It's when your spirit senses a change around the body it comes back quickly so it is prepared for any eventuality."

"Like what?"

"Well maybe you are going to be woken up or a noise has disturbed you."

"I see, so what about the people in hospitals why do they come back? Some of them say they have seen their loved ones and have been sent back."

"Yes it is not their time, or they are not as ill or badly injured as first thought."

"First thought by whom?"

"By their spirit or their guides. You see what with modern medicine and the progress mankind has made, there are many illnesses and injuries that can be dealt with by your hospitals which couldn't be cured in the past. We have to keep up to date with new discoveries as well you know, we don't always get it right straight away."

"That's interesting does that mean spirit makes mistakes?"

"No we always double check, although we want you to come home, we also want you to complete your journey and achieve as much as you can."

"Ok thank you for talking to us we will let you go now god bless."

"It's been a pleasure god bless."

Jan came back and we talked about how much we didn't know it seemed we were on a roller coaster. Things were happening all the time and we were struggling to keep up.

About a week later Jan woke me up in the middle of the night and said.

"I was laying here trying to get back to sleep, something woke me up, when I tried to move I couldn't."

"What do you mean you couldn't move?"

"It was like I was paralysed all over, I thought I had a stroke or something. It lasted quite a while, I tried to call you but couldn't speak, I could think but that's all."

"That must have been frightening, how did you get the feeling back in your body?"

"I don't know it just went away and I could move again, so I woke you up."

"How do you feel now?"

"I feel ok, just a little bit jumpy."

"Why don't you go and have a cup of tea, I will come down and keep you company."

"Yes that's a good idea it will help me to calm down."

We went down stairs and while Jan made a cup of tea I checked on the kids to make sure they were alright. They were, so I went and sat with Jan and we went over it again. We wondered whether there was something wrong she said she would see how she felt in the morning. If she didn't feel alright she would make an appointment to see the doctor and get checked out. The following day Jan felt fine so we did nothing more about it, we just thought it's one of those things that happen now and then. We were doing as we had been told by our guides, look to the earthly for an explanation before we blamed spirit. Although we couldn't think of a reason for it to have happened we decided to wait and see. As our guides have told us they will never allow anything we couldn't handle, we thought we would be ok.

A few days later it happened again this time it lasted longer and Jan was in a bit of distress over it. She felt as though she couldn't breathe and this caused her some concern. We decided to see the doctor and get her checked again. On seeing the doctor she did a full check-up including blood tests. There didn't seem to be anything wrong but we would have to wait for the tests to come back, these would take about a week. We were quite busy that week so didn't get a chance to have a chat with Jan's guides. It happened again during that week, each time it seemed to be longer and it didn't matter what Jan did the only thing she could do was grunt. Fortunately I was listening out for anything unusual and heard her. I woke up and tried talking to her but she couldn't reply. I thought she may have had a stroke or something, and then I thought maybe its spirit. I remembered what I had been told about bringing someone back if they were under spirits control. I did as I had been told and Jan was able to move again, it had gone away. Now we knew it was spirit and it couldn't be her guides because of the way it was being done and the worry it was causing. As it was about 5am we decided to stay up. We talked about what had happened and Jan said,

"It was like the last time only quicker, I was dozing, all of a sudden I couldn't move. I think because I was awake and realised what was happening I was able to make a noise sooner. It still took a while to wake you; I thought you were never going to wake up."
"I woke up as soon as I was aware something was wrong."
"How did you know what to do to get me out of it?"
"I remembered what your guides said about talking to you and holding your wrist, I tried it and it worked. To me that means it was spirit doing it."
"That makes sense but it wasn't my guides, it looks like they are stepping up the attacks again."
"Yes, but you weren't being attacked before."
"No, so this must be something different. "
"Yes, we had better try and find out what's going on."

Jan was alright after we had sorted out what we thought was going on. We decided to talk to her guides that night. There obviously wasn't anything wrong with her medically. Later we got the kids sorted out and then Jan got comfortable and I watched closely. We didn't know what to expect so I said to Jan,

"Let me know when you can feel one of your guides close, I will try to check them out before you go into trance."

"Yes alright I can feel someone here it feels like Richard."

I relaxed and was able to sense a man with something on his head like a band around the forehead.

"I'm sensing Richard let him come through, if it doesn't feel right don't wait for me just chuck him out."

"Ok."

"Good evening Richard"

"Good evening."

"Things have been going on with your medium and we would like to know what it is."

"What's been happening?"

"Don't you know?"

"There are a lot of things going on with my medium it is part of her development."

"During the night she has been getting some kind of attack, she can't move or say anything, it's like she is paralysed."

"Yes that is what happened."

"Why? Who's doing it?"

"As we have told you there are bad spirits that want to stop you working.

They are trying to control my medium to stop her from working with us."

"Why are they attacking her I thought they couldn't get through to her?"

"Because my medium goes into trance with us it has made it easier for them to force their way in when she is not on her guard."

"So it's only trance mediums that have that problem?"

"No there are many people who have the same problem but they don't talk about it as they think it is a dream. My medium is more sensitive and knows something is not right, that's why she fights it."

"So lots of people experience it but they don't have any problems?"

"Yes as I said they think it's a dream."

"So how come they can get through to your medium? She is used to going into trance won't she automatically protect herself?"

"It's easier for them to get to her when she is dozing, she will have to make sure she is protected before she goes to sleep."

"Will that stop it?"

"Yes she was not expecting to be attacked during the night so my medium was vulnerable."

"Is this a common thing?"

"Not necessarily some are just open and easy to get at."

"Why does spirit let it happen?"

"We can only help if we are asked, as most people are not aware of their guides they don't ask for help?"

"So it's free will again, what about your medium if she asks you for help if it happens again?"

"If she hasn't stopped it then we will help."

I thanked Richard. Jan came back and said,

"Well I suppose I couldn't get away without aggravation all the time. At least we know there's nothing wrong with me."

"Looks like something you're going to have to work through. Can I talk to Richard again?"

"Ok let me have a cup of tea first."

While Jan was having a cup of tea we talked about the pros and cons of what we had learnt so far. She settled down again and asked Richard to come through again.

"Hi Richard sorry to ask you back again, is Clair going to get the same kind of attacks as your medium?"

"No we will make sure that doesn't happen."

"Why couldn't you stop your medium from getting it then if you can protect Clair?"

"My medium needs to overcome this type of attack herself otherwise when you start working they will try to control her."

"How do you mean?"

"Well when you visit people that are having problems, one of the things my medium will have to do is bring the bad spirits through, so that you can talk to them."

"Why do we need to talk to them?"

"As we have said, some of them will want to get away from their situation, unless you talk to them how will you know? They will then need rescuing the same as those who are lost. You will also need to control the bad spirits and the best way of doing that is for my medium to bring them through."

"Sounds like we have a long way to go, before we are ready for that."

"Patience, you will get there you are already well on the road. It's no different than when my medium gets the wrong one through and you throw them out."

"Oh, it's that easy is it?"

"Not quite but you will learn."

"You know that car we bought, well I'm going to have to replace the head gasket, I think it's been low on water at some time I noticed some water in the oil the other day."

"You are able to do that yourself aren't you?"

"Oh yes it should be no problem I'm going to do it tomorrow. I will probably give it a service at the same time, like you said they never topped the oil up so I don't think it got a service either."

"It would be a good idea then you will know its ok."

"Yes well thank you for coming back at least we don't have to worry about Clair getting paralysed, god bless."

"God bless."

Jan opened her eyes and said,

"Well at least that's one worry we won't have. You didn't say anything to me about the car."

"No, but it's no big deal it will only take a couple of hours, I've got the parts."

"So I just ask my guides for help, if it happens to me again?"

"Yes, at least you won't have to try and wake them up."

169

We went to bed feeling a lot happier, knowing that Jan was alright. The next day I got on with the car and when I had finished I tried to start it, but it would just turn over. I checked all the electrics and fuel and made sure everything was as the book said it should be and tried again. It just turned over again but wouldn't start. I checked the points then made sure all the plugs were getting a spark. Double checked the fuel was getting through and tried again, same thing. By now I was getting a bit frustrated, Jan came out and said,

"What's wrong?"

"I don't know I have double checked everything but it just turns over."

"My dad used to work on his cars and he had the same sort of problem."

"How did he fix it?"

"Something to do with the plug leads I think."

"I've checked them they are in the right order but I'll check them again." It still wouldn't start.

"Do you want to ask Richard? Maybe he can tell you what's wrong"

"It won't hurt to ask although what would he know about engines they never had them."

We went indoors and Jan asked Richard to come through. "Hi"

"Hello you seem to be having some problems?"

"Yes and I can't work out what's wrong, have you got any mechanics around who can have a look and tell me what I have done wrong?"

"Yes we have my mediums father here and he says the plug leads are in the wrong order."

"But I did what the book says."

170

"Yes we know but someone has altered the firing order he says it needs to be 1342 not 1243 try it."

"Ok I will give it a try thanks for helping, hope Bill is ok, and maybe we can talk to him soon."

I went out and rearranged the plug leads turned the key and it started, it ran just like it was supposed to. I made a note of the firing order for future reference and tidied up.

Over lunch we talked about the car and the fact that her dad had been on hand to help me when I needed it. He had passed about 5 years earlier, and that's the first time any reference had been made about any of our relatives in spirit. We hadn't thought about finding out about them, in fact it wasn't even considered that we could with everything else going on.

That night we settled down to have a chat with spirit and we thought we would ask about our dads and Jan's mum. So Jan closed her eyes and asked one of her guides to come forward.

"Good evening Richard"

"Good evening how's the car going?"

"It going fine thank you, we never expected your mediums dad to be around is he always here?"

"No he was visiting just to see how you are all getting on. Your parents visit quite often you know."

"We never thought about that aspect of things, they are alright then?"

"Of course why wouldn't they be?"

"Well with what you have told us and the dangers, we wondered if it was too risky for them to be around us."

"As we've said before they come in groups or they are escorted for safety, they can come as often as they wish providing they come together."

"What if we are being attacked at the time?"

"It makes no difference they will not be attacked, you are the targets."

"So they won't attack them to get at us then?"

"We wouldn't let them and there would be no point, you wouldn't know they had been attacked."

"No course we wouldn't I wasn't thinking it through. "

"You can't think of everything."

"The other day we were talking and I mentioned to your medium about how I felt when I went into the dining room; you know the empty one we are using as a workshop?"

"Yes what about it?"

"Well I was saying about how I felt the hairs on the back of my neck tingling and it felt as if it was full of bad spirits. If I'm right do they hide in there?"

"They use that room to carry on their training where they won't be disturbed."

"Why do they need to use that room what about the rest of the rooms?"

"When they are ready to do something else they send those they have trained out to attack you. It's easier to work in there without you distracting them and interfering with the training. As you hardly use the room they can retreat into it without worrying about being detected. Especially when you're,trying to get rid of

172

them. By going in there they can make you think they have gone."

"I don't understand why do they need a room in the house when they are in spirit?"

"It's their base, it's where they regroup and plan the next move undisturbed."

"Is that common?"

"Yes in a lot of the houses you will visit you will find a room that isn't used much where the atmosphere is uncomfortable."

"So why don't we go and clear them out and put protection round it to stop them coming back?"

"It's better to know where they are at all times that way we can keep an eye on them. You are also learning to build your defences, there will come a time when you stop feeling anything. When that happens you will know you are protecting yourself properly. If you like we are making use of their presence to help you to progress."

"I suppose we should thank them for helping us to learn?"

"They wouldn't be very pleased if they knew they were helping you. If you like they are helping you to defeat them."

"Yes I see what you mean, by giving us the practice we get stronger. So once we don't detect them anymore that means we have overcome them. Is it the same as what Sheena said about different levels? When we overcome one level we are attacked by the next?"

"No when you overcome that room you will be able to protect yourselves against all but the strongest."

"What about the strongest then how will we overcome them if they are not around?"

"You will meet them as you go about your spiritual work and together you will be able to deal with them."

"I see, well I think it's getting late so we had better say goodnight."

"Good night god bless."

Jan came back and we were pleased our relatives could come and see us when they wanted to, they could watch the children grow up and be a small part of their lives even if the kids didn't know. We talked about the dining room and what was going on in there. Jan said,

"Are we supposed to go in there occasionally to check it out to see if we are still able to feel anything?"

"No when we go in there we will now be aware of what it is we are feeling I suppose we will get the practice like that."

Chapter 21

We called it a night and went to bed. The next day we had a day out at Brighton and browsed in the antique shops or bric-a-brac shops. Jan was looking at some rosary beads and crosses when she jumped and dropped it.

"What s wrong? I said"

"It felt like the spare room does, all the hairs on the back of my neck went up. You try it."

I picked it up and looked at it and said,

"I don't feel anything are you sure?"

Jan picked it up again and immediately dropped it she said,

"It feels horrible, like when you feel bad spirit around."

"But it's a cross why would it have bad spirits around it?"

"I don't know but I'm not touching it again."

We left the shop a bit puzzled how a cross could feel like that. That night after everyone was settled we asked spirit if Samuel would come through.

"Good evening you're Richard aren't you?"

"Yes good evening."

"Where's Samuel?"

"He's busy sorting something out for my medium, you shouldn't ask for a particular guide as we are not always here. We may be working somewhere else on your behalf. Or we may be learning something new."

"Are there always some of our guides with us?"

"Yes of course but you must remember we are not as individuals always here, we have other things to do on your behalf."

"Like what?"

"Well we have to make arrangements so that you will meet the right people at the right time for your progression. We need to talk to their guides to make a mutually beneficial meeting for you both with their mediums."

"So everything is planned then?"

"As much as we can, providing you are in the right place things will go according to plan."

"So in future we just ask for one of our guides?"

"Yes you will get one of those you know most of the time. When it is time to meet a new guide we will be here as well to introduce you."

"I was wondering about that. We were out today and your medium picked up a crucifix with a set of rosary beads attached. She felt very uncomfortable with them and put them down immediately."

"Yes I know."

"Ok so you were with us did you enjoy the beach?"

"I'm more used to soft sand but it was nice to see people enjoying themselves."

"Yes, but why did the beads feel so bad?"

"Because they have been used for the wrong reasons and they carry the vibrations of the bad spirits on them."

"What do you mean the wrong reasons they are religious items?"

"That doesn't make any difference they are objects and they represent religion to you but not necessarily to spirit."

"Why not?"

"The cross is representative of the Christian religion which has only been around for 2000 years or so. Even I was here before that, and the cross does not represent anything sacred to those who were on the earth before that. In fact the cross was originally an x shape rather than a tee. The reason they changed the shape was when they crucified their victims they died too quickly. The x tended to be unstable and collapsed killing whoever was tied to it. When they started using the tee shape they found the victims lasted longer. Because Jesus was crucified on the tee shaped cross it is used as a religious symbol. But there are other uses for the symbol."

"What other uses?"

"It is used in devil worship, that's why the rosary my medium picked up felt uncomfortable."

"So does that mean when a symbol is used for the wrong purposes it carries the vibrations of what it was used for."

"Everything absorbs vibrations some good where good has been and bad where unhappiness has been or bad things have been done. When you do a psychic reading on an object you are picking up the vibrations the item has absorbed."

"Is that why when we were looking at houses, when we were going to move your medium said some of the houses we went in didn't feel very nice?"

"Yes there had been unhappiness in them and she could feel it in the atmosphere of the house."

"So everything absorbs emotions and feelings?"

"Yes, thoughts are things in our world and bad thoughts will stay around your earth plane until they are covered up by happy thoughts."

"Does that mean when that happens the bad thoughts are gone?"

"No they are still there under the happy thoughts. When you take hold of an object to sense the vibrations you will pick up on the most obvious feelings. If you study it more you will pick up on other vibrations that are not so obvious."

"So every item tells a story?"

"Yes but if you try to sense an abject more than once, you will not necessarily home in to the same vibration. It is like an onion the vibrations are in layers, depending on your ability will depend on what you sense."

"So that's why when people go to places where prison camps were during the war they can feel the pain and sadness from what happened there?"

"Yes."

"So all items are covered in these vibrations?"

"Yes, you will find some foreign carvings have bad feelings around them."

"Well I suppose so after all they are objects as well."

"That's not what I meant; when the natives are carving them they may chant over them while they are working. You have heard of black magic or voodoo, some of the chants are not very nice."

"Why would they do that?

"To protect their work from evil spirits, sometimes the only way they believed they could do that, was to put a stronger evil spirit to guard it."

"So belief is what makes those chants work?"

"Yes but not necessarily belief by people. There are those in spirit that will attach themselves to these objects, in the thought they are protecting them for the maker. They are usually spirits with the same belief as the people that do the chanting."

"Does voodoo really work?"

"Voodoo is just another belief system and yes it works."

"I know there have been cases where the locals have a curse put on them and sometimes they die. But I thought that was because they believed it, until I heard about people who are not locals getting sick or having bad luck. How can they be affected if they don't have the same beliefs?" "Because the locals grow up in that culture the belief is second nature to them. If someone puts a curse on them it will have the desired effect because they expect it to. The mind helps to make the curse work better. There are those in spirit who will take on the role of distributing the curse where it is intended to go. When a local starts feeling pains, (much like you have) they believe in the curse and that makes them more susceptible to it."

"What about people who don't believe?"

"The bad spirits who take on the role can also affect them, you have already experienced it, why should they be any different?"

"So it's bad spirit that makes it all work?"

"Yes there is nothing mysterious about it. If you understand how they work not much will surprise you."

"So when they know they have a curse the locals go to a witch doctor to try to counteract the spell or curse that's been put on them. Does that mean they are asking their guides for help even if they don't know it?"

"Yes the witch doctor is a type of medium within their beliefs, and they will cast a spell asking the good spirits or their guides to help."

"Speaking of spells what about pagans and the like is that the same thing?"

"Yes all spells work in the same way, be they for good or bad."

"So all that sort of thing from everywhere around the world works in the same way?"

"Yes of course there is nothing new in your world just different ways of looking at it."

I thanked Richard for coming as time was getting on and we said good night. When Jan came back she said.

"That was interesting now it all makes sense, the feelings I get when I go in some houses and the spells and stuff. It all joins together doesn't it?"

"Yes they are a busy lot those bad spirits aren't they. It's like we have been living in half a world."

"Yes it's taken me long enough to get used to this world and now the goal posts have been moved."

"Yes I know the feeling."

We called it a night and went to bed. Over the next couple of days we were very busy getting on with everyday things. Jan seemed to have stopped getting attacked now we knew what was causing it. I hadn't had any aches and pains for weeks now so things seemed to be going in the right direction. Then I had a weird experience, I was asleep in bed when I was woken up by a feeling of pressure going up and down my body. It felt like a magnetic field circling my body, even underneath me it was like rings of energy. I felt ok I could move and I knew where I was, but I had never experienced that feeling before. After a few minutes it stopped and I thought about it for a bit then fell asleep. The next morning I was full of energy it was the best night's sleep I had for ages.

That night I talked to Jan about it and we reckoned it could have been my guides giving me some healing. When everything was sorted we sat down to ask Jan's guides about it. She asked one of them to come through and I must be getting used to them because I knew it was Richard.

"Good evening Richard".
"Good evening"
"I had an experience last night it was like I was getting my batteries topped up is that right?"
"Yes you have been working hard in your job and also in spirit while you have been asleep. We thought you were getting a bit low so we gave you some healing. It's not usual that the recipient feels it because we usually do it when you are fast asleep. But you needed a strong dose so that's probably why."
"How often does that happen?"
"It is quite rare for us to administer such a strong dose, but because we didn't want you weakened and therefore vulnerable we did what was necessary?"

"If I was working in spirit why would I be using my physical energy?"

"You weren't but because of the interference you have been getting and the work you have been doing both in spirit and in your job you were getting worn out."

"So was it my guides who gave me healing?"

"They were there but in this case they had a spirit doctor who specialises in that sort of thing to administer the healing."

"Does that mean I will need it again in the future?"

"That depends on how you settle down to dealing with the interference you get."

"If it's rare I must have been getting a lot of aggravation, what about your medium?"

"My medium has not been attacked as much as you. Although you are both important for the work you are going to do, it is you that will have to control the proceedings, you have to learn a lot more about what you need to do."

"Maybe I should slow down a bit in spirit until I have managed to sort out the aggravation?"

"You're almost there but you must try to stand back a little and not take on other peoples lessons. You try to protect everyone and they need to learn as well."

"Even the children?"

"Yes you will have to let them deal with their own problems, just be there and advise."

"It's easy for you to say but I have to get used to the idea that they are not children in this situation. I have always tried to help and protect them."

"Yes we know you are the sort of person that is hands on but give them space they will learn."

"If you say so I will try."

That explained why I couldn't get rid of the feeling that I wasn't in control of what was happening around me as much as I usually was.

"On another subject, your medium has a great interest in Egypt is that her interest or is she being influenced?"

"My medium is picking up on one of her guides who comes from there; you will have noticed you have an affinity with certain places also."

"Yes there are some places that I feel as though I have been to before, even without going there. Is that the same with people you know when you feel that you have known them before?"

"Not quite you may have known them in spirit or sometimes you are of like mind and blend well together."

"Do we ever meet loved ones from a previous life?"

"It is very unusual there are so many different pathways and you have already learnt from them the last time you were together."

"I was driving through Kingston the other day and I saw a man limping. I wondered what was wrong with him, and then I felt a pain in my leg for a moment and then it was gone. Why was that I hadn't hurt my leg?"

"You wanted to understand why he was limping so we showed you."

"Do you mean you can give me other people's ailments?"

"When you are healing sometimes you will pick up others pain so you will know where to place your hands."

"I thought I was directed by my guides."

"It can be done either way. When you are communicating with a loved one they will sometimes give you their pain when they were on the earth so you can describe them better to the recipient."

"Why do I need to feel their pain? Can't they just tell me/"

"Yes they can but you have to let us know how you want to work."

"Well I'm telling you now they can tell me, I have enough with aggravation and my own pains I don't want theirs as well."

"Ok you have made that clear."

"Does that mean when I start working clairvoyantly I can tell you what I want and you will give me the information?"

"When you are communicating you will need certain information so that the recipient will recognize the communicator. You will ask questions of spirit to get these answers."

"Is that how it works?"

"There are many ways it can work it depends on the medium and how they have been taught."

"When we saw that medium a little while ago I thought he was quite rude and didn't have a lot of respect for either the recipient or the communicator, is that how all mediums work?"

"No as I said it depends on how they have been taught and what they expect, if you remember he believed his mother was his guide."

"Yes that's right and from what you said he was stopping his guides from working with him."

"Yes we can only work with our mediums if they will let us."

"So how does it work if you do it properly?"

"In the early days of your development you will be working with your guides. This is because you are used to communicating with them and we will pass on the information from the communicator to you. As you progress you will start to communicate directly with the person who is giving the information. When that happens, you will have to learn how to speak to people who come to you from spirit. It is then that you will have to set up the rules for spirit to talk to you."

"What do you mean rules?"

"Some of the people in spirit will be talking to their loved ones for the first time, they will be very emotional and excited. Because of this they will be all over the place. This will not make your job easy so you will have to give them guidelines on how they are to communicate with you and what information you want from them."

"How do I do that?"

"First think of what you would need to know about someone so that you will recognize them. Then write a list and memorise it, in that way you're putting up a notice saying to spirit this is the information I will require should you wish to work with me. They will then know what is expected of them and you won't get them shouting at you from all directions. It will also give us your guides the authority to organise them into an orderly queue."

"Why do you need them in an orderly queue surly I will only hear one at a time?"

"Think of it like this, if you are the only one who is communicating they will push and shove and shout to be heard. Not only will it be confusing for you, but the recipient will be getting bits of information from a number of people, which won't make any sense to them. By giving guidelines and a list of questions you will be more efficient and so will they. Not only will the recipient know who is there, it will make it easier for those in spirit to get their message across. You will also be able to bring more people through to the recipient."

"That makes sense will they agree to it?"

"They will if you don't listen to those who push in or shout."

"I suppose that will come with practice won't it?"

"That's what development circles are for practicing and refining your art."

"So first we have to find a development circle?"

"When the time is right you will be guided to the right circle."

"Ok well time is getting on thanks for talking to us it looks like we have a few things to think about good night."

"Good night and god bless."

We discussed what we had heard and Jan said.

"It seems we have got to be in charge of any communications when we are doing clairvoyance and feelings when we are healing"

"Yes that's the way I see it, it's early days yet we can't even do it."

"No I wonder where we are going to find a circle to sit in."

"I don't know I suppose that's one of the things our guides are arranging."

"I think from what was said you better back off a bit when it comes to protecting the kids you don't want to get ill."

"I didn't realise I was so busy with it."

"I wonder where they do this clairvoyance; I can't see us doing big demonstrations like the one we went to?"

"I don't know well have to wait and see."

We called it a night and for the next few days were quite busy preparing the kitchen floor. We were going to lay a screed over the central heating pipes and Arthur and Brian were coming to help.

Chapter 22

When we had everything ready I called Arthur and arranged for him to come over to give me a hand. When they arrived next day they both looked around and Arthur said,

"It feels very busy here are you still getting aggravation from Kay."

We looked at each other and Jan said,

"Not any more it seems to have stopped. Maybe she gave up after we moved down to Bob's house."

"Must be your guides then, how are you getting on?"

"We do a bit of meditating and Mike is starting to get a few things. We also practice a bit of healing."

We didn't want to say too much in case they wanted to see what we were doing. It wasn't for any other reason than Arthur is a bit of a know it all when it comes to spirit. Although we were grateful for his help we didn't want to get confused with his beliefs and what our guides were telling us.

We got on with laying the floor and Brian said,

"Have you been to the spiritualist church yet?"

We looked at each other and I said,

"No we didn't know there was one, where is it?"

"There's one in Camberley and another in Fleet, they have services on

Sundays and one night during the week."

"Do you just go there or do you have to join, or what, how does it work?"

They laughed and Arthur said,

"You just turn up, it is in a small hut in Camberley why don't you come with us next time we go?" I looked at Jan and she said,

"Ok when are you going?"

"We will probably go tomorrow."

"What Sunday morning?"

"No it's in the evening and it starts at 6.30 we usually get there about

6.15."

"How much is it to get in?"

"Nothing, you just give a donation when the collection comes round."

"What do they do there, is it the same as the time we went to Bournemouth?"

"No that was just a demonstration this time there will be a few hymns and prayers then the medium will try to prove survival like Roy did."

"Alright will you come here then and we can follow you?"

"Ok are you taking the kids?"

"I don't think so well go and have a look first."

We finished the floor then we all went down the pub for a couple of hours then they went home. On the way home the car just stopped, I tried starting it again but it wouldn't turn over. We left it for a while and I checked the battery and cleaned the connections it all seemed ok it just wouldn't start. We talked about what could be wrong and after about ten minutes I tried it and it started. I don't know what was wrong but it seemed ok now so we drove home. We talked about what we had been told and it all started to fit together. We thought we would talk to one of Jan's guides so we sorted out the kids and settled down. I gave Jan healing without touching and could feel that magnetic feeling again and Jan asked one of her guides to come forward.

"Evening Richard."
"Good Evening>"
"Now we know where we are going to find a circle. We have been talking to Arthur and he was telling us about a spiritualist church in Camberley did you know about it?"
"Yes we have been checking it out and arranging things for when you were ready."
"Ready for what, to see other people doing clairvoyance?"
"Yes we that is your guides decided it was time for you to see how others do it."
"So we can talk to some mediums and see how it's done?"
"Yes but be careful they may not think the same as you."
"What do you mean?"
"Don't go in there all guns blazing be quiet and listen to what others have to say."
"You mean don't say anything just listen?"
"Yes you don't want to upset people by saying the wrong thing."
"You are saying treat them the same as we would Arthur?"
"Yes remember you have learnt from us but most of them will have learnt from mediums. They will have beliefs and understanding that has been passed from one medium to another."

"Ah I see what you mean they haven't been taught by spirit."

"That's right there will be some strange beliefs, it's not for you to judge their beliefs just listen."

"Ok by the way the car broke down this afternoon I couldn't figure out what was wrong, but it seems alright now any ideas?"

"We wondered whether you would have any problems with it."

"What do you mean?"

"Because we helped you with it we wondered whether the bad spirits would interfere with it."

"Why would they, is it another piece of property we need to protect?"

"We wondered if they would consider it to be fair game to them."

"Why is that?"

"Because you had our help with it you see, if we hadn't been involved they probably wouldn't have interfered. But you will protect it after a while."

"What are they doing, is it the energy to energy thing again?"

"Yes they are interfering with the electrics they won't be able to cause any harm just the inconvenience of stopping now and again. If you leave it for a few minutes like today it will start again."

"Well I guess it's just another of those things that are sent to try us."

"You will overcome it very quickly."

"When Arthur and Brian came over they said they could feel something in the house was that our guides or aggravation?"

"That was interference they were feeling."

"How come they can feel it and we can't?"

"That's because you are protecting yourselves and they are not."

"I see so we have progressed then?"

"Yes we told you that you had, you don't feel much interference anymore do you?"

"Well a bit now and again but I just close down to it and ignore it."

"Why don't you try opening up for moment and see what you feel?"

"Ok, it feels cold and the hairs on my neck are tingling."

"Yes now you can see how far you have come."

"It's a gradual thing isn't it, we don't realise until we go back how far we have come."

"That's right now you know you can close down again. Remember that feeling, that's how you will know when someone is having problems at home or around them."

"When you say around them you don't necessarily mean in the house do you?"

"No I wondered if you would notice."

"What did you mean then?"

"There are those that stay in the house to cause problems and those that follow you around. They are there for much the same reason but they are different groups."

"Is that like possession?"

"No they just make you feel unwell and moody when you are out, it's just another way of wearing you down."

"Do they work with the ones who stay in the house?"

"Sometimes but usually they are separate groups working for different reasons."

"So not only do they attack us at home but they also go with us. We can't even go out to get a bit of peace then?"

"It's not often you will get both."

"Just as well otherwise we would get no peace at all. I think it is time to call it a night thank you for talking to us and good night."

"Good night and god bless."

Jan came back and we talked about how crafty they were not telling us about spiritualist churches. Now we had an idea where we were going to find a circle so that we could learn about clairvoyance and things. The following day we went along to the spiritualist church with Arthur, Brian and Penny. When we arrived we saw an old tumble down shed in between two blocks of flats backing on to the main railway line to London. I don't know what we were expecting but this wasn't it. Maybe if it had been in a hall in a proper building we would have felt more encouraged. Anyway we went in and it was laid out with about 80 chairs in the hall bit with two toilets on the right as you came in. There was a platform at the far end and on the other side opposite the toilets was a small kitchen. Although the place had been carpeted and the inside painted it still looked a bit rickety. There were about ten people there and we sat down near the front and looked around. I saw a cross on the front of the platform and wondered if it was an ordinary Christian church. A man came over to us and welcomed us. He asked whether we had been before, we said no, this was our first time, he said well enjoy the service. If you have any questions come and see me afterwards. While we waited for it to start I asked Arthur,

"How does it work then?"

"We start with a hymn then a prayer then another hymn then a talk then another hymn then the medium gives clairvoyance. After that they say a prayer then it's finished."

"Does the medium give clairvoyance like we saw at that demonstration?"

"Yes just the same although we don't know who the medium is yet they might not be as good as Roy was."

"When you say not as good, how do you mean?"

"They might not get as good evidence."

We sat and waited for it to start and then two men went onto the platform, one was the chairman the same man that welcomed us and the other I suppose the medium. There were about 25 people in the hall and they had a woman to play the organ. We had the hymns and the medium told us all about how he had got involved and how he had got ill if he did too much work for spirit. He said it was spirits way of slowing him down. Then it got to the clairvoyance and he gave some people a relative and a message. I listened and thought, how do these people know it's their mother or father, he hasn't told them anything about them all he said was I have your mother/father here. Looking at the people he was talking to I could have said the same thing, it was a safe bet that given their age their parents had to be dead. Anyway it came to an end and the others had a cup of tea and we left. Arthur said,

"Well what did you think of it?"

Jan said, "I got a bit confused at first when he asked if they could take it until I realized he meant did they understand, other than that it was ok. I don't really know what I was expecting but it was interesting."

We talked a bit more and then we went our separate ways home. Jan and I talked about what we had seen and decided we would have to go again and see what else they did. The next service was on a Tuesday night so we arranged to go and see what happened at that. We went and it was called a demonstration, less hymns and more clairvoyance. When we got there we were surprised to see it was a different medium. When we asked afterwards they said they had different mediums each time. It seems there are a lot more mediums about then I thought, I asked about circles and was told they were just going to start an open circle. If we would like to come along we would be welcome.

Chapter 23

We went to the open circle and there were about ten people there. They did a meditation and then the man who was in charge asked if anyone wanted to give off anything. I wasn't sure what he meant until a lady said yes I have something for that man there and then said a few things that he understood. There was nobody else who wanted to say anything so the man who was called Tom said ok, we will talk about the difference between psychic and spirit.

He said. "Psychic is where you pick up information from the person and spirit is when a loved one tells you something which you then pass on to the recipient. When you work on the platform you mustn't do psychic readings it must be from spirit, the idea is that you are proving survival of someone's loved ones. A psychic reading is when you use your intuition or pick up feelings from the recipient. For instance you might get the idea that they are feeling down or particularly happy today, the only way you will know if you are right is to tell the person what you are feeling. Now is that clear, good then are there any questions? No ok then I will ask one of you to start who wants to go first?"

A lady said she would start and gave some information to another lady who said she understood some of what was said. A few other people had a go and then Tom said now we are going to have a go at psychometory. That is when you hold an object that belongs to someone and see if you can pick up their vibrations. I thought we know a little about that and Tom asked Jan if she would like to

196

try. Jan had a go after saying she had never done it before and got some information for a man sitting next to her who had given her his watch to hold. I thought she did quite well for a first time but what did I know some of the others had a go then it was my turn. I thought now let's see if I have learnt anything, I told the lady sitting next to me a few things but she said she couldn't take anything so I stopped. Tom said don't worry it's your first time it takes time to tune in. Then it was time to stop so they said a prayer then had a cup of tea. We talked to a few people and found out that some of them had been going to the church for quite a while and it was the first time they had sat in a circle. They told us there were other churches all over the country and we should go to some of them to see what they did. Then it was time to go as they wanted to close up so we went home. On the way we talked about the circle and Jan said.

"What did you think of the circle then?"

"I thought it was interesting, when Tom spoke about psychic I was expecting him to show us how to do it. When I did psychometory on that ladies bracelet I think I was trying too hard. I couldn't seem to tune in to her it's not easy is it?"

"I just felt something, I wasn't sure if I was right or not so I thought I would tell him and see. It was like when I picked that cross up but not horrible."

"We will have to go again and see what else they do."

We picked the kids up from their friends and went home and put them to bed. Then agreed we would have a little chat with Jan's guides, Jan closed her eyes and one of her guides came through straight away.

"Hello Richard."

"Good evening did you have a nice time?"

"It was interesting I'm beginning to see why you never told us about churches before."

"Yes it's not often we get the chance to educate our mediums before they get tainted with man's beliefs."

"No I suppose most people have to go to churches to develop before they can talk to their guides."

"That's not what I mean, there are a lot of people who can hear us but they are not always able to ask questions like you are, or if they are they don't want to do anything with it."

"I don't think it's a case of getting into this so we could work, it's not as though that was our intention. We just got in a situation where we needed to know more to protect ourselves."

"I know it's funny how things work sometimes, but we are only guiding you along the pathway you have chosen."

"We have worked that out for ourselves now, anyway it looks like we have a lot to learn from these churches and the people in them."

"Yes you will hear some strange ideas just listen and again accept what you can and dismiss the rest. Don't try to educate anyone with the knowledge you have been given at this time just go and see. You will learn more about how they go about development and what works and what doesn't."

"Ok, you never told us about psychic readings on people."

"We did all you had to do was think it through if you can pick up on objects what's so different about reading people, after all they are spirit as well you know. It's like doing clairvoyance only your subject is still in your world."

"Yes I hadn't thought of it like that so it should be easier than communicating with your world."

"There are many different ways of working as you will find out in due course just enjoy the journey."

"Ok, were thinking of going to a different church to see what they do what do you think?"

"It will be good experience for you the more you see the faster you will learn."

"Why didn't Tom show us how to do psychic readings all he did was tell us what we were supposed to do?"

"You will find a lot of circle leaders will tell you but very few will demonstrate."

"Why is that?"

"If they get it wrong they will lose their credibility, if people see that they won't go to the circles."

"So although they know what to do they can't always do it?"

"No and that's where you will be different because you will show people how to do what you are asking them to do."

"Well in that case we had better get some practice in."

"You don't need to worry you have plenty of time it will come as you work with us."

"Ok well we better call it a night I have an early start tomorrow good night."

"Good night and god bless."

Jan came back and said,

"Looks like we got a whole new world to explore, it seems never ending doesn't it."

"Yes still it appears we've got plenty of time, I guess it's a case of taking things one at a time."

"Yes do you think there are many people that trance? I was talking to a lady at the church and she said she had never seen anyone. I thought everyone did it."

"I don't know well have to have a look around and see what people say."

We left it there and went to bed. The next day I checked the local phone book to see if there were any churches listed. There was one in Woking which was not far so we gave them a call to see when they were open. It seemed all the churches were open on Sunday nights, so we decided to go and see what they did on the coming Sunday. When we arrived we were asked if it was our first time. When we said we had been to another church a couple of times we were told we should be going to our own church and supporting that instead of going to lots of different ones. That didn't make us feel very welcome but we stayed and they had a service just the same as Camberley but with a different medium. After the service we got talking to some people who said they were healers at the church. They had healing sessions twice a week and after the service if anyone wanted. That kind of surprised us we didn't realize how popular healing was or that you could just turn up and ask. We thought healing was only done in circles but then thinking about it they didn't do it at the open circle at Camberley. We wondered whether they had healing sessions as well, we would have to ask. The people we were talking to said they did colour healing on Thursdays, when we asked what that was they said they shine a coloured light on the patient and give them healing. I couldn't see the point in shining a light on someone but didn't say anything. I thought it would be better to ask our guides. They also talked about how they never had an open circle so they were not able to learn about clairvoyance. We told them about the one at Camberley but they said it wouldn't be right to go to another church. This puzzled us we thought they should be able to go where they liked, anyway they wouldn't so we left it at that and went home. We had left the kids at home and when we got there the kids were saying the dogs had been cowering in the corner. We asked what they had done to them and they said nothing they just started growling and then went to the corner of the room and cowered. They also said the dogs were yelping so they gave them a cuddle and they were alright after that. We wondered whether the bad spirits could attack the dogs and thought we would ask later when the kids were out of the way. We asked the kids if anything else had happened and Clair said there was a man who came into the room, he just stood there and looked at them so she ignored him. She wasn't frightened of him, Jan asked what he looked like and she described her grandfather. That was a surprise and we were even more surprised when she said she had seen him before. I had never met him so I didn't know what he looked like but Jan said it was definitely him. The kids seemed ok so when they went to bed we sat down to talk to Jan's guides. I thought I would get some practice with healing so I placed my hands on her shoulders then put them either side of her head. Jan said.

"I can feel a lot of heat from your hands and my head is tingling,"

"I can feel a lot of tingling too I must be getting better at this, I feel I have got to move my hands to your neck is it hurting?"

"Yes it's been aching all day, I have got Samuel here do you want to speak to him?"

"I have got a few questions I would like to ask."

"When don't you, ok I will bring him through."

"Good evening Samuel."

"Good evening."

"I wanted to see if I could sense you coming through."

"Could you?"

"I knew there was someone there but if I was to guess I would have said

Richard is he here as well?"

"Yes he is my backup tonight."

"Ah that's why I thought it was him, why couldn't I sense you?"

"You are getting used to sensing him and that's who you look for. That's why I came through to give you both more practice with someone else."

"Alright I'm just going to finish healing then I have some questions for you."

"We can talk while you are doing that, who have you got with you?"

"I have Rosy with me I can feel her swaying."

"Good and who else is there?"

"I think its Elijah because my head feels different."

"Yes you are right, how does your head feel different?"

"It feels as though I am bald you know a bit of a draft round the ears."

With a chuckle Samuel said. "He doesn't have much on top, what about Rosy how long is her hair?"

"It feels as though my ears are covered but I don't think it's longer than down to my neck."

"That's right well done."

I finished healing and I was feeling quite pleased with myself until

Samuel said,

"Why have you stopped healing you haven't finished yet?"

"I thought I had, shall I come back?"

"No it's alright we will finish off for you but you must try and sense when your guides step back."

"I will try but I think I was too busy trying to see who was with me."

"Never mind it will come its early days yet."

"It seems sometimes like it's going to take forever to get the hang of this. When we were talking the other week we talked about different types of healing. Nobody said anything about colour healing, how does that work?"

"Colour healing is when you use a coloured light so that you can use the vibrations of the colour to enhance the healing."

"Does it work?"

"It makes no difference to the quality of healing but psychologically the patient thinks it is more powerful and so they feel better for it."

"So the use of these lights makes no difference to the healing. Why do they use it then?"

"Because as I have said it has psychological value, the healers believe it makes a difference as well. It's just another way of attracting patients."

"Were the dogs being attacked by spirit?"

"Yes they were being pinched and pushed around."

"How can we stop that, they aren't involved in any of this?"

"They are your pets, anything that gets to you will be done to upset or interfere with your concentration."

"We weren't even here."

"No but when you got back you found in your absence there had been interference. The idea is to stop you going to the church, if you think something is going to happen, then they think you will stay at home."

"Well their wrong they will not control our lives by attacking us or the dogs."

"You don't need to worry about the dogs they are old souls, we wouldn't have let you choose pets that couldn't deal with interference."

"So animals progress the same as us then?

"Yes of course, they have their journey too, not in the same way you do, they don't choose guides or lessons they just learn by experience."

"Isn't that a bit haphazard surely there is someone looking after them?"

"When they are in the company of yourselves they are looked after by both you and your guides."

"At least they are not left to fend for themselves. What about non domesticated animals do they get interference?"

"There would be no reason to interfere with them as the only object is to use your pets to get at you."

"We better stop now as it's getting on a bit thank you for talking to us good night."

"Good night and god bless."

When Samuel had gone we talked about what he had said and we both thought it was a good thing we had the opportunity to get answers. We called it a night and went to bed.

Over the next few months we attended the church in Camberley and got to know a few people. While going to church we also continued practicing at home and got to know a few more guides. This was useful not because we were able to have more conversations, but so we could practice recognising when a different one came through. I was able to identify all of my guides first time until it no longer mattered which one it was. All that mattered in the end was that it felt right, I trusted the right one would be there when they were needed. I have never been let down by them, although on occasions I let myself down, usually by trying too hard to get it right. We found we were getting hardly any interference, although there were plenty of spirits in the house they were not able to bother us anymore. They started a discussion group at the church which we went to but over the months we had found there are so many different ideas mostly without any basis of truth. For instance there were a lot of people that believed you had a doorkeeper who was in charge of your guides. So every time you wanted to do something spiritually the doorkeeper would select the guide for that particular activity. We couldn't see the point in this, if all our guides have been chosen for their expertise then they ought to know who was needed and when. We didn't say anything just looked and listened. We also went to other churches where they held open circles and found a great difference in the way they did things and the beliefs of not only the circle leaders but not surprisingly the sitters too. One circle we went to had about 35 people sitting in chairs placed round the outer edges of the room. This is how it worked. First we were told to meditate and find the light. Then when we had found it we were to ask for a message for someone in the circle. At the end of the meditation we were each asked in turn if we had anything, if so to tell the person it was for what we had got. Naturally there were the circle leader's favourites who were asked first, and they would spout on about all sorts of unrelated trivia which some people were too polite to say no to. Then after congratulating them on what they had said, she would ask everyone in turn if they had anything. Almost all said they had nothing but if someone said something she would say well done and go to the next person. There was no teaching, just sit and get what you could if you didn't get anything then it was not your time yet. At the end of this a prayer was said and the circle closed. On talking to some of the sitters a lot of them thought it was a good circle, we were at a loss for words. This wasn't teaching, no one was shown how to do anything or corrected or even encouraged to stretch themselves. We went a couple of times to see if that's all they did and it was.

On the way home after the third time we discussed what we were going to do next. We decided to search for other circles and see if they were any different.

We found another and went along the next week, there were about six sitters and were told the lady would only allow seven and no more. So you had to get there early to make sure you were not turned away. Fortunately we were early and managed to get in, I thought as there were so few of us maybe we would be taught something. When the circle started we were welcomed and then after a prayer the lady told us about doorkeepers. She said they were in charge and they would invite the spirit guide to come forward when we were working and we needed to get to know them first. I asked if we had only one guide and she said, yes you only need a doorkeeper they will get the spirit with the right knowledge to come when you need them. We had a meditation. The lady turned on some music and said now I want you to go into the quiet and ask your doorkeeper to come forward. Well I did as she asked and the thought I got back was.

"As you haven't got a doorkeeper, who would you like to come forward?"

I said "Anyone will do I don't suppose she will know anyway."

Well my Red Indian guide came and sat with me and we had a chat while the meditation was going on. When the music had finished we had been meditating for about half an hour and apart from having a chat I was getting bored. The circle leader then asked everyone if they had their doorkeeper with them and everyone said yes so I went along with it. She then said describe who you have

207

got and I will verify what you say if you are right. When it came to me I described my guide and she said,

"You are wrong it is not a Red Indian it is an old woman."

Well I looked at her and said,

"I don't think the old woman is with me she is with the lady next to me. I am aware of my Red Indian guide."

She said, "You are wrong and I am not going to argue with you when the circle closes don't come back. I am here to teach and if you don't want to learn then don't come."

I thought I wonder if it's the first time she has thrown anyone out of her circle, anyway Jan played the game and she said Jan was right she had done very well. The circle was closed after she had verified or denied what people said. I found it interesting that those who she said were wrong accepted what she said although she didn't give them proof. We left and Jan had a go at me for getting thrown out, she said,

"You have got to play the game if you go round upsetting people then they won't let you come back."

"Well what do you expect she didn't have a clue who was with me/"

"That's not the point it's her circle and you have to obey the rules, even if she didn't know what she was talking about. Richard was with me and he said watch and learn."

"Ok I won't argue next time, I don't think that was the circle we are looking for do you?"

"We are not going to learn much from her except what not to do. I didn't like the music it kept distracting me, I suppose that's because we haven't meditated to music before, I wonder how many circles do?"

"I think we will find out, if we find another circle to go to."

We talked a bit more about doorkeepers and what they were and why did people think they had only one guide. From what we had been told it didn't make sense maybe we were wrong, we had heard other people talking about their doorkeeper so it seemed like it was quite common.

When we got home it was late so I just wrote down some questions to ask next time we spoke to spirit.

We carried on going to the circle at Camberley and the discussion group and in the circle they were still doing psychic readings and psychometory. We were getting quite good at them both but we thought we should keep looking around to see what else was going on. In the discussion group I asked about doorkeepers and was told much the same as the lady had said so that confirmed for me it was quite a common belief. Until we had time to sit down and talk to our guides we would have to try and work out who was right. We thought we were as our guides had been right on everything else so far, but remembering what we had been told we thought we would wait and see what they had to say.

Finally we had an evening free so we sorted the kids out and settled down to talk to Jan's guides. I no longer gave Jan healing unless she needed it and sat opposite her while she brought a guide through. Someone came through who I didn't recognize, it had happened before so it was not too much of a surprise and I said,

"Who are you?"

"I am one of Jan's guides"

"No you are not, what do you want?"

"What makes you think I am not one of her guides?"

"In the first place you weren't introduced and secondly her guides don't refer to her by name."

"Well this time we are."

"Correct me if I'm wrong but you don't know her as Jan you know her as the spirit."

"That's her name isn't it?"

"That the name I know her by but that's in this life."

"I can answer your questions just as easily."

"Maybe, but you are not right now leave."

"No I think I will stay for a while."

"Jan throw him out."

Jan did and opened her eyes.

"That was interesting."

"Why what was so interesting then?"

"I could pick up what they were going to say before they said it."

"How did you throw them out?"

"I just said bugger off and opened my eyes."

"Shall we try again?"

"Good evening Richard."

"Good evening."

"We have been to a few circles and they don't appear to be teaching anyone, they mostly just sit there and say what they have got if they get anything."

"That's why we didn't want you to find out about churches too soon."

"How do you learn to do clairvoyance, if there is no-one to teach you?"

"You go to your local church haven't you learnt anything there?"

"Yes we have we are getting on quite well with psychic and psychometory but what's the next step?"

"Some of what you have been getting is clairvoyance, just be patient you will find another circle where you will find out more."

"Why can't we learn it here?"

"You need sitters who you don't know anything about."

"Of course never thought of that, what's a group soul?"

"What do you mean by group soul?"

"Well what people are saying is they are part of a group soul, one part stays in spirit another comes here and other parts of the soul inhabit other people. They say that's why we have an affinity with people when we first meet them because we are part of them. They also say their doorkeeper is part of their group soul."

"The soul is an individual; it can be in spirit or on the earth. It does not split into pieces. Each person has their own soul that is their life force there is no sharing or division."

"That's what we thought what about doorkeepers?"

"Each of you have many guides who look after your progress and protect your soul or spirit. Some people don't like the idea of many guides looking over their shoulder. They are more comfortable with one whom they call a doorkeeper."

"Does that mean the other guides can still work with their medium?"

"Yes but it also means one guide is on duty all the time, at least while the medium is awake."

"So that guide has to stay with them all the time they are conscious. Does that mean they can't go and do other things for their own progression?"

"No it means they can only go when the medium is asleep."

"If I remember correctly we were told if you feel as though you have known someone before it may be that you met in spirit or just have like minds?"

"Yes that is correct, although on rare occasions you may have met in another life."

"What as part of a family from before?"

"No just that your paths may have crossed at another time."

"I see those other circles we went to, how do they learn anything?"

"They don't, there are a few that can get little bits but until they are taught to focus and helped to speak of what they get they will only progress slowly."

"Is that why they say it takes many years and dedication to develop?"

"Yes that's why we held you back we knew how frustrated you would be."

"What about those people, do they know when bad spirit is there?"

"No they don't believe in bad spirit they think like attracts like. They wouldn't even consider they might get interference. Usually they don't as they won't be a problem for bad spirit."

"How come people who aren't developing get interference then?

"Just because they aren't developing doesn't mean they are not aware. There are many people who are aware of spirit but choose not to do anything with it. Also remember there are those who are not aware who desperately want some kind of attention, they will be forced open by bad spirit."

"Can you force someone open if you needed to?"

"We can make ourselves heard in an emergency if we need to."

"Yes I was wondering about that. We have to stop now thank you for talking to us good night.

"It's been a pleasure good night and god bless."

Over the next few months we found a few more circles to go to but apart from the odd strange ideas were much the same as we had already been to. The strange ideas included one man having a grizzly bear as a guide, another person had Joan of Arc and still others had Jesus, Winston Churchill and the like. Another circle we went to, one of the sitters asked after the opening prayer if he could reach outside the circle to get his glass of water. At that circle it was different to the rest in that if someone got something during meditation, they would tiptoe across the circle to whisper what they had to the recipient. Other than that it was the same as the others.

We heard about a well-known medium who was going to give a deep trance demonstration at Reading church so we made arrangements to go along. When we arrived there were about twenty people there and the medium had a friend who was going to look after her. We were asked to sit quietly while the medium tuned in and went into trance; this took about five minutes with a little heavy breathing. Then the friend welcomed the spirit and after a short speech from the spirit we were told we could ask questions. While people were asking questions I listened carefully to the answers and realised they were not full answers. I whispered to Jan that I didn't think this was right and she said she didn't either. We both sensed a woman with the medium but they thought it was a man. The medium was speaking in a deep gruff voice like a woman trying to talk like a man. When the session was over and the medium came out of trance she was tired and needed to be helped into a backroom for a rest. The friend of the medium came back and answered a few more questions then closed with a prayer and that was it. I was surprised that no-one else seemed to have noticed that it wasn't her guide especially as there were a few experienced mediums present.

We talked about it on the way home and decided that just because these people were well known didn't make them any good at what they were doing. When we got home we had a chat with our guides about it and this is what they said,

"Good evening Samuel"
"Good evening"
"We have just come back from watching a demonstration of deep trance and were not impressed as we didn't think

the medium had her guide with her. Why didn't she or her friend know it was an imposter?"

"The medium thought it was her guide but didn't know it was an imposter. The friend can't tell the difference and just works on trust. They both believe like attracts like and it never occurred to them they might not get her guide."

"What about the other mediums present couldn't they tell the difference?"

"They were not looking they took everything on face value, it was assumed as the medium was well known and had written books about mediumship she knew what she was doing."

"Why was she talking like a man?"

"Because she believes her voice should change to represent a man talking it is allowed to happen."

"How would she know anyway, as she was supposed to be in deep trance?"

"The medium asks her friend if it went alright and because she knows no different she would tell her what transpired."

"It seems to me there are a lot of mediums out there that need to learn the difference between good and bad spirits. Why don't they talk to their guides like we do and not just listen to others?"

"Most of the people who have the opportunity to converse with their guides don't. They seem to think we are just here to give teachings. It is rare for spirit to have a conversation like we do."

"That's a shame it would get rid of a lot of misconceptions about spirit and how we work together, it would also help people understand more about the philosophy."

"We live in hope that there will be some changes in the near future."

"The way things are going it won't be the near future it will be the distant future. Thanks for explaining that we have to go now god bless."

"God bless."

Chapter 24

We spoke to our guides quite often and found we were getting more information about our guides without asking Jan's. I was seeing pictures just like watching television which made things easier in one sense. But harder in another, as I still had to sense who was with Jan, I couldn't see her guides. Our guides took us on journeys in spirit while we were meditating and showed us different places in the spirit world. We never once went to the realms surrounding the earth. Most of the time we went with our guides, sometimes we were taken on the same journey. When we finished the meditations we would chat to Jan's guides about what we had seen. This is how the conversation went.

"Good evening Richard."

"Good evening."

"I have just been shown a hospital in spirit why do you need them you don't have bodies to heal?"

"No but we have people coming over with all sorts of problems, although they have come straight over they are not aware of what has happened to them. This is why we let them think they are in hospital, it's where they expect to be and the surroundings help us to get through to them, so that we can help them understand what has happened. We are not healing the body but the mind, by allowing them to think they are in hospital we are able to talk to them. Once they come to terms with the fact that they have passed then it is easy for us to explain the illness they have suffered is of the body not the spirit. They then go on their way, some will come back and help, others will go on to help in other ways. Some of these ways we have already discussed."

"What about the schools of learning?"

"We have talked a little about the opportunities there are for progression. The schools are for that purpose or just for learning something that may have interested you while on the earth plane."

"What if you don't want to do anything?"

"Then you don't, not until you are ready."

"How about those people who thought they had animals or famous people for guides, do they?"

"If you have an animal for a guide how will you communicate? You will only have guides who have inhabited human bodies. Otherwise as you saw he made himself look silly to the other sitters. Remember if you are not credible you will not be taken seriously just like he wasn't. As for famous people it's the same thing, credibility. It is very important that you are respected otherwise you will not be accepted as someone who knows what they are talking about. What chance do you think there is of a famous person from your world being a guide."

"What about Roy having his mother for a guide? I know she wasn't famous or anything but even so."

"That wasn't his mother; one of his guides had to pretend. When you pass you will want to make sure your loved ones return home safely. By loved one I mean siblings, children, grandchildren and even their children. That can take up to a couple of hundred years so you won't want to go anywhere until they are safely home."

"So does that mean none of our guides will have been in spirit for less than 200 years?"

218

"That's right and probably much longer, it takes a long time in your years to gain the skills required to be a guide."

"By which time unless they are historical figures like say Henry 8th or somebody like that they couldn't be guides anyway even if they wanted to?"

"You will find if someone is of that nature they will use a different life as a guide. Just because they are well known in your world doesn't mean they are in the world of spirit."

"Do you mean you can choose anyone of your lives to portray yourself?" "Yes again we are concerned for your credibility. You should also remember you choose your guides from your friends or from recommendations made by your friends here in spirit."

"So all our guides are known to us before we are born?"

"Yes how else would you be able to plan your journey?"

"That makes sense to me. What is it like in the realms surrounding the earth?"

"It is permanently twilight and cold."

"What can you see?"

"We can see everything because we use our senses."

"Ok what I mean is what can be seen by those who are lost or confused?"

"They can see others wandering around, they will also see people in your world. They can see your houses, some of which will have lights over them like beacons. They will see other houses that are dark and they will see others like themselves."

"Don't they talk to each other and try and work out what has happened?"

"Sometimes but don't forget they are in a strange place and don't know how they got there. Because it is dark and cold they tend to keep to themselves if you like as a way of protecting themselves."

"What are they protecting themselves from? If they don't know where they are how do they know there is any danger?"

"They will have seen people dragged off by the bad spirits who go around in gangs, so they will be dubious about whom they talk to or show themselves to."

"Does that mean they have to hide from the bad spirit?"

"It means they will go in the other direction if they see bad spirit and try to avoid being noticed. Some will go to houses with lights over them in the hopes of being able to communicate with someone who can help them. If you like it's like moths being attracted by the light."

"Why do some houses have lights over them and what is the purpose of them?"

"Those who work with spirit in your world will have lights over their house, it's an extension of the aura of the medium. The aura of the medium grows as they develop and we make use of it in that way. The idea is to attract lost souls so that they can be helped either by the medium or by their guides. Your house has a big light over it but it can also attract unwanted guests which is why you have had interference."

"So if we move the light goes with us? What happens to the house when new people move in who are not aware?"

"Yes as the light is an extension of your aura it will be over whichever house you are living in. The house you have left will have a signpost to show where you have gone to."

"What's the point of telling the lost souls where we have gone if they didn't know we were there in the first place?"

"It's not the lost souls you are redirecting it is for those of us that go and rescue them."

"Can't you just tune in to where we are?"

"Your guides can as we have an affinity with you, but there are many other spirits who rescue lost souls and don't have the same connection we have. They will want to find you quickly sometimes to bring people into your light."

"Does that mean we are providing a sanctuary for them until they are acclimatized to their new surroundings?"

"Partly but it is also so they can get used to seeing you working and open their minds to their circumstances. If you run a rescue circle then many more will be brought to your light."

"What about those mediums who just do healing or clairvoyance?"

"All spiritual work produces a light, although they may not be aware of the lost souls, their guides are, and are often able to take them on the next step in their journey to the spirit world."

"If there is a signpost telling anyone who can read it where we have gone then aren't we going to get the bad spirit coming as well?"

"Yes you will but they will only follow if they have a good reason."

"Do you mean if we are going to cause them problems by interfering with their little empires?"

"Yes they will not usually follow healers or clairvoyants as they are not interfering with them."

221

"So by doing healing does that give the lost souls comfort?"

"They will feel the energy from the healing which will not only heal them but show them there is something different about them."

"How do you mean?"

"All of their aches and pains will go and even where they have been maimed they will benefit. If you go to a healing sanctuary like your churches where they have healing, you can tune in and be aware of them."

"So although we are giving healing to the patients we are also helping those in spirit?"

"Yes there will always be excess healing rays. That's what makes the healing sanctuary so peaceful for the patients. The guides of the healers will prepare the sanctuary, before the healing starts, to build up the energy, so the healers can work in the right kind of environment. It's the same when you run a circle the room has to be prepared before you start. If you run more than one circle then it is prepared in advance of each circle. The protection is different for each type of circle."

"There's a lot more work goes in to starting a circle than most people think."

"Yes we like to make sure you have the best conditions to work in."

"How much notice do you need to clear the way before a circle can be started?"

"Usually it takes a little while for sitters to be gathered together and it gives us plenty of time. After all we know when our medium is going to run one, we usually discuss it with them before-hand."

"What about bad spirit we have talked a little about them but I know there is a lot more?"

"That will have to be for another time, my medium is getting tired"

"I didn't realise what the time was, good night and thank you for talking to us."

"Good night and god bless."

We talked about what Richard had said briefly then went to bed. The next day we sat again as there were more questions to get answers to. I asked Jan,

"Are there any questions you want me to ask or anything that Richard talked about last night?"

"Yes ask about the houses that don't have lights, I presume they control them."

"Ok let's see who comes through it was going to be one of my questions anyway."

We didn't meditate or do any healing Jan just closed her eyes and went off into trance.

"Good evening Richard."

"Good evening."

"I thought you might want a break after last night."

"We talked it over and it was decided that I would come and finish what we had started."

"Ok first question you have told us about the houses with lights, what about the other houses?

"Most houses have lights over them but where they are controlled by bad spirits the light is very dim."

"Why is that?"

"While the bad spirits are there their energy is dull and the light from the people who live in the house is dimmed by their bad energy. Because there is so much negative energy in and around the house the light tends to get covered up by it. The best way I can put it is positive energy burns brightly and negative energy is dull."

"What if you have a working medium in the house?

"The light is constantly being replenished by the work the medium is doing so stays bright."

"How can we tell the difference between the houses controlled by good spirits and bad if sometimes the light is bright but there are still bad spirits controlling it?"

"You use your senses when you enter the house, you will always pick up the negative however they try to hide it. It's those who are lost that get drawn in, when you see spirit in energy form instead of people like you do now, you will see the light that is your guides is bright and the others are dull."

"We have only seen you as people, when are you just energy then?"

"We only show ourselves as people when we are working with you, otherwise it would be more difficult for you to recognise us."

"I suppose it would be difficult for the mediums that see spirit but what about those who just sense you. I can't see how it would make much difference to them as you still feel the same don't you?"

"Yes but it is easier for you to associate with us, don't forget there is often more than one medium present and not all mediums sense."

"We talked about what the bad spirits do in houses that they control, but is that all there is. Surely they are not restricted to houses are they?"

"No there are many who don't use houses they just take over an area around your world or travel between one job and the next."

"Do you mean they move from one place to another annoying people?"

"Not exactly what happens is if someone who controls a house needs a particular skill they will send out a thought and someone will come and bargain with them for the use of that ability. As you know there is no money it is about power and the bargain will be struck on what favour's or people those who want the skill are prepared to offer. Depending on what is required depends on how many of these contractors are needed."

"Are you saying that there are bad spirits who specialise in certain things that travel from one place to another when they are needed?"

"Yes for ease of understanding we will call them contractors which are essentially what they are. These are very experienced in what they do and are constantly practicing to get better and move on to the next step which is an independent."

"So if I have this right there are three different types of bad spirit so far, the ones who control houses, the contractors and the independent's.?"

"Well the contractors work for a group who hire out their skills for more power which means territory or people. When they have completely mastered their particular skill they will usually break away from the group and go out on their own. When they become independent of the group they will tout for business just the same as you do when you go after a new contract. With the independent working in a house you know there is going to be trouble for those who live there."

"What like major upheaval?"

"Not necessarily, because they are more skilled at what they do they are more subtle in their approach. It may take longer but there is a guarantee they are going to get results. It could be they have been asked to make someone feel unwell with constant headaches or upset stomachs. The person they are working on may be subject to depression or guilt about something. The independent and the contractor will make these feeling seem constant which would drive anyone to withdraw from those around them."

"Can they make anything happen to us?"

"No they can only bring back the memory of whatever you have naturally suffered. For instance if when a child you broke a limb they can remind you of the pain you suffered, only because you haven't broken the limb again you will not understand why you are getting the pain. It won't be a constant pain but sharp twinges at awkward moments or headaches when you have something important to do. The idea is to inconvenience you as much as possible. Take for instance a relationship, if you are feeling on top of the world so to speak and your partner is feeling low you will become subdued because of your concern for them. The next day they will switch it around so you are feeling down and your partner is feeling happy. With this going on all the time you will very soon get fed up with each other, and separate, in the hope of finding a happier life maybe with someone else. The job is then done."

"Why would the bad spirits want to separate couples?"

"They don't always want to separate them, just cause them misery, it's how they get their kicks and also gives them something to do."

"So they can only give you the memory of what you have had before, like when I was getting aggravation it wasn't real it was just memories of previous discomfort.?"

"Yes when you realize you haven't caused the pain you are suffering then usually it will go as subconsciously you realise it is not your pain. The problem is there are so many people who get attention from those around them when they are suffering, like sympathy and being looked after that they enjoy the attention and don't realise what's going on. You have met people who wallow in their misery and are always complaining that they are unwell, it's another form of attention."

"So they do all this for kicks is that the only reason?"

"Sometimes they just want the house to themselves and whoever is living there is just in the way."

"Are there any other reasons why they do these things?"

"Yes there are people like you who get attacked because they want to stop you becoming a nuisance later as we have discussed."

"What happens after you become an independent what's next?"

"There is nothing else, it takes many of your years to reach such a position."

"So what do they do after that, do they just carry on forever?"

"No after a while they become bored they then decide to come home as there is nothing left for them on the dark side, they have done it all."

"They can just swap sides whenever it suits them?"

"Yes of course as you know we never judge, sometimes it's a bonus for us because they will work with us to stop other contractors from working. With all they have learnt by keeping themselves safe they are in an ideal situation to assist us. What could be more useful than someone who has as you say worn the tea shirt?"

"Does that mean they then work with the good spirits to rescue people that are lost, how do you know you can trust them?"

"They don't come over and start straight away it can be some years before they offer their services. Usually things are too tame for them and they want to make amends for what they have done."

"If they are independent why would they want to work for the people in the houses and get paid with people? Surely they wouldn't want to be tied down with keeping an eye on and training them."

"It's not only people that they bargain for they may want to learn a new skill and will trade for someone to show them how to do something else."

"That makes sense I suppose the more they can do the more in demand they are?"

"Yes and your thinking do women do that as well aren't you?"

"Well it did cross my mind."

"Don't forget they are all spirits they only have a gender in your world even if you are aware of them as women they are as capable as anyone else."

"Yes I guess you are right what about the good guys do you have a structure like that only for the benefit of people rather than for your own ends?"

"When you say a structure how do you mean?"

"I mean as I understand it you work together in teams for the benefit of others. Although you progress while you are working that's not the prime reason for helping is it?"

"No we help where we can for all to come home safely the fact that we progress at the same time is a bonus."

"So who is in charge of the good guys, I don't believe it's a dictatorship which it would be if one person was in charge?"

"No one spirit is in charge we work together for the benefit of all. You are avoiding the use of the word god why?"

"Because if there was a god he would have to be a dictator however benevolent he was and I can't see that working. You have also mentioned the source which we call god. That tells me there is no individual but rather an energy that we all come from, which is managed by the good guys for the benefit of all spirit whether on earth or in between. Is there a group of spirits that oversee things and coordinate everything?"

"There are groups of spirits that look after different aspects of our work."

"How do you select them do you vote them in and if so for how long?"

"They are chosen for their skills by those they are going to oversee much the same as you choose your guides. When the job is done they will go their separate ways. Some of them may be asked to sit for another who is on a journey, others may be asked to teach. It is usually those

229

with the skill that is needed who will be asked. As you can imagine they are all well versed in what they do."

"I see that makes far more sense than one person be they spirit or what knowing everything. It's time to say good night thank you for talking to us but I am afraid we live in a world where time is important."

"Yes we are well aware of your restrictions, I will say good night and god bless."

Jan came back and made a cup of tea and we talked about what had been said. We decided that god had to be whatever the individual felt comfortable with as we had no definitive answer, or did we? It's interesting that spirit allow us to believe in things that are not necessarily factual but close enough to enable us to work with them. It seems there are a whole lot of things to do with bad spirits that are rarely talked about. We were to find out the truth to that at a later stage in our development. We went to bed with a lot of things going round in our minds, about what was true and what we had been led to believe during our upbringing by those in churches when we were young and later at school. Although neither Jan nor I attended church any more than we had to as both our parents were not church goers. Over the next few weeks we went to Camberley church and continued to attend the open circle, although we felt it was getting a bit stale. We were not in our opinion learning anything different than we had been since we started. To be fair though we were getting quite good at psychic and psychometory but we felt we needed more. Then we heard about another open circle that was going to start at a church not too far away and decided to go and have a look.

Chapter 25

When we arrived at the church which was in Hampton Hill we found it was run by a couple called Ann and Mike. They were both working mediums who had been and done courses at a place called The Arthur Findlay College near Stansted Airport. It turns out this college is a place devoted to teaching mediums. We sat in the circle with about 20 others and Mike went round and asked everyone their names and what they had been doing. He then said we will try to show you the next step on your pathway, please be patient as we will need to work our way through things you may already have done. We are going to start with a meditation which will last about 20 minutes and I am going to talk you through. This he did and when he brought us back he then asked each of us how we felt and what we had seen. One particular part of the meditation was about going over a bridge. He never described the bridge just said go over the bridge, what was interesting was that lots of people saw a bridge but they were all different. He also asked us if we had met anyone and those that had he talked to them about who they had met, and confirmed whether they were right or not, he also corrected them if they got something wrong. This was what we have been looking for we said to each other, now at last we may be able to find out more. After that he gave us a little talk about spiritual philosophy and we did psychic readings. We stayed in the circle and each had a go and Ann helped to draw out what we were feeling. With this kind of encouragement most people who had never done it before got something. We stayed and had a chat with a few people and found they had been looking for an open circle for a long time and thought this one would be a good place to learn. On our way home we talked about what we had seen and felt we had finally found a place where we might progress. Over the next few days we tried meditating one at a time without the light on, while the other tried to sense who was there. Jan was tuning in to me with her eyes open when she started seeing little round coloured lights rolling up my arms and over my head, some lights were yellow and others were a deep electric blue. When I came back she told me about it and then she meditated while I watched her. Although I was able to tell who was with her I never saw any lights. After Jan had finished meditating we thought we would have a chat with one of her guides so she closed her eyes and Richard came through.

"Good evening Richard."

"Good evening."

"I have some question for you."

"That will make a change."

"Yes well, while we were meditating just now your medium saw little round lights rolling up my arms what are they?"

"They are spirits in their natural form."

"Why are they so small?"

"How big do you think we are?"

"I hadn't thought about it I suppose I always thought you were the same size as us. That's how I see you as people."

"Yes we show ourselves like that so that you can associate better. But our natural state is energy so we can be any size we desire."

"Thinking about it we were told before that you were energy and didn't need bodies. I just never thought about how you would appear in your natural state. What about the different colours do they mean something or is that your choice?"

"You may also see oblong shapes as well. As you know we can read each other's aura, and the colours tell us what the individual spirit is capable of. The different colours also let us know how advanced each spirit is."

"Are they always bright colours?"

"For your guides and helpers yes, the bad spirits also show colours but they are dull much like the light around the houses they control."

"I suppose that's because they are tainted by the things they do?"

"Yes in just the same way as the lights over their territory."

"Are you able to show yourself when you want or can you stop us from seeing you?"

"We are able to hide when we choose, you will also find the bad spirits can hide from sight but not from senses."

"Why would they want to hide?"

"They only want you to see them when it is convenient to them, they will show themselves as people almost all of the time. Don't forget their objective is to frighten."

"So when do they hide?"

"When you go to someone's house where they are being interfered with they will sometimes hide in the hope that you will miss them."

"What happens if we miss them will they be able to carry on with what they are doing?"

234

"Not only will they carry on but any that you have thrown out they will be able to bring back."

"So when we start doing that sort of work we will have to be able to find them?"

"By the time you start working you will be ready for most possibilities."

"We have found a circle where they appear to know what they are doing we think, anyway we are going to keep going and see what transpires." "The circle you have found will help you to progress but be careful what you say. They are good people but they have their beliefs just like everyone else."

"I suppose you know about the spiritual college like you knew about the churches?"

"Yes of course but as you have found out, there are things you needed to know before you found the churches, it is no different with the college."

"Okay we better go now it's getting late again thanks for talking to us good night."

"Good night and god bless."

We talked over what had been said, it seemed we were going to have to play hide and seek with the bad spirits sometimes. It was getting more and more complicated and that's without learning to do clairvoyance.

Chapter 26

The next day Darren came in looking a little worried. When we asked what was wrong he said,

"My friend was lying in bed this morning when his duvet started to slide down the bed, it went over the end of the bed then slid up the wall until it was hanging there about a foot off the floor."

"What has he been doing I asked?"

"Nothing we had a go at the Ouija board last night that's all."

"Why did you do that?"

"Well we got talking about what you do and thought we would have a go."

"Did you get any results?"

"It went to some letters but didn't spell a word then stopped, we just thought it was a game because it's made by a game company you know like a board game."

"Where is the game now?"

"It's at my friend's house."

"Okay let me explain about Ouija boards. Suppose you pick up a telephone and dial a number, any number what will you get?"

"Someone will answer it."

"Yes but you won't know who they are. That's the same as a weeja board you are dialling a spirit, you don't know what you are going to get. There are good and bad spirits as you know from the aggravation we have had in the house. If you get a bad spirit they will play games with you to try to frighten you, and that's what has happened."

"Can you do anything to stop it?"

"The first thing he should do is throw the game in the dustbin. Does he want to come round and speak to us?"

"No he's too frightened he thinks our house is haunted."

"Okay tell him we will sort it out before he goes to bed tonight and he has nothing to be frightened of. We will get rid of it but he must not use the weeja board anymore tell him to throw it away."

"Okay will I get things happening to me?"

"No we will stop that from happening too."

"Alright I'm sorry I didn't know."

"That's ok, but remember, not to play with that type of game again, if you're other friends do then you must leave the house."

"Don't worry I'm not getting involved with that again."

That night we asked one of Jan's guides to come through so we could sort out Darren's friend.

"Good evening Samuel."

"Good evening."

"I expect you heard about Darren's friend, can we clear his house from here?"

"Yes how do you want to do it?"

"What do you mean? I thought you would just get rid of the bad spirits for us?"

"This would be a good time to practice what you have been learning all this time."

"Apart from a couple of rescues we did with Arthur and you know how that turned out, we haven't done any yet."

"I know so let's start by bringing the bad spirit to my medium and when they come through you can talk to them like you are talking to me."

"Okay but I want to talk to your medium first."

"Jan are you ok with this?"

"Yes it should be interesting they can't be any worse than the ones who pretend to be my guides. Anyway our guides wouldn't suggest it if they thought we couldn't handle it."

"Alright just wanted to make sure you were alright with it. If you get

Samuel back and we will go from there."

"Just let me get comfortable he's just behind me."

"Hi Samuel how is this going to work?"

"Talk to them and see what they want. Remember what we have talked about and decide what you are going to do with them and do it. I will be close by and will come back when you have finished, listen to your guides and your senses."

Samuel stepped back and after a moment there was someone else there. "Good evening."

"What's good about it?

"Well we have got a chance to talk, why did you frighten my son's friend?"

"Because I wanted to."

"That's not very nice is it?"

"Who says I have to be nice it's not very nice here."

"Do you want to go somewhere nicer where you can be with your family and friends?"

"No I'm quite happy here away from them goody goodies."

"Well you can't stay at that house you will have to leave."

"Why I was there first I'm staying."

"I'm not going to argue with you I have given you a choice you either leave the house or I will throw you out."

"Oh really do your worst."

"Ok Jan throw him out."

Jan opened her eyes and said,

"It was just the same as the ones who try to pretend to be my guides, when I threw him out he was covered in what I can only describe as a red net. He was in an awful hurry when I let him go."

"Do you think there are more, if I remember rightly they wouldn't be able to do that with a duvet by themselves?"

"I think we should have a look and see what else is there."

"Alright off you go then."

After a few moments someone else was there so I said,

"Hello what have you been doing?"

"It wasn't my fault they made me do it."

"What wasn't your fault?"

"I didn't want to frighten him they made me."

"So they have been keeping you there to do nasty things to my son's friend?"

"Yes there are five of us they make us do all sorts of things."

"Like what for instance?"

"We have to move things and hide them, they get other people to make him feel ill and then they made us move his bedcovers."

239

"Would you like to get away from them?"

"We would if we could but they just catch us and bring us back."

"We can help. We will take you to heaven they won't be able to get you back from there."

"Can you do that?"

"Yes get your friends together and we will get started."

"Okay we are all here now. We are frightened they are watching us."

"Okay we'll put protection round you so they can't get to you."

"Is that that blue glow?"

"Yes now open your eyes and tell me what you can see."

"I can see a light it looks like a tunnel with a light at the end."

"That's right the light is where heaven is shall we go?"

We took them to heaven and when they were safe we came back. I was able to sense what was happening while Jan says she could see everything. Jan came back for a moment and we thought we might as well try to get rid of the others that were in the house. Jan went back into trance and brought someone else through.

"Good evening."

"You think your smart don't you messing up our little game?"

"What you are doing is not nice so we are going to stop you."

"You have no right to interfere it's not your house."

"Actually we were asked to help. That gives us all the authority we need to deal with the likes of you."

"Well we are staying and there's nothing you can do."

"Ok if you say so, we are going to put protection round the house so you can't get back in, then we are going to banish you from here. All of you can go together, good bye."

Jan opened her eyes and said,

"Boy were they angry, you should have heard the names they called you."

"I did they called me some pretty rude things, anyway was it easy to control them?"

"I think I had a lot of help from my guides they didn't feel very nice at all, but I was able to keep the feelings they were trying to give me at a distance so it wasn't too bad."

"So how do you feel now, are you alright?"

"Yes I feel fine, were you able to sense anything?"

"Yes it was like being there with the kids almost, I could see them all go to heaven and I was able to see who was waiting for them. Shall we ask Samuel back?"

"Ok I will ask him."

"Hi Samuel, how did we do?"

"You did very well for a first time we didn't expect you to go and get the others we were going to clear them out when you had finished with the children."

"I suspect we had a lot of help from our guides, it's interesting it was like
I knew what to do."

"Your guides were telling you what to do."

"I never heard them."

"No as you said it was like you just knew. That's how you guides communicate with you they feed thoughts directly into your mind."

"Is that how clairvoyance works?"

"That's how it will work for you. Different people will work in different ways depending on how far they have developed. Some will hear and others will see, gradually as they progress they will get thoughts and impressions and then they will just sense or know."

"That's interesting when we went to that new circle they said first you sense then as it becomes clearer you will see and hear. That's backwards isn't it?"

"Don't forget you are used to seeing and hearing, these are the senses you use most so people will naturally think that is the best way to communicate. They forget how we communicate so they expect us to work their way. You are all spirit and the most natural way for us to communicate with you is by sense. It is a much faster way of passing on information."

"Does that mean the way we communicate is very slow and we have to speed up by using our thoughts to communicate with spirit?"

"Yes we do not slow down for you even when you first become aware we still work at the same speed."

"Why don't you slow down until we get used to talking to spirit then gradually speed up when we are used to it?"

"If we do that then you will progress much slower in your development, there will be those that are a little lazy who will not accept anything but words or sight."

"I see so it's up to us if we want to be any good at this communicating lark we have to keep working on our development?"

"Yes you will see as you go around the churches and see different mediums work. Some will tell you they hear and see and others will say they don't see anything. Take notice of the information each gives and you will see the difference in how much each type of medium gives."

"Ok Darren's friend's house is clear now isn't it?"

"Yes he won't have any more trouble providing he does not invite others in."

"How could he invite them back?"

"He can't invite them back but he might just open the door for others to get in."

"How would he do that?"

"By using the game again or thinking are they still here."

"So how does he stop them from coming in?"

"By getting on with his life and forgetting all about it."

"That's easier said than done, when you have a frightening experience like that you are not going to forget it easily."

"We know that, his guides will protect him until he has settled down don't worry he will be fine."

"Ok thanks for your help tonight we will have to stop now good night."

"It's been a pleasure good night and god bless."

Jan came back, she was a little worried about Darren's friend, so we telephoned him and told him it was all gone now and to forget about it. We also told him to get rid of the board game, to throw it away. He said yes, Darren had told him what we said and he had already thrown it in the dustbin.

We were quite pleased with our first attempt and decided we would wait and see if Darren's friend had any more problems. That would prove to us that we were working the right way. It's not that we didn't trust our guides but we wanted to understand it for ourselves.

Chapter 27

We went to the circle at Hampton Hill each week and it was interesting to see the different ways they showed us how to do things. We weren't doing so much psychometory now as we were getting better at psychic readings. We did colour readings with lengths of different coloured material which was picked out by the recipient and given to the person who was to do the reading. Really it was another way of doing psychic readings, but by doing it that way it was more interesting. After we had done that a few times we then discarded the material and just said a colour. Some of the people there were able to get bits of clairvoyance when they were doing psychic readings. We were told this was the way we would gradually pick up more clairvoyance. It turned out that when you thought about what you were getting you tend to rationalise it and that's when you get it wrong. By doing psychic readings we weren't thinking so it made it easier for us to give some information from spirit. We were told all the while you kept talking it would come through. What Mike said was think of it like a tap, when you turn it on it flows, it's the same with clairvoyance all the while you talk spirit can feed you more, when you stop they have to wait for you to start again. Often when you stop, you then start to think and that's when it goes wrong. He made it sound so easy. When he asked us to do something either Ann or Mike would show us how. Jan and I found we could get little bits of information and we were told to keep practicing it would come gradually.

We asked about The Arthur Findley College and were told you had to join the Spiritualist National Union as a B member and then all the courses were open to us depending on our ability. We thought it would be a good idea to join, then after we had we were given a list of courses which we could attend. The courses usually lasted for about a week and the idea was it was like a hotel we could stay for a week full board, and attend the course we had chosen. As it was quite expensive we would have to save up for a week there which we did. Over the next year we attended a number of courses and managed to pass them. Courses could also be done at home these were more on the administrative side of things and theory. Once we had done the theory we would then set about the practical side which ranged from clairvoyance to speaking and healing and many more.

During the time we were doing these courses we attended the circle with Ann &Mike and when they started an open platform we went there as well. An open platform is where budding speakers and clairvoyants got the chance to stand in front of people and practice whatever they were working on. We went to another church where they were running a speakers philosophy class. This is where they taught us how to address a congregation and how to speak about a subject which was to do with spiritualism. Naturally we got to know quite a lot of people and we heard some weird stories about what people believed.

The open circle at Camberley closed because Tom was ill. When he got better he said he wanted to start a closed circle would we like to join. We said yes we would like that and a few weeks later we started sitting. We sat in a little room at the back of the church. We would say a prayer and then Tom would ask us to try and get a communicator for someone in the circle. We took it in turns with varying success. Sometimes we were able to recognise who was there and sometimes even get a bit of a message. With all the practice we had had we were getting more than most but felt we had a long way to go yet. After about six weeks Tom said we are going to have a physical circle tonight was everybody happy with that. We thought why not and we all agreed to give it a try. The room we were sitting in had heavy curtains over the window to block out the light. There were seven of us and we had an infrared light which was directed at the small table in the middle. On the table was a trumpet and a small bell, the trumpet was the shape of a witches hat made of aluminium with two bits of luminous tape circling the bottom. This was held in front of a normal light for a while then put on the table where the tape glowed in the dark. The idea was that if the trumpet moved we would see it and the bell was there in case spirit wanted to ring it.

When the circle started we would sing a couple of songs, we were told this would raise the vibrations and then sit quietly talking about spiritual things. We did this for about four weeks but nothing happened. We were then told it could take years for anything to happen as spirit wanted to see if we were dedicated or not. It was decided by Tom that we should all concentrate our energy on him to try to get things moving.

247

Jan and I discussed the physical circle and thought we would have a chat with our guides about it one night. While everything else had been going on we were still chatting to our guides on a regular basis at least twice a week.

The next time we had a chance to sit we wrote down some questions we wanted answers to and Jan asked one of her guides to come through. By now it was second nature for me to sense who was there and fairly rare for me to get it wrong.

"Good evening Richard." I said when he came through.
"Good evening."
"As you know we have been attending a physical circle at the church."
"Yes how are you getting on?"
"Although we would like something to happen we don't think it will, why is that?"
"When you start a physical circle the sitters have to be of like mind. If one sitter doesn't want anything to happen then it won't."
"How are we ever going to know if someone is not in agreement? If they say that's what they want we have to believe them?"
"The circle was set up as a closed circle which is why everyone wanted to sit, when it was changed into a physical circle they didn't disagree because they thought it would be changed back again if nothing happened. The other reason why nothing will happen is because the

protection was set up for a closed circle. You can't change the purpose of a circle without closing down the previous one first."

"So that means if we want to start a circle we have to give you notice so you can put the right type of protection round it?"

"Each circle has its own type of protection, we can set it up at a moment's notice but each sitter needs time to prepare in their own mind for the circle. This means talking with their guides and deciding if it is the right circle for the individual. It is the circle leader's guides who are responsible for setting up the protection. We will discuss with the rest of the sitters guides about their mediums situation and what it is they want their medium to learn. If we are working for the same reasons then we will sit together and work out an agenda for the circle. We then have to arrange for another group of experienced spirits to oversee the circle and advise us of any unforeseen circumstances as they come up."

"So it's not just a case of sitting in a circle there is a lot of work to be done behind the scenes, why do you need a group of overseers can't you keep an eye on things yourselves?"

"The reason we have another group of spirits watching is as we are involved with our mediums we can only look after the immediate situation. The overseers can see the bigger picture and advise us if things are not going to plan. Also don't forget we are often going about your future business or doing healing on your behalf so will not always be at the circle. All circles need continuity to progress at a steady pace rather than in fits and starts."

"Sometimes it appears to us we are not getting anywhere is that because we aren't sitting in the right circle?"

"That may be the case, but for you, we wanted you to sit in as many circles as possible so you would get a good idea of what others were offering. In that way you would see what worked and what didn't."

"So the physical circle isn't going to do anything? What's the idea of the trumpet and bells?"

"The trumpet has been used in other circles for spirit to talk through they will talk through the large end. You will if you sit in one of those circles hear the voice coming out of the smaller end. The bells are so that those who are unable to speak can let their presence be known. That particular circle won't have anything happen because as we have said it isn't set up properly."

"Why do we have to sit in the dark with an infrared light?"

"The infrared light is used as the frequency of the light is lower than your normal light and it will make it easier for you to see the phenomena that they hoped for. They say you can't see ectoplasm in ordinary light because it is too delicate and dissolves before it gets a chance to form. Sometimes you will get one of the sitters transfiguring in a physical circle and you won't see it in normal light."

"Why would anyone want to sit for years to get something to happen, I can't see the point it must be pretty boring?"

"It takes a long time for sitters to become as one and blend, until that happens nothing else will so the sitters have to be dedicated."

"I have read about things happening in broad daylight, how is that, if you have to sit for a long time in the dark?"

"Like we said before it's the tried and tested method, we progress too you know and we are always looking for new ways of doing things. We spoke a while back about thinking outside the box, we are just waiting for you to catch up."

"Does that mean you are always looking for better ways to communicate?"

"Yes you will be aware that in the past most of the communicating was done either by knocks or by trance mediums in deep trance. Well as people have become educated we have been working more on mental mediumship, the same as you are doing, it's quicker and doesn't have the restrictions of physical mediumship."

"So the future is in mental rather than physical mediums? If that's the case why do we still have physical mediums?"

"It's another way of showing you that spirit is here although there won't be so much of it there will always be a place for the dedicated to display it. There are many in your world who are interested in that form of mediumship."

"In the early days when mental mediumship was first getting off the ground they had mesmerisers to get them started why was that?"

"They used hypnotists to put them into trance but not for mental mediumship. Trance and hypnosis are very close together in the mind, if you like when you go into trance you put your mind in a state similar to hypnosis."

"You mentioned transfiguring just now can you explain more about that?"

"We have touched on it before, it's the easiest form of physical medium- ship. What happens is again you can use an infrared light and you allow spirit to build up a face of someone in spirit on your face. For this you don't have to go into deep trance but many do as they are trying to get a voice as well."

"Why can't it be done in light trance?"

"It can but you will always get those who want to be sure it's not them speaking much like deep trance and light trance, as we spoke of before. The guides will work with their medium and once they have blended, they will produce ectoplasm and mould it on their mediums face to show someone else."

"Is that similar to the cobwebby feelings I get when my guides come close?"

"Yes it's the same sort of thing only more so."

"You suggested the infra-red light was not needed for transfiguring is that right?"

"Yes it can be done in normal light but people don't believe it, it may take a little longer for you to see but it will happen."

"We were talking to someone the other day and they were talking about walk ins, apparently the Americans seem to think it's normal."

"What exactly do you mean by walk ins?"

"Well they believe if you are fed up with life you can leave your body and another spirit will come and take over for the rest of the body's life."

"I wonder sometimes at what people will think next, as you know you inhabit your body for as long as it functions, when it no longer works you pass over to spirit. Can you imagine what it would be like over here we would have no end of problems trying to keep tabs on who is here and who is there." (*This was said with a chuckle*)

"That's what I thought there are some very strange ideas going around, another thing someone told me was the open circle they attended, which was run by the president of the church, the sitters had guides from
Disney."

"What do you mean?"

"Their guides were Goofy and Pluto and the like, it's no wonder people think we are cranks."

"Some spiritualists don't do themselves any favours do they?"

"Well I guess on that note we will have to say good night."

"Good night and god bless."

Chapter 28

We talked about what had been said about physical circles and decided we wouldn't go to the one at Camberley anymore and would let Tom know when we next saw him. When we went to church the next time we were asked if we would be willing to stand for the committee, we thought about it and said we would. Over the next month or so the church had its AGM and we were both elected to the committee. We were asked to run a discussion group in the church and agreed. This was attended by about 25 people and went well for a while until we were asked if we would turn it into an open circle. We put the idea to the committee who agreed and so set it up for the following month. We were lucky that we had attended courses at Arthur Findley College because they had taught us how to run workshops. With the experience we had gained from other circles and our guides we planned how we were going to run it. The first week we had about 15 people and over the next few months as we found our feet it went up to an average of 30 each week. We ran it on similar lines to Ann & Mike as we had found that a good circle and added a few other bits we had learnt from other places. It was from that circle we started getting enquiries about haunted houses. People had heard about some of what had gone on with us and asked if we could help.

We heard a lot of ghost stories from people when they told us about their experiences and also a lot of rubbish. The problem we found was deciding who had a genuine problem and who was blaming spirit for their own failings. We visited quite a few houses before we started to understand what was spirit and what wasn't. It was a good lesson as we found theory and practice is not always the same. Where we had learnt to deal with bad spirits at home we knew what was going on. When we went to other people's houses we had to listen to their experiences and at the same time tune in and check to see if it was spirit or their imagination. Quite a few times it was the people in the house blaming spirit for things they were not doing, for instance like losing things or moving things. We found it wasn't difficult to tell who was telling the truth because as soon as we walked into the house I could feel bad spirit if they were there. Sometimes it was the individual who was having mental problems and it was difficult to explain to them that they should consult their doctor. After all we were not medically trained and people wanted it to be spirit otherwise it would mean they had a mental problem, who wants to admit to that.

During the winds of 1987 the church at Camberley which was an old scout hut had taken a battering and was leaning dangerously to the side.

We propped it up and made it safe but the committee decided we would have to look and see about rebuilding the church. It was put to the members and I was designated to sort out the building of a new church. The first job was to get a design and then put it to some builders to get a price. A few of the committee including myself drew a design of how the church was to look and these were put before the members to vote on their preference. As it turned out they chose my design so I was asked to get an architect to do some proper drawings which they did. We then had to apply for planning and building regulations from the council and that took three months. Once we had got the permission we were able to go ahead and get prices for the work to be carried out. I went to four local builders to get prices. We settled on one builder who could build it in the time frame that we wanted the price quoted was £98,000.00p and I visited their offices to see if I could reduce the price in some way. I managed to knock £10,000 of the price just by substituting the doors for a cheaper wood and putting nice but cheaper fittings on the doors and a cheaper kitchen. I also managed to get them to reduce the price by £8,000 so we were now at the figure of £80,000.00p. Then we had to get the money for the project, we couldn't go to an ordinary building society as they would not lend to us so the only place we could go was the SNU which had a trust property who would lend to churches. They are like a building society except their funds come from the surplus of other spiritualist churches who save with them much like an ordinary building society. The first thing they wanted to know was could we afford to borrow £80,000 and how were we going to pay it back. I put this to committee and proposed different ways of increasing the church income on a regular basis, so that we could afford the mortgage. We planned a lot of events through the coming year to raise the profile of the church and to increase the income. One of the things we did was introduce a Saturday night special which I was put in charge of as I knew a lot of the top mediums around the country. I managed to book 12 for the coming year and the first one gave us a profit of £200.00p. I then had to write a business plan showing where we were going to get the money from and present it to the trust property committee. All this took about six months so we were fairly sure of our income by then. The trust property passed the business plan and we were on our way. The next thing was to arrange a start date and an alternative venue whilst the building work was going on which I did. When the builders pulled down the old church they just pushed it with a bull dozer and it fell down. When they started clearing the ground the bulldozer sank in mud which was under the church to a depth of four feet so the first thing they had to do was dig the mud out and take it away and then lay a concrete foundation. While they were digging the mud out they found a water pipe that was leaking, they said if it had gone on for much longer the church would have sunk into the mud. I guess we were lucky it had stayed up as long as it had, anyway they got on with it and I had to visit two or three times a week to sort out interim payments and any other problems that arose. We managed to keep to schedule and when I visited one time there was a big wooden cross nailed to the inside of the back wall. When I explained to the builders that we were spiritualists and not Christians some of them looked a bit worried I laughed and explained what we did and then they were alright. Next time I went they had put the cross back up, I just left it. Finally the building was finished and handed over to the committee not without some dramas though. They had to dig up the road because the levels were wrong to connect the sewage and for that they had to get council permission and this delayed the final connection for a week. Fortunately they were able to get on with other things and still finished a week early. I was able to get a large supply of carpet tiles from one of my contracts for free so we had carpeting which I laid. Our circles were putting a pound a week in a kitty which we used to purchase material for curtains which Jan made and what with one thing and another we were able to get the church up and running. We were short of hymn books and managed to get some from another church who were updating theirs and we used what was left in our circle kitty to buy about one hundred new chairs. Now we were all set for the inauguration of the church and I had two hundred chairs to fill. I arranged for the president of the SNU Gordon Higginson to came and officially open the church and a couple of well-known mediums to support him. When the night of the inauguration came there were a lot of well-known mediums there so those I didn't know I got their telephone numbers for future reference. It all went well and everyone was pleased with the night and we were up and running, all we had to do now was pay for it. We had a mortgage over 25 years which was costing £800.00p per month so we had to work hard to produce that kind of income. We fell short the first few months but then we got in our stride and managed to meet our commitment. All the while this was going on we were still visiting people and helping them with their problems. We were running the circles except the open circle until the church reopened and we were doing services so we were quite busy. Fortunately the kids were more or less independent now and were able to take care of themselves.

Chapter 29

"One house we went to had already had a vicar go and splash holy water around and say a few prayers. That didn't work so the couple had gone to their local spiritualist church for help. A 'medium' had visited and when he got there he asked for a bowl of water. He proceeded to take off his shoes and socks and stepped into the water, he then said a few prayers and informed the couple the spirits had gone. It's no wonder people think we are cranks sometimes when you get people like that wandering around. Anyway we talked to the people in the house, a young couple, and they explained about the noises and things that had been moved. We asked if I could check the house out and upon walking round all the rooms I could feel the unwelcome presence of bad spirits. When I sat down again I was able to describe a lady that they had both seen one night and we explained how we worked and then proceeded to bring the spirit through Jan. The lady was quite nasty and rude, fortunately Jan managed to stop her swearing and we had to throw her out as she wasn't interested in being taken to heaven. When Jan came back we explained what had been done to get rid of her. The couple said thank you and they thought we had finished. I said there will always be more than one to deal with and there are some children here too.

I asked Jan to get one of the children and this is how it went,

"Hello what's your name?"
"Jane"

"Hello Jane my names Mike and I am here to help you. You've got brown hair and your 6 years old aren't you." Yes nearly 7."

"Do you know where you are?"

"No I am lost, it's all dark and there are horrible people here."

"Yes I know but they can't hurt you now I will look after you. Do you know what's happened to you?"

"No it just went black and I was here."

"Okay what's the last thing you remember?"

"I was playing in mummy's room and I got tummy ache, I lay on the bed and went to sleep."

"Did you find some pretty sweets in mummy's draw?"

"Yes you aren't going to tell me off are you?"

"No of course not tell me what happened next?"

"I don't know I woke up and it was night time."

"Those sweets you had were mummy's pills and they made you ill. Do you remember going to the hospital?"

"No I saw an ambulance and they put someone in the back and mummy and daddy got in as well."

"Where were you?"

"I was standing next to the ambulance with mummy."

"Did you see who they put in the ambulance?"

"Yes it was a little girl."

"She had brown hair and she was about your age wasn't she?"

"Yes I think it was me."

"Yes it was so what do you think happened to you?"

"I don't know."

"Does your tummy still hurt?"

"Yes and I feel sick."

"Okay I'm going to take the pain away now and you won't feel sick anymore. How's that are you feeling better?"

"Yes my tummy isn't hurting anymore. Am I dead?"

"Yes I'm afraid so, but it's not so bad you are still talking to me. Where do people go when they die?"

"When granny died mummy said she had gone to heaven but if I'm dead is this heaven?"

"No you got lost, would you like me to take you to see your granny and granddad?"

"Yes please."

"Good now I see you have got some friends there with you, we are going to take them to heaven with us alright?"

"Yes alright the nasty man isn't coming is he?"

"No just your friends, open your eyes and tell me what you can see."

"I can see a tunnel with a bright light in it. It's a long way away."

"That's right that's the entrance to heaven let's get everyone together then we can go there."

"Ok were ready but don't go too fast little Jimmy has got a bad leg and he can't walk very fast."

"Ok well make his leg better then he can keep up how's that?"

"He's jumping up and down his leg must be alright now he said thank you."

"Yes I heard him ok shall we go, doesn't that feel nice and warm?"

"Yes it's much nicer here I can see people."
"Yes so can I and I can see your granny and granddad over there, look they have got their dog Spinks with them."
"Yes can I go to them I love playing with Spinks?
"Yes you will be safe now bye."
"Bye thank you."

Jan opened her eyes she had a few tears which had smudged her mascara. "You will have to wear waterproof mascara in future." I said
"Yes I wasn't expecting that, what a tragedy for the mother."
"Yes now we can get rid of the other lot. How are you doing?" I said to the couple who lived there.
"Were alright, we didn't realize there were so many."
"No, most people don't, we just have to deal with the others and things should be ok then."

Jan wanted a comfort break so I explained to the couple how it took more than one to move things. I told them that the children were safe now but the people who were in control were still in their house. I told them we had put protection round their house before we came, otherwise the bad spirits would have left and come back when we had been. By doing that we could clear the house of all of them. They asked would they come back and I said not if you don't invite them. I then went on to explain that just by looking or thinking of them it was like an invitation, so the best thing was to just get on with their lives and forget it ever happened. They would not get past the protection as it would be left around their house until they no longer needed it.

When Jan came back we settled down again to deal with the others. I told Jan there was an old woman in the house and described her so she could tune in and get the right person which she did.

"Hello what are you doing here?"

"I was just minding my own business and you interfered with everything, you have no right."

"Well actually we do the people who live here asked us to help them so that gives us the authority we need to clear their house."

"Well I'm not leaving."

"What's your name?"

"Marilyn, why do you want to know?"

"It's always nice when talking to someone to address them by name I'm

Mike. Do you know where you are?"

"Yes I'm what you call dead and I live here, things were going fine until you came and took the children."

"We couldn't leave them here they were upsetting the people who live in the house."

"They were just playing it wasn't doing any harm."

"Maybe not to you but the children were frightened and we needed to take them to heaven where they are safe with their loved ones."

"Do you know where heaven is then?"

"Yes would you like to go and be with Frank he's waiting for you?"

"How do you know about Frank he's my husband?"

"Yes I know and he says the kids are there with him and he loves you."

"I wondered what happened to them can I go and see them?"

"You can go and stay with them."

"Will they let me into heaven I haven't been a very good person?"

"Yes of course, I'll take you if you want."

"How can you? You're not dead."

"No but I know the way. Shall we go and see?"

"Alright but if it's a trick I am coming straight back."

"Okay, open your eyes and tell me what you can see."

"I can see a big light it's very bright."

"Yes that's the entrance to heaven shall we go and have a look?"

"Alright but no tricks."

"How are you feeling now?"

"It's a nice warm feeling, it's like being cuddled."

"Yes what can you see now?"

"I can see people lots of people."

"Yes they have come to welcome you home. There's Frank and your two children can you see them?"

"Yes can I go to them?"

"Yes go in peace and be happy."

"Thank you, bye."

She was gone and Jan came back again with a few tears of emotion. I told her there were a couple of others that needed getting rid of so after I described a man to her she tuned in and got him through.

"Good evening what have you been doing here?"

"Mind you own business."

"But it is my business we were asked to come and get rid of the spirits in this house and that's what we are doing."

"Well you won't get rid of us so easily."

"By that I take it you know what's happened to you and you don't want to go to heaven?"

"Yes we know were dead and no we don't want to go to heaven."

"Okay then we will have to throw you all out, we are going to brand you and send you away from here."

"We will just come back."

"No you won't we are sending a couple of our guides to see that you go far away from here. You won't be able to come back because we are leaving the protection round the house. As you know you couldn't leave till we let you and you will not be able to get back in through the protection."

"Just get on with it."

"Ok good bye."

The couple were a bit unsure until I went around all the rooms again with them and showed them the difference in temperature and atmosphere in each of the rooms where they had had problems. They hadn't told me which rooms were giving them problems so when I told them it gave them more confidence that we had got rid of their problem. Jan was waiting downstairs when we had finished going round the house and they asked her a few questions about how it felt getting those different people through. Jan said it was fine they were gone now. They had a cup of tea and we chatted for a bit then we left and went home.

We talked about what had gone on. Jan said,
"When you went round the house could you tell which rooms they were in?"
"As soon as I walked in the house I could feel the bad spirits. When I walked round it got stronger when I was in the room where they were. I could also tell who was there so I knew who to ask you to get and what they looked like. You didn't seem to have any problems getting them either."
"No I just pictured the people you described and then I felt them near me and kind of grabbed them."
"Did they struggle to get away?"
"The last one did but I just ignored him. He tried to give me a headache I think it was so I would throw him out."
"Well I thought they might attack you to try and stop us."
"You might have told me I wasn't expecting it."
"Sorry I wasn't sure anyway we seem to have managed to do the job."
"I hope so they were a nice couple they didn't deserve what was going on."
"No how did it feel when you got the child through?"
"It was much different from when I get my guides the children were frightened. I could feel the difference when they went to heaven there were a lot of emotions and laughter."
"Yes I'll bet, it's a shame they prey on the little ones."

"The woman wasn't sure about you but once you told her about her husband she seemed to settle down a bit, but she still didn't know whether to trust you or not."

"Have you any idea why?"

"Yes I felt she had been taken to heaven before and ended up where we found her."

"No wonder she was suspicious, anyway she's ok now."

"What's this about a brand what's that for?"

"I have no idea I just felt I had to put a brand on them before I let them go."

"We'll have to ask about that, it's a good job they never asked us what it was for."

"If they had asked I expect we could have asked one of your guides to come through and explain."

"How did you know there were so many of them?"

"I didn't I just knew when they had all gone."

We talked a bit more about what had gone on and realized we had quite a few questions to ask. There was a lot that went on that we didn't know anything about. We were glad we were able to listen to our guides otherwise we could never have cleared the house by ourselves. When we got home it was late, fortunately the kids were staying round friends so we didn't have to worry about them. The next day was a Saturday so we got on with things around the house and we both kept thinking about the previous night and what we wanted answers to. During lunch we wrote down our questions ready for a chat later.

The children were staying round their friends again so we settled down to have a chat with Jan's guides.

"Good evening Richard."

"Good evening."

"As you may imagine we have a number of questions for you."

"Yes we thought you would what's your first question?"

"What's a brand?"

"A brand is a sign that we put in the aura of the bad spirit so that everyone they come in contact with knows what they have been doing. It also tells other spirits who caught them and it stops them from doing it again."

"How does it stop them?"

"Those who might give them work will see that they have been caught and rather than allowing unreliable spirits to work for them they will chase them away. It also makes them a target for ridicule as they have been foolish enough to be caught."

"Does it stop them forever?"

"No but it takes a long time for them to cover up the information. You remember we talked about the aura being like and onion? Well it takes a while to put another layer over the top."

"What is a brand exactly I know you have just said it's a sign but is that all it is? Surely if they want to muscle in on someone else's property it won't stop them?"

"It's an energy and depending on what they have been doing depends on how much we neutralize their abilities."

"Can't you just stop them all together?"

"No they still have free will, eventually they will see sense and move on, until then we can only make it difficult for them to carry on with their little games. As we have said they are lazy they will not try to do things if they have to work at it."

"What about the protection that was put round the house who did that and how did I know it was there?"

"We put it there when you were asked to help, otherwise you would have got there and there would have been nothing to find. They would have left until you had gone and then gone back."

"So when they found they couldn't leave they must have known what was going to happen?"

"They knew there was a possibility that they would have problems but you are unknown. They thought that by being quiet and hiding either you wouldn't find them, or the couple would have told you not to come as it had all gone away. You were able to detect the protection because you have been putting it around your own property for quite a while now that's one of the reasons you are not getting so much interference."

"I thought we had become stronger than them, that's why we weren't getting interference?"

"Yes, but without the protection that you have built up, you would still get sudden attacks which would get through briefly."

"I see so they never give up?"

"It's not just one lot there are others who will try to get through to you. If you like they are competing to see who can get through."

"So we are a target for anyone who wants to try and get at us?"

"Because of my mediums vendetta there will always be someone who will try to get at you. Don't concern yourselves you are strong enough now to deal with most things. If you weren't we would not have arranged for you to go to that house."

"How was I getting all the information when I was talking to the children and the woman?"

"Your guides were feeding you as you went along. You have succeeded in sensing your guide's thoughts."

"It's not the same as clairvoyance is it?"

"Yes it's just the same, the difference is you were not trying you were concentrating on what was going on rather than trying to get information about someone. Your focus was on what was happening instead of what you were doing."

"So if I can focus more on what is happening rather than what I am trying to do I will be more accurate?"

"You both will but it isn't as easy as that you have to learn to let go."

"I see what you mean, it's not easy to let go when you are trying."

"It will come give yourselves time."

"The little girl who took her mums pills I suppose that happens quite often does it?"

"More times than we would like but there are so many hazards in your world and parents don't always realise the dangers to their children."

"Were all the children suffering from the same problem?"

"No, similar problems, that's why we were able to deal with them all at once."

"Ah you mean like the plane crash they all died the same way so they could all associate with the one who came through?"

"Yes you will find when you run a rescue circle we will collect people with the same experience so we can help more people at the same time."

"Wait a minute who says we are going to run a rescue circle we don't even run an ordinary circle yet?"

"It's all being arranged you have already agreed to it."

"Not that I can remember."

"We discussed it a few times when you were asleep and it was your idea not ours."

"Did we both agree?"

"Yes it won't happen if you are not in agreement. If you are going to go to people's houses then you need to practice and you will need others to sit with you so you might as well teach them at the same time."

"Another case of making use of the situation."

"Your time is short compared to ours we try to make the most of the time you have."

"You sound as if we're about to join you over there I'm not in that much of a hurry."

"That's not what I mean you have much to do and we want to make the most of your time."

"I was joking anyway how does the protection stay around the house when we have gone do we leave some guides there to maintain it?"

"You have a dry sense of humour sometimes I'm not sure. Some of your guides will stay and show their guides how to maintain the protection.

Once they have got the hang of it they will re-join us."

"Can't everyone's guides put protection up for their mediums?"

"Only those who specialise in that type of work. If the medium isn't going to be active in a particular field they will not be required. If there is a problem they can always ask for help like in that case."

"So did we do the job properly?"

"You did a good job but one was hiding and you missed them. You will have to go back and finish what you started."

"How did we miss that one?"

"You weren't expecting them to hide so you never looked for them."

"But when I checked round afterwards I couldn't feel anything."

"No they were moving round the house to get away from you. Don't worry, it will be sorted out you can't be expected to get it right the first time."

"It's alright for you to say but we have got to face them and admit we got it wrong."

"There is nothing wrong with making a mistake if you own up, then put it right. You did a better job than the medium that stood in a bowl of water didn't you?"

"I hope so, can you believe that, I wonder where they get their ideas from the bad sprit must have been laughing their heads off."

"Unfortunately you will find many strange ideas out there. Just learn your trade and do it to the best of your ability."

"Thank you for your help we will have to stop now it's getting late again good night."

"Good night and god bless."

We were disappointed that we hadn't done the job properly and decided to give the people a ring and arrange to go back and finish the job off. So the next day I spoke to them and they said it was all quiet and that they hadn't noticed anything. I explained it was the first time we had someone hide from us and that we didn't know and hadn't got all of them. Although it was quiet now I said it would start up again and if it was ok we would like to come back and finish what we had started. They said that was fine and we arranged a date when it would be convenient. When we went back I checked the house and discovered there were three spirits in the house. Jan sat down and I described a man to her and she got him through.

"Hello thought we had missed you did you?"

"You did didn't you, what you going to do now because we are staying?"

"No you're not we've come back to finish the job."

"Really if you couldn't get rid of us last time what makes you think you can now?"

"Well for a start we have got you where we want you and you can't hide, secondly we are going to brand you all and send you on your way."

"Do your worst then."

"Okay Jan, throw them out and brand them at the same time."

Jan opened her eyes and said,

"They were pretty nasty I had a bit of a job holding on to him the others were attacking me."

"Well they are gone now I am going to check round again I don't want to make any more mistakes."

I walked round the house and try as I might I couldn't find any more of them, I wanted to be sure so I asked Jan to bring one of her guides through to double check. Jan said it wasn't necessary she had already asked and we had got them all. That pleased us and we explained to the couple that we had just started working although we had been developing for the past three years and had lots of spirits in our own house. As we couldn't find anyone to get rid of them for us we had to learn how to do it ourselves. They said they had trouble finding someone too and after the vicar and that other medium they thought they were stuck with it. It was only by chance they were talking to someone we had met at an open circle who told them about the problems we had had and that we had got rid of them. They thanked us and we left them to the rest of their evening and went home. We were feeling much better about things now we had finished the job. It was like we just had a feeling of completion, I can't put it any other way we just knew it was done. It didn't matter that we had double checked with Jan's guides that was just reassurance I think.

Chapter 30

We were back at the open circle that we were running the next night and we were getting an average of 35-40 people coming. We decided to change the format a bit and after the meditation we split people into groups of the same ability and had some of the more advanced run the groups. We circulated round the groups and helped where we were needed and everyone got more opportunity to have a go. At the end of the circle before we closed we asked if they thought it was better that way. One of the group leaders said they found they were getting more information when they were running the group than when they were sitting in the circle. I explained that as they were running the group their guides were feeding them the information so they could help the sitters. As it seemed to be a success we said we would run the circle after the meditation like that in future. If anyone wasn't happy would they let us know and we would assess the situation again. As it turned out everyone was happier with the new format so that's how we carried on. We started to go to an open platform which was being run by Ann & Mike and I had the opportunity to get up and try clairvoyance on some of the others who were there. It wasn't anything like sitting in a circle I was nervous of standing in front of all those people. Still I had a go and I went to a man at the front and gave him some information which he said he understood. Then I carried on telling him about his youth and his grandparents. I didn't give him a chance to say yes or no I just carried on talking. Finally Mike stopped me and explained that I should give the recipient a chance to reply. Everyone laughed, so did I and the man explained that he could understand most of it but not about his grandparents. Then Ann came over and I don't know how but said some of what I had and then explained to the man exactly where to look in his life. When he did he remembered bits and Ann then said to me, I was allowing myself to be side-tracked by my own thoughts and that's where I went wrong. I apologised to the man and he was fine, it turned out he was the president of the church. I thought I need to practice this on the platform because if I can't do it how could I teach others.

Mike said I should be more gentle, try not to force things on people but not too bad for the first time. Jan did a reading so that she could get used to standing in front of people. It's not easy to talk in front of people and the idea of the open platform is so that budding mediums can get over their nerves. We found another church that had an open platform and took advantage of the opportunity to get as much practice as we could. We met some people at this church who asked us if we sat in a closed circle. We said no and they invited us to their church to sit. A closed circle is where the sitters are invited and you sit every week and you make a commitment to do so. Whereas an open circle you can go when you like and there is no commitment, you also don't need an invitation. While sitting in the closed circle we found the development more intense which was just what we needed to push us on. What with the open circle that we ran and going to Ann & Mikes open circle two open platforms a month and a closed circle once a week we were quite busy. We still found time to chat with Jan's guides and we found the information invaluable as it helped us to understand more quickly the lessons we were being given. After a few months of this we were at Camberley one night and the medium didn't arrive. I was asked if I would take the service and with knocking knees I said I would give a talk and answer questions if they wanted, but I wasn't ready to do clairvoyance. This they agreed to, and so that was my first experience in front of a full church on clairvoyant evening. Afterwards some of the committee said it had been an interesting evening which helped me to feel better about my presentation. Jan said we would have to start doing services as we can't tell others how to do it if we can't do it ourselves. So we both agreed we needed to get working but how. We went to a service at the church where we sat in closed circle a few weeks later and one of the sitters was doing his first service. The information he gave was very good and afterwards I asked him if he would like a booking at Camberley church. He said that was his first time and he felt he was ready and yes please if I could arrange it. When we next had a committee meeting I brought the subject up and everyone agreed to let him have the next cancellation. He came and I chaired for him and the evening was a success, it was his second service. We booked him for a couple of cancellations later in the year and about six months later he asked me if I would like to do a service with him. I said I would and he said you got me started now it's your turn. I was to do a talk on the reading he was going to do and then share the clairvoyance. I have never been so nervous in all my life my fifteen minute talk I managed to do in about three minutes. I talked so fast I'm not sure if anyone understood what I was saying. He then started the clairvoyance and after doing a couple of readings asked me if I was ready. I got up and managed to slow down a bit and gave a couple of readings and then he took over and finished the service. It was a new experience for me but at least I had done my first one, now I had to get my head down and practice more. On the way home Jan and I chatted about the service and she said when we do services I would have to do the talk and she would do the reading, we could share the clairvoyance. She said all I needed to do was slow down and I would be fine.

We went to AFC on a few more courses and they gave us the opportunity to practice our clairvoyance on a class of about 20 and gave us advice and constructive criticism which helped enormously. When we came back we thought it was time to start working so we asked at Camberley if we could do the next cancellation , they said yes and so that's how we started working on platform. We knew a lot of people from other churches and when we asked them they started giving us bookings. The first thing we found out while doing services is that once you learn to do clairvoyance, you then have to learn how to get out of situations where the recipient doesn't know the communicator, and carry on and prove survival, and give a meaningful message that is not only relevant but understood. Many are the times I would say something only to find the recipient has no idea what I'm talking about. Once I learnt to rephrase what I was saying they could then understand. The real learning starts when you start getting on platform we found out, but with perseverance and good old hard work we found ourselves quite busy with services, doing about two a month building up over a year to three or four. We observed there are two ways of finding your recipient one is to let spirit guide you to who you want to talk to and the other is to throw it open and see who puts their hand up. The mediums that throw it open say they want spirit to find the recipient. I thought if they guided me to the recipient then they were finding them, but the mediums say their way is better because they don't choose. Much like a deep trance medium I think who wants to be taken away so they can't influence what is said. I found it to be quicker to go to an individual as I had their attention and I didn't have to wait for someone to recognise what I was saying and put their hand up. Also by throwing it open you could get more than one recipient and it then takes time eliminating those it is not for. Consequently you can't get round as many people as when you go directly to them. Another lesson you can't learn until you get on platform.

We gave up the open circle with Ann & Mike and the closed circle and started our own closed circle. It was a rescue circle and once we found the right sitters we set about teaching them everything we had learnt. While doing the services we got chatting to the chairperson at the churches and mentioned we ran a rescue circle. We started getting asked if we could help people who were having problems at home. We said we would go and see them and see what the problem was. That's how we started going to clear people's homes of unwanted spirits, with the people in our rescue circle we used to go out about twice a week to clear houses. We continued with the open circle at Camberley and started an open platform once a month. With experience we had gained by doing services we were able to give the sitters in the open circle the chance to practice from the platform. Running an open platform was much different from running a circle and I asked a lady who was very experienced whom I knew if she would coach me on how to chair and help people. She agreed and came to the open platform each time for about six months until she was satisfied I was running it properly. When running an open platform I found by tuning in to what people were getting I could draw them out and get more information than they thought they had. It was a case of teasing the information from them, no-one was left to struggle and almost everyone was pleased with the results they got. It didn't matter whether they were reading, giving a talk or giving a communicator they all managed to get something. It had taken some time for us to learn but we had finally got to a stage where we could help budding mediums to progress.

Jan decided to do a course to become a spiritual healer, which meant when she was qualified after two years we would be able to clear people if we came across anyone with problems around them at a church. We were able to clear them anyway but with Jan being a healer we could pretend she was giving healing and no-one would be the wiser. It's all about the law you have to be qualified to get insurance and work in churches as a healer. While she was going to the healing group at Camberley I was busy teaching gymnastics.

When you clear someone, first you have to tune in to the bad spirits, (there's always more than one) and then with the help of your guides they are extracted and branded then sent on their way. With practice all you have to do is touch the person and you can pick up the bad energies around them. It's quite amazing the difference the person feels after it has been done, although it can take them a while to settle down to not having aggravation all the time. They are happier and often not tired all the time, if they were getting aches and pains they will be gone also. Although Jan would do the healing I was able to hold the patients hands and talk quietly to them during the extraction. This gave me a chance to help when the spirits were being a little stubborn. With all the practice I had giving Jan healing during my development I was able to heal as well but in the eyes of the law I wasn't qualified. If someone asked me for healing I would always say I wasn't qualified and if I gave healing it was always by request and in private. One time I was visiting my mum and her friend had glaucoma, when she found out I could heal she asked if I would give her healing. I explained my situation and she said that's ok so I gave her healing on her eyes. After a couple of days my mum telephoned me to say her friend's eyes were fine now and thank you. I never expected to get a result like that but was pleased I was able to help. I also had a friend who was blind in one eye, she had been unable to see out of it since birth, but the doctors couldn't find anything wrong with it. As an experiment before circle each week I would give her healing. After about a month she was able to see shadows but unfortunately circumstances changed

281

and the opportunity to continue was lost, I will never know whether the healing would have made her eye better or not. There was another man called Bruce who sat in my clairvoyant circle and when he came one week he said he was having trouble with his eyes. It was suggested he see an optician to see if there was a major problem or just new glasses were needed. When he came the following week he said he had glaucoma and I mentioned the friend of my mums, he asked if I would try it on him. I gave him healing and it seemed to cure him anyway he never had any problems after that.

Although healing the psychical is not my first love I am always happy to help if asked. I felt there are plenty of healers around but not many who could heal those who had passed and were lost or confused. This was and is my priority because there are so few of us they can turn to for help.

We went to a house in Basingstoke where they were having problems and while we were talking to the man and his wife his hand started to swell up. He said look at my hand they are doing it even while I am talking to you. I placed my hand on his and the swelling went down immediately. It was all the encouragement he needed to ask us to clear his house. When we had finished he asked if there was anything he could do for us and we said go to the local church and become a healer. A few weeks later he turned up at Basingstoke and joined the healing group, he became a good healer and has been healing ever since.

When we were going to people's houses we discovered there were lots of different things happening but there were only a couple of things happening at each house. It's not like you see in films where they put lots of things together to make it more exciting. There were those who controlled the house and there were those who were lost. There were also those who followed people about. So the idea was to rescue those who were lost and get rid of those who controlled the house. We would travel all over the south of England from the south coast to the east coast and up as far as Hertfordshire. We went to one house in Fareham where they were having a few problems with their new baby.

Chapter 31

When we arrived we asked what was going on and they said,

"The baby goes to sleep for about half an hour and then wakes up screaming. When we go to see what is wrong we get a terrible cold feeling on entering her room. The covers have been thrown out of the cot and we have seen indentations on her nightwear, it looks like someone is pressing down on her. When we pick her up it stops and gradually she calms down, we know somebody died in the house but why would they hurt the baby? The room is very cold even when we have the heating high it makes no difference"

"Can I go and see the room?" I asked.

"Yes well take you up the baby has just gone down."

I went in the room quietly so as not to wake her up and it felt like the room was full of bad spirits. I knew we were in for a fight as soon as I opened up I was attacked quite viciously so I closed down quickly so they couldn't get at me. We went back down stairs and I said,

"There are a lot of nasty spirits in that room as well as around the house; we will start by explaining to you what we are going to do and if you're okay with that we will get started."

"Shall we bring the baby down?"

"No she will be fine she will stay asleep and won't be disturbed while we are working, they have got enough to worry about with us being here. What we are going to do is Jan will go into trance and bring them through and I will talk to them and help those who need it and get rid of those who don't. There is nothing to worry about all you will see is Jan with her eyes closed. You will be able to hear what they have to say but it will be

Jan's voice you hear we don't go in for funny voices."

"In our experience we have never had someone who died in a house come through when we are clearing it."

"What happens to them then?"

"Almost everyone goes to heaven there are only a very few that get lost and that is usually because of their beliefs or the way they died."

"Have you seen this before?"

"Not quite like this but let's see how we get on shall we, please don't speak while Jan's eyes are closed as it may distract her from what she is doing. If you have any questions feel free to ask when her eyes are open."

"Okay we won't see any spirits will we?"

"Not unless you are clairvoyant, while we are working I will be keeping an eye on you both. If you feel uncomfortable or in pain let me know straight away so I can stop it. They may try to distract us by attacking you."

"Are we going to be alright?"

"Yes I'm just warning you of the possibility, okay Jan you ready?"

"Yes I am aware of a women dressed in black about 50."

"Okay can you bring her through? Good evening what are you doing here?"

"I was minding my own business till you showed up."

"Well what do you expect you can't go around frightening people and hurting children?"

"I'll do what I like it's got nothing to do with you."

"Obviously you know what's happened to you why are you attacking the baby?"

"None of your business I told you to go away."

"So it's got nothing to do with your baby being taken away from you?"

"How do you know about that?"

"It's my job to know about the people I'm talking to. You never saw the baby again did you?"

"I don't want to talk about it."

"Okay well you can't take it out on this baby so either you go to heaven or we will brand you and throw you out."

"You can't do that I was here first."

"Maybe, but you don't belong here, and you certainly are not going near the baby again."

"I don't need to I have others to do that for me."

"Not anymore we are going to brand you and the five people you have got helping you and throw you out. You can't get back in because we have put protection around the house so be on your way. Throw them out Jan."

Jan opened her eyes and said,

"She was very nasty but she has gone now and so have her gang."

"Now we need to help the people that are lost, can you get one of the children?"

"Okay I've got a little girl about 5 years old."

"Okay hello what's your name?"

"I'm Allison has she gone?"

"Yes your safe now, we are going to help you, how did you get here?"

"I don't know I was playing with my ball and when I chased it I was here."

"Can you remember where you were playing?"

"Yes I was playing outside my house."

"Did your ball roll into the road?"

"Yes I ran to get it and it went all black."

"So the next thing you knew you were here? What do you think happens to you when you run into the road?"

"You might get run over, is that what happened to me?"

"Yes I'm afraid so."

"I'm dead aren't I?"

"What happened next?"

"It was all dark and a lady came and brought me here, she was nice at first then she made me do things to those people over there. I didn't want to so she hurt me and said if I don't do as I'm told I will go to hell. I was frightened so I did what she told me to, I'm sorry"

"That's ok the people are alright there are some more children there with you aren't there."

"Yes but they are hiding we didn't know what you were going to do." "We're going to take you all to heaven, you will be with your mummy and granddad."

"Is mummy in heaven she was alright when I was playing?"

"Yes but that was a long time ago would you like to go to her?"

"Yes please what about my friends?"

"We're going to take you all to heaven so let's get everyone together then we can go. Is everyone alright?"

"Yes we are ready."

We took them to heaven where they met their loved ones and we knew they were safe. Jan opened her eyes and said she watched the children go and they were all happy and laughing.

The lady said, "How many are there we were told there was just one?"

"It takes more than one to do what's been happening here we just have a couple more to sort out and then it will be done, are you alright?"

"Yes the baby hasn't woken up either."

"No she will be fine now, ok Jan there is an old lady there she is a nun can you get her through?"

"Hello how are you feeling?"

"Apart from the usual aches and pains alright, I'm glad you got the children away from here they were real nasty to them. I tried to help but they were too strong for me."

"That's ok I take it you know what's happened to you?"

"Yes I died and I have been wandering ever since."

"Are you in pain?"

"A little my legs hurt with all this standing up."

"Alright we will take the pain away there, how's that?"

"That's much better you don't realize how bad it's got until it's gone, how did you do that?"

"The pain was in your mind, you thought you were still suffering but once you realised you haven't got a body the pain goes away it was only a memory."

"I think I'm going to like it here, where is he?"

"Who were you expecting?"

"Jesus was supposed to come and meet me and take me to heaven."

"He won't be coming."

"What do you mean he will come soon?"

"I know you have spent your life in service to the church but what they have told you isn't true."

"But we were taught that if we gave our lives to god we would be met by his son and taken to heaven."

"Yes I know what you were told but because you have been looking for Jesus and not found him, you have not seen those of your loved ones who came to get you. You see the bible was written by man and is not the truth, it was written to keep the people in fear of god so they would do as they were told. You have been misled, the truth is everyone eventually goes to heaven to be with their loved ones."

"Does that mean my life was a lie?"

"No you have done many things to help people when they have needed it and that's all any of us can hope to do in this life. Would you like us to take you to heaven?"

"Yes if you can, I don't want to stay in this dark place."

"Alright open your eyes and tell me what you can see."

"I can see the light at the end of what looks like a tunnel."

"Good that is the entrance to heaven and we will take you to meet your loved ones are you ready?"

"Yes there are a lot of other nuns and religious people here from all different faiths."

"Yes we have collected them together so that we can take them with us with your help, is everyone ready?"

"Yes they say they are ready."

"Ok let's go, tell me what you are feeling as we go."

"It's feeling warmer and getting lighter."

"Good what can you see now?"

"I can see shapes of people, now I can see them clearly its mother superior and she has got some of my friends with her."

"Yes and if you look over there you can see your parents and brother."

"So this is what heaven is like, I think it is time to go they are calling me."

"Okay go in peace."

"Thank you and god bless you."

"Goodbye and god bless."

Jan opened her eyes and said,

"That was an awkward one is that the lot?"

"I will have a walk round and check if that's alright?"

The couple said ok so I did. The lady came with me as she was more sensitive than her husband and when we came to the baby's room it was warm and the baby was awake giggling and waving her arms. The lady smiled and picked her up and gave her a cuddle. We carried on round the house with the baby and when we got downstairs her husband smiled and asked if she was alright. The wife said yes and the room feels much better now and thanked us for helping. I said.

"Now they have gone you should forget about all of this and get on with your life. You must not think to yourself are they still here as that would be an invitation for others to come in."

"What about the protection you've put round the house won't that stop them?"

"The protection is there now to stop anyone coming in and doing the same thing again, but if you invite them in you will neutralise the protection, the best thing is to try and forget all about it."

"How much do you charge?"

"We don't do it for money we do it because we have been there and we couldn't find anyone to help us. We had to learn about it to help ourselves and decided there must be others out there with similar problems."

"That's very kind of you we hope you are able to help lots of people like you have us." said the woman.

Once we were sure they had no more questions we said good night and left. We were feeling quite pleased with the evening and the fact that the baby was going to be alright now. Jan said.

"That must have been horrible for them it's lucky we were in that church when we were."

"Yes I think our guides may have had something to do with it. Why don't you want to check the house out before we start?"

"I find it easier to work if I don't go looking for them but just get the one you ask me to its less confusing. If I had picked up the children I would have wanted to help them first."

"Yes I see what you mean I suppose one of us has to control who comes through and when, as I'm looking after you when you're in trance it makes sense that I should be the one controlling the evening."

"What do you do when you go round?"

"I sense which rooms have got what type of spirits in them and make a mental note then I deal with the worst room first. They haven't twigged that yet, I wonder if I will be able to find them if they hide in another room?"

"I should think your guides will help you after all we are working as a team and they can easily direct you to where they are."

"Yes we're the earthly part of the team and without them we can't do it."

"Why didn't you say a prayer before we started?"

"Well we don't usually when we are talking to your guides. I figured it was no different. Besides we don't know what religion the people are going to be and I think it is better not to get involved with faith. I just ask my guides to help and protect me to myself and then get on with it."

"We'll have to ask if saying a prayer makes any difference."

"There are a few questions that have come up from tonight, I'll write them down when we get home."

It took us about one and a half hours to get home so we had plenty of time to think things over. When we got home it was about midnight so we went straight to bed after Jan had a cup of tea. The next night we settled down to ask some questions. Samuel came through and I said,

"Good evening Samuel."

"Good evening."

"We got this one right didn't we?"

"Yes you cleared them all out."

"After last night we have a few questions to ask, the first is about saying prayers. Do we need to say a prayer out loud or don't we need to say one at all?"

"You are right not to say a prayer out loud, some people are not religious and it will make them feel uncomfortable. It is a good idea to say a prayer to yourselves. What you are doing is talking to your guides and anyone that is listening will know where your allegiance lies. This will strengthen the bond between us and show those who are listening that we are working together."

"So those in the house who are causing trouble can hear what we say even if we don't say it out loud?"

"Yes because you think it and when you send out a prayer it will be heard by all around you in spirit."

"So can they pick up all my thoughts?"

"No only those you want them to you are able to block them from thoughts you don't want them to be aware of, you do that automatically."

"Does that mean we can also block our guides when we want to?"

"We are only interested in the thoughts you send to us we don't pry."

"That means we have our privacy even from our guides?"

"Yes you automatically close your mind when you are thinking privately."

"Okay what about going round the house, why is it a good idea for just me? Were we right in what we said last night that as I was controlling the proceedings it should just be me?"

"Yes it is easier for my medium to just get those you describe it helps her to focus and ignore anyone that doesn't fit the description you've given."

"I see, at first I didn't know what to say to that nun I was trying to be diplomatic and not upset her and her beliefs."

"I think you have a saying you can't make an omelette without breaking the eggs. Sometimes you will have to go against some ones beliefs to help them you did fine."

"Why would the baby's guides allow that to happen to her?"

"You are forgetting the baby is a spirit and she has chosen her journey, it wasn't for very long before you got there, she is fine now."

"It still seems cruel to attack a baby."

"She was looked after by her guides no real harm would have come to her."

"Hello Richard that was sneaky swopping over in the middle of a conversation."

"Just testing we don't want you getting complacent do we."

"I'm getting used to your little tricks now it's not that I don't trust you but I am aware you will test me sometimes, just not when I am working please."

"Even when you are working you must be aware of what's going on all the time never assume anything."

"We're thinking of starting a closed circle for clairvoyance what do you think?"

"If you are both in agreement and you have time why not."

"Ok we have decided to start it next Tuesday will you set it up from your side?"

"We are already working on it."

"We will have to stop now I can hear Darren coming in thanks for talking to us good night."

"Good night and god bless."

Chapter 32

We started the circle the following week and as usual I was circle leader. I found I was able to tune in much easier than usual and was sure I was getting help from my guides. It was a whole different ball game being circle leader I had to think of what we were going to do and how best to encourage people without putting them down or making the feel inadequate. As the night progressed it was as though I was being guided as to what to do and say so I stopped worrying and just enjoyed it. Everyone thought the circle went well, to be fair I had been running the open circle and the rescue circle for a while so I wasn't surprised although I felt my guides deserved the credit. On the Friday when we had the rescue circle we had a man come through Jan who needed help, I said,

"Good evening."

"Hello can you hear me?"

"Yes what's wrong?"

"I have been wandering around trying to talk to people and everybody is ignoring me."

"Tell me what's happened."

"Well I woke up this morning and said good morning to the missus, she just got out of bed and went down stairs. I got up and went down and asked for a cup of tea she ignored me. I thought I might have upset her so I said I'm going down the pub for a beer and a pie. When I got there they wouldn't serve me, they just took no notice. I was getting fed up by now so I went home and the missus was in tears. The neighbour was there making tea so I asked if I could have one and tried to find out what had upset the missus. Next thing I know I am here what's going on?"

"So before you got up what was happening/"

"I don't know I was asleep."

"Does your wife get upset easily?"

"No even if she is annoyed with me she doesn't ignore me she tells me off."

"What if she couldn't see you?"

"Well I was standing in the same room."

"How do you feel do you feel anything different?"

"Well I do feel better than I have for a long time and I feel lighter."

"How do you think you got here?"

"I was brought here by a man."

"What did he look like?"

"Now you mention it he did have weird cloths on like something out of a history book."

"What can you see now?"

"I can see you but you don't look normal."

"Thanks what's wrong with me?"

"You seem to be what's the word shimmering."

"Why do you think that is?"

"Am I dead?"

"Yes you died in your sleep."

"No wonder nobody could see me what happens now?"

"When people die they go to heaven do you want to go there?"

"I never believed in heaven is there really a place like that?"

"Yes shall we take you and you can see your parents and your brother and sister."

"Can I get a pint there?"

"Yes if you want."

"Hope the missus will be alright."

"You will be able to visit her and keep an eye on her until she comes over."

"You aren't dead are you?"

"No we are sitting in our circle to help people who get lost like you."

"How do you find us?"

"We have guides. That is people who are dead like the one that brought you here to help us."

"That's good because I was getting a bit confused."

"I expect you were, would you like us to take you to heaven then?"

"Yes please can't wait to see the family again."

So we took him to heaven and he was fine, one of the things we were told in the early days was not to tell people they had died, but to help them come to that conclusion. It is not always easy to get them to realise what's happened to them but it can be an awful shock if we just told them they were dead. Then there are those who know they are dead but expect certain things to happen like the nun who expected Jesus to come and get her. Then there are those who believe when you die that's it there is nothing else. Imagine their surprise when they find there is. Mostly though people get to where they need to without any problems, we just deal with those who can't get there by themselves. What with running three circles a week and doing what we call house clearances and services we had become quite busy. We were training the other sitters in the rescue circle to clear houses and took a couple with us when we went.

Especially if we knew it was going to be interesting or different so they could gain the experience. During our visits we came across some strange ideas, for example one house we went to they had someone else go before us. They went round the house sprinkling holy water and saying prayers. But before they did that they went into the loft and covered the loft hatch with tin foil. They said that would stop the bad spirits from getting into the house again once they had cleared them with the holy water and prayers.

The problem with holy water is the spirits have to believe it will stop them, if they don't then it is just water and will have no effect. It's the same with quoting passages out of the bible or saying prayers. If the spirit doesn't believe it, it will not do anything. One of the things about films like The Exorcist is they went around saying prayers from the bible. The spirit wasn't a Christian and so they had no effect. What I am saying is you have to work within the belief of those you are trying to help or get rid of otherwise you might as well go home. One house we went to the lady had poured salt across all the doorways of the house, internal as well because she had been told spirit couldn't cross salt as it was pure. Needless to say it didn't make any difference to her problem. When we visited some of the Caribbean community we found a popular belief was to have a salt bath to get rid of the bad spirits, the very fact that they had asked us to visit was proof it didn't work. We came across people who had a feud going on with rival families; these had been going on sometimes two hundred years. The people that had started them were in spirit but were still plaguing those left on the earth. They believed quite rightly that their family was cursed and we had to talk to those in spirit and try to get them to see reason. Most times we were successful but sometimes we just had to brand them to stop them. We met people who said they were being haunted and could hear lots of different voices. Some were being haunted but others were schizophrenic and there was nothing we could do but suggest they might see the doctor as it wasn't a spiritual problem. Some of the houses we visited had problems in the house and a few when they went out as well. There are those in spirit who will haunt a house and others who will just work on an individual wherever they go. They are different groups who specialise in their particular skills and will not usually work together. So although one lot may be attacking the people in the house they will not be working with those who attack them when they leave the house. We saw one couple who were afraid to go home because the wife was getting attacked. They ended up staying in a hotel when we got to them. What was happening was the wife was getting clawed across her back, this was happening under her tea shirt and even when her husband put his arms around her to try and protect her. There was no way she could have done it herself even if she were double jointed she couldn't have reached. We managed to clear her and they were able to return to their home in peace, I have to say it was a difficult one but in the end it is the same type of spirit just a different way of giving people problems. Some of the bad spirits we have come up against have been really evil and when we have thrown them out they have vowed to get us back. I suppose they will try when we go back home but until then we will carry on.

We settled down one night to have a chat with spirit and Jan asked one of her guides to come forward,

"Good evening Richard."

"Good evening."

"Can you tell me how the good and bad spirits find their way to the rescue circle, is it our light that attracts them?"

"The light that is over the house and which goes with you attracts good and bad spirit. We then sort out those who need help and those who don't, when you are working in your circle we encourage those in need of help to come forward or make you aware of them. It depends on the lesson you are learning as to who comes forward. There are many different lessons you need to learn in your circle to prepare you for your house visits. We will use the appropriate spirit good or bad for you to learn from."

"What about those times when we are aware of lots of spirits who need help?"

"We try to get as many people who are lost together with similar problems. When you speak to one the others are listening and can associate with what you have said in this way you can rescue many lost souls at the same time. This is one of the reasons why it is so important for us to be able to work with you in this type of work."

"So it's back to what you said ages ago, when they realise the difference in how they feel by coming through a medium they are able to grasp their situation quicker and pass on that feeling to those who are watching?"

"Not quite it's more a case of them realising the difference and then because they can accept what is being said those who are watching follow along."

"Why is it sometimes we get the odd one left who don't go with the crowd?"

"Occasionally there will be one who needs individual attention they may have other issues they need to resolve."

"When you say other issues do you mean beliefs?"

"That is one issue but each one will be different and it will be up to you to find out what is troubling them and resolve it for them."

"Nothing in this work s straight forward is it."

"No that's why you are the one doing the talking, my medium doesn't have the gift of the gab as you say that you have."

"I'm not sure if that is a compliment or not."

"It is always good to have someone who has the ability to be flexible when they are talking to someone who is in pain or confused. It's not that my medium can't do it but you are more used to it."

"So I suppose from what you've said you bring the bad spirits for the same reasons, to teach us how to deal with them?"

"Yes sometimes we will bring a whole house full when we are taking back control from the bad spirits. As we have said we monitor the houses we have allowed them to take over, when it starts to get too active we will bring them all to circles like yours to sort them out."

"So you don't go trawling the realms around the earth for lost souls you just bring a house full to us?"

"We do both it depends on the lesson and who asks for help."

"Are the houses local or can they come from anywhere?"

"As you know there is no time or distance in our world so we get them from wherever is appropriate at the time."

"When we are rescuing someone I find I am able to tune in to what they are seeing and feeling as well as where they are going, I am also aware of what's going on with the other sitters in the circle, how do I do that?"

"We help you to be aware of everything that is going on but you have developed sufficiently to be able to do most of it yourself."

"I just wish it was as easy when I'm doing clairvoyance."

"You will get there just be patient."

"Thank you for answering my questions we will have to go now good night."

"It's been our pleasure good night and god bless."

We chatted about what had been said and both agreed it shed some light on the mechanics of running the circle. It appears they work a lot harder than we imagined making sure the circle ran to plan. It's never as simple as it appears at first glance. We wondered how much work went into running a clairvoyant circle probably just as much.

During the next few weeks we were busy doing services and circles but we got the chance to go to a Saturday special that I had arranged with a well-known medium. While we were there we got talking to one of the people who went to the open circle and they were telling us about someone they knew in New Zealand who were having problems. They asked if we knew anyone over there that could help, we didn't but we said we would see what we could do at our next circle. I asked a couple of questions about the problem and a brief description of the people and their house as something to tune in to make sure we had got the right house and said I would let them know how we got on. I explained we wouldn't be able to do anything until the following Friday but in the mean time we would put protection around the house. Usually this quietened things down because the bad spirits in the house would be aware of it and try to get out. When they found they couldn't they would get their heads down and hope it would go away. Sometimes they would get angry at being restricted and bang about a bit but most of the time they tended to lay low in the hopes that the people in the house would think they had gone. As he said he was going to be telephoning them on the Sunday we asked him to explain what we had done and to be patient until the following Friday. They were not to do anything on the Friday just carry on as normal and let him know next time they spoke of any change in the situation.

On the Monday at the open circle he said he had told them what we said and they said they would call him on the following Saturday and let him know what had happened. During the week we sat and talked to Jan's guides to see if there was anything we needed to be aware of to get the job done successfully. They said just do what you usually do and things should be fine. So the following Friday we sat and I asked the sitters to tune in and tell me what the house or the lady who lived there looked like. I didn't tell them where the house was I just asked them to tune in to the lady whose description I had been given. Well after a couple of false starts one of the

303

sitters described the house down to a specific room with a particular type of wall covering. Once I was satisfied they were in the right house I asked the others to tune in and try and get some information on the lady. They then started to describe her and other parts of the house. I asked where the house was and someone said I don't know but it's not this country. Once we had established we were in the right house I asked them to tune in to a man whom I described and got one of them to bring him through. It was interesting to note he didn't know he was not in the house or that we had moved him halfway across the world. We dealt with him and his cronies and rescued the lost souls and when we had finished, I explained to the circle including Jan where it was and what they had got right and wrong. We all felt the job was complete and I told them the guy was going to ring me when he had spoken to them the following day. I would let them know how things had gone at the other end. The following day I received a phone call to say everything seemed to have stopped. I said give it a week and we'll see how things are then. I spoke again to the guy later in the week and he said he had an e-mail saying things were quiet now and they had no more problems. On the Friday I told the circle what I had heard and we were all pleased we had got it right. This of course meant we could help people all over without having to go there. We decided that if it was possible we would go but didn't think anyone would want to fly us around to solve their problems. So that was our first of many remote clearances.

We sat down one night to have a chat with Jan's guides and I said,

"Hello Richard."

"Good evening."

"I was wondering what happened to the spirit when someone is in a coma. I know it leaves the body when we die but where does it go in a case like that?"

"When you are in a coma the spirit stays with the body until you either get better or the body dies."

"Well if the spirit is there why don't they come back?"

"It depends on the condition of the body; sometimes the brain is too badly damaged. With your modern medicine and technology you are able to keep the body alive even though the brain is hardly functioning. At other times although the body heals itself the shock of what happened stops the spirit from returning."

"So the spirit could come back in some cases and the person would wake up?"

"Yes what sometimes happens is the spirit has been so badly traumatized it won't go back to the body, even if the body has healed. The person's guides try to persuade the spirit to return by explaining everything is alright but we can't make it. If the body is maimed or too badly damaged the spirit won't want to carry on a life with such restrictions and refuses to come back."

"Is that why loved ones are advised to talk to them, sometimes the people wake up and say they have heard every word that was said?"

"Yes the spirit can hear what their loved ones are saying but you must remember if they are in shock they don't realize their spirit is separate and think they can't wake up."

"So that's why some people wake up after some years have passed. It takes that long to persuade them to come back?"

"Yes but it is always worth talking to them from your side you never know."

"Can a medium talk to them by bringing them through in trance and explaining what is going on?"

"It's possible but to our knowledge it has never been tried."

"Can we bring the spirit to our circle and talk to them?"

"Again it's possible but never been tried."

"Why not I would have thought someone would have thought of the possibilities?"

"Even if someone had it would be difficult to approach someone whose loved one was in a coma and give them hope when you don't know what the condition of the brain or body is in. You would also have to try and persuade the medical profession and they are only just coming round to accepting healing. Maybe in a few years they will be open to the possibility."

"We were talking to a couple of people and they were telling us about their previous lives. Remembering what you said about blocking off our spiritual memories how would they know. They said they had been and had regression and they were taken back to before they were born and into another life. Thinking about it they said they were hypnotized and taken back. If I remember correctly they used to use hypnotists in the early days to go into trance. What's the difference between hypnosis and trance?"

"You have been thinking haven't you, let's see first of all hypnosis is very similar to a trance state. The only difference is with trance it is self- induced and you are making contact with spirit. With hypnosis it is done by somebody else with suggestion and you are just opening your mind to further suggestion. When you are guided back through your life you will automatically delve into your subconscious to the particular time of your life the hypnotist suggests. When you get to a stage prior to your birth you will have nothing in your subconscious to pick up on. That is the time when a wandering spirit can impress you of their life. As you know there are two kinds of spirits and it is pot luck which one will impress you. Some will play the game as they have an opportunity to talk to the living, others can be rude or downright unpleasant. In neither case will the sitter be caused any harm as if the session is not going according to the hypnotist's plan they will bring the sitter back. When the hypnotist asks questions about your previous life they will tell them about their own. Most people believe it is their previous life as they have no reference or proof it isn't and they want to believe."

"So what about a trance medium won't they know the difference between the spirits that come forward?"

"Most trance mediums are deep trance and won't have the same kind of experience my medium has as they are not aware of what's going on while they are in trance. It's only people who have trained to tell the difference who will notice."

"I think we will have to give it a try and see for ourselves."

"Why not, it will be interesting."

"Do we need a hypnotist or can we do it without?"

"If you take someone into a deep meditation without them going into trance first you should be able to achieve the same state."

"As the meditation is not for spirit communication it can't be the same type can it?"

"No you will have to go down instead of up when you meditate to contact us you always raise your vibrations. In this case you will need to go within rather than outside the mind."

"Yes I understand what you are saying, well give it a try when we have an evening to spare."

"It should be interesting."

"Thank you for talking to us well let you know how we get on, good night."

"We will be watching good night and god bless."

That answered a few questions for us, we chatted about what had been said and we both were looking forward to the experiment. We talked about coma and we would like to give it a try but we were both aware of the complications of finding someone and approaching their loved ones. We decided we would talk to our rescue circle and see if any of them would like to try regression as they all did light trance we would be able to compare notes. I have not mentioned it but up to date, I haven't had the chance to try going into trance. I have been too busy teaching others so I don't know whether I can. That would be an interesting experiment also.

Chapter 33

I was busy building a double garage with an office in the loft so I didn't have a lot of spare time and was quite tired over the next few weeks. I wanted to get the walls up and the roof on before the weather changed so I was hard at it when I wasn't working for a living or spirit. Eventually we had the time to try things out and all of our rescue circle wanted to be involved so we arranged a suitable evening and gave it a try. The first thing I did was ask for a volunteer to go first, they all wanted to so I had to pick one. We had decided it wouldn't be Jan as I wanted her to tune in while I was taking them back and to tell me if I missed it when spirit came in. We hadn't told the others what to expect or anything about what we had spoken to our guides about. We wanted to have a clean slate and see what happened. I explained how the meditation would be different and the reasons why and then went ahead as everyone was happy to get stuck in. I had chosen Carol as after Jan she was the most experienced at trance and also thought she would be a good subject for what we were doing. The first thing I asked was were there any times in her life she didn't want to go back to, she told me to miss out her 30s otherwise it was fine. I took her through the meditation and then started to take her back at 10 year intervals. I was a surprised as anyone else when I asked her what was happening ten years earlier, as it was as though she was there. It was one day that we were talking about just normal day to day stuff. I took her back another ten years and asked her more pointed questions about what was going on in her life nothing personal just life in general.

We were all surprised how detailed she was, then I took her back to the age of 8 and asked her to describe where she was and what the room looked like. It was amazing the detail so I took her back to the age of 2 and asked her what was going on. She said she was sitting on the floor playing and mummy was doing the washing. I took her back to 6 months and asked her what was happening. She said she was lying in the pram and mummy was talking to daddy about his job. It was as I suspected, babies could understand what adults were saying they just hadn't learnt to talk so could only grunt and gurgle. Carol said she could see other people in the room but they had been there all the time and she could talk to them. I said what did they look like and she said they looked different from her mummy and daddy. I said in what way were they different, she said they could float in the air and they had bright pretty colours round them. We realized she was talking about her guides and it made sense as we knew babies were still aware of spirit for the first few years. I took her back another 2 years and asked her what was happening. Carol said it was like she was floating she couldn't see anything but felt she wasn't alone. I said we are going to go back to your previous life tell me who you were and where you lived. After a minute she started to tell us about a farm, Jan whispered to me that she had a lady with her. I tuned in to what was going on with Carol and sure enough there was a lady there. Jan and I picked up some information about the lady then I asked certain questions to verify what we had picked up. Sure enough she answered the questions as we had expected her to. I then told Carol I wanted her to go back another two years and this time we got a man. Some of the others tuned in to him and were able to get enough information for me to verify which I did. I then asked Carol to come forward 6 years and tell me what was happening, after a moment she said it is cold the fire isn't on. I brought her forward to the age of ten and she said it was her birthday and she had a new dress because she was having a party. We moved forward through her life back to the present, I then reversed the meditation and she came back. When we asked how she felt she said very relaxed she hadn't felt so laid back in ages. On talking to her about her previous lives she said she knew what she was saying all the time but when she went back to before she was born it felt like somebody else was talking like when she was in trance. The difference was she knew exactly what was happening when we were talking to her about her childhood but when she was talking about her previous life it was as though someone else was talking. They all had a cup of tea and then we thought we would try again with someone different. I was not short of volunteers so I asked Derek if he would have a go. He said ok and got comfortable on the sofa. (I had them lie on the sofa so they would be comfortable) I went through the meditation again and took Derek back to before he was born with the same results as we regressed back. When we got to before he was born I asked to speak to his spirit. Someone spoke to us and said hello I asked them to wait a moment after I said hello and checked with everyone to see if they were picking anyone up with Derek. No-one was so I said who is speaking, they said we don't have names here but you know me as Derek. I said are you the spirit that inhabits the body you are talking through. He said yes so I asked him to tell me about a particular event that had happened a few days earlier that only Derek and I knew about. I was suspicious because nobody was picking anything up and we should have picked up the feeling of Derek like we did in circle. They gave me some story which wasn't true but I just said thank you and gradually brought Derek back to the present. The others asked if what we had been told was true and I said, no that wasn't Derek's spirit but it was worth a try. We asked how Derek felt and he said much the same as Carol except he had noticed when we took him back before he was born he was more aware of spirit and what was happening around him. He said he was surrounded by spirit and could only assume it was his guides as it wasn't an unpleasant feeling. We had a chat about what had happened and I told them about our conversation with our guides and they all agreed we would not be able to access our previous lives. We decided to have another go only this time the intention was to talk to someone's spirit if we could. When they said you have tried that I said this time I'm going to take Jan back if she is willing as I know some of her guides. I am also used to her when she is in trance more so than anyone else and I think I might be able to tune in better. I want to try and sort out why we couldn't pick up on that spirit who was with Derek. I took Jan back through her life to before she was born and then asked for her spirit to talk to us. A very gentle voice replied and it said how can I help you? I tuned in and all I got was Jan with Richard and Samuel who were also there but they were standing back. I knew it wasn't a guide because there were no feelings of character or personality, just a peaceful voice. Because the voice was coming from Jan it sounded female I asked,

"Who are you?"

"I am known by you as Jan."

"Can you tell me about a previous life?"

"As you know we block off our memory of our past so that it doesn't interfere with our view of our present. If we were aware of past lives we would not be able to experience the present one in the right perspective. Therefore I cannot tell you anything about my past."

"Are you on track as far as your intentions were in this life?"

"Yes so far I have achieved many of my goals some a little later than expected but I am on schedule."

"Where are you now?"

"I am here as always it is just that my consciousness has been subdued for this experiment."

"Are you able to communicate with your guides at this time?"

"I am able to speak with them at any time but due to the busy lives you lead it doesn't always filter into the conscious mind."

"How do I know you are Jan's spirit and not someone interfering with us?"

"You are unable to tune in to me because you are finding it difficult to get past the woman you know as your wife. You will not be able to isolate me from her because you are used to tuning in to her as a whole person."

"Can anyone else here detect this spirit?" I asked the others.

They all said they couldn't pick up anything except the guides who were around us. They all agreed the room seemed very peaceful and they were not able to pick up any other spirits.

"Thank you for giving us this opportunity I will give it some thought no doubt I will have some questions to ask."

"I am sure you will."

I brought Jan forward until she was back to the present and asked her, "What could you feel when I was talking to that spirit?"

"I couldn't feel anything but a beautiful peace, I could hardly hear what you were saying but I knew what the spirit said."

We had a cup of tea and talked about what had happened, everyone agreed it had been interesting and some of it unexpected. For instance they were surprised that a 6 month old baby could understand what was being said even if the baby couldn't speak. We decided it was because the baby hadn't learnt to form the sounds to make the words. All in all it had been an interesting evening. We knew someone who was a hypnotist and we were going to conduct another experiment with them to see if we could tune in to what happens when somebody is hypnotised. This we would have to arrange, I had already suggested it and they were willing to give it a go. The following few days I thought about what had happened and Jan and I discussed it and came up with some questions for her guides to answer when we had the chance.

Chapter 34

It was another week before we had a chance to talk to Jan's guides; we sat down and asked one of them to come through.

"Good evening Sheena."

"Good evening."

"It's a while since we spoke how are you?"

"I am fine I have come to introduce you to another of my mediums guides."

"Who would that be?"

"If you tune in she is standing behind me and once you have located her I will step back."

"Would that be the nun who is dressed in dark blue about 5"3?"

"Yes I will step back now god bless."

"God bless. Hello it's nice to meet you what is your name?"

"I am called Sister Mary."

"Where do you come from?"

"I was in |France about 400 years ago."

"What did you do?"

"I spent a lot of time tending the vegetable gardens and distributing food to the poor."

"You must have had a large garden."

"The monastery had a lot of land and there were many of us working in the gardens."

"What are you helping your medium with while she is here?"

"My interest is healing the body and the mind."

"Do you help with rescues?"

"Yes that is when I help to heal the mind."

"So you also help when your medium is giving healing to somebody here as well?"

"Yes I am one of her healing guides."

"How many healing guides has she got?"

"More than enough to cover all eventualities, both in the body and when you are doing rescues."

"Can you tell me whether that was your mediums spirit or someone messing us about the other day? I wasn't able to tune in to them in fact none of us were?"

"It was her spirit you were talking to we had to take her quite deep to enable her to let go of her conscious mind so that you could converse."

"So that's pretty unusual then?"

"Yes it is unusual but we thought it might be interesting."

"We were surprised a baby could understand what the adults were saying."

"Why, they are still the spirit and being very close to our world they have not yet settled into the body so much that they can't still remember who they are."

"Never thought of it like that, how long does it take for the spirit to forget about your world?"

"That depends on whether the spirit has decided to be aware all of their lives or maybe later in their life. As you know some will never be aware of us it just depends on the pathway they have chosen."

"Ok supposing the spirit has decided they don't want to be aware in their early years when do they forget about you?"

"Usually by the time they are two or three."

316

"Why is that?"

"They are becoming more focused on their surroundings and if they are playing with or talking to spirit the parents who are not aware tell them there is no-one there. In the end the child will believe the parents because they are usually right. Gradually the child will stop playing with spirit because they are told it is their imagination."

"So if you have more aware parents it is more than likely the child will still be aware of spirit?"

"Not necessarily you have to remember when they play with friends they want to join in and children can be quite cruel if someone is different."

"Yes I see what you mean shame though there would be a lot more enlightened people around if that didn't happen. And it would make your job easier when you are trying to show people there is no death."

"Yes but there will always be someone whatever the situation that fears passing, it's the fear of the unknown."

"What's this I keep hearing about the Age of Aquarius, people say we are moving to another phase in human enlightenment. What do they mean by that?"

"Humanity is becoming more aware of spirit, as they become more educated they are able to think further than the indoctrination they were subjected to as children. There is a different general awareness in your world than there was a hundred years ago."

"I see that makes sense, well it's been nice talking to you but we will have to go now so I'll say good night and thank you for talking to us."

"Thank you it's been interesting good night and god bless."

Jan opened her eyes and said,

"I have been aware of her for a few days now I wondered if she was going to come through."

"That's another one I have got to recognize. Ah well I seem to be doing alright with the others so I don't expect it to be a problem."

"When you consider you are able to recognize the other guides in the circles I should think it will be quite easy for you."

"I was just kidding when you look back it's surprising how far we have come in our development."

"Yes when you consider some of the people we talk to who have been sitting for years they don't seem to have got very far."

"I think we have an advantage because we are able to talk to spirit and not only get answers but help when we don't understand something."

"Just as well really what with all we've been through."

Chapter 35

We called it a night and went to bed. The next day we were going to

Reading to be assessed for speaking and demonstrating by the West London Council if we passed we would be certificate holders and then if they changed the law we would be able to carry on working. Jan was demonstrating her clairvoyance and I was to speak for 15 minutes or more about the reading and bring in some of the seven principles. We had both done about 10 written exams and passed them and now we had to do the practical. We had also been assessed by 3 different mediums that came to our services incognito. After each service they asked the recipients if we had proved their loved ones to them.

We went to Reading and took the practical exams and I am pleased to say we passed so all the hard work had paid off.

We were now diploma and certificate holders of courses run by the SNU. This made us legitimate in the eyes of the churches which gave us the opportunity to teach and run all day workshops if we wanted. Of course we couldn't teach people about rescue circles, because most mediums believed like attracts like and they tried to ignore the other side of spirit. Consequently most people didn't believe or want to know about bad spirit and how to deal with them. After all if you attracted bad spirits they believed you must be bad also. Over the years we did quite a few workshops mostly to do with developing clairvoyants. We found when we were going to house clearances people were insisting they paid us for our time. We said we would only take what was offered if they were happy for us to give it to a children's charity. They all agreed so we saved it up and gave it to the Charity for Terminally Ill Children and it was used to give them a holiday of a lifetime. We were now getting referrals from the SNU and the Spiritualist Association of Great Britain or SAGB which is the Christian spiritualist arm of spiritualism in this country. The British Psychological Society in London were referring people to us as well as many of the churches we went to, so we had to step up our visits to people. Fortunately we now had four or five of us doing it and were able to cope with the increased demand. As far as we were concerned they were all people whatever their beliefs that needed help. We never heard of or met anyone else who did the same as us but we heard of a few who tried from the people we went to help. We did a few remotes in Europe and Scotland and quite a few in England when they were too far to travel to. We even went to a church in St Albans where they were having problems and cleared the bad spirits from there. One of the things we discovered on our travels was that it wasn't only people that were haunted. There were a few cases where carvings mostly from Africa had been chanted over during their creation and we had to clear them before the house felt peaceful. If a house was really bad then it usually took a week to settle down again, this was because the people who lived there took a while to get over their experiences. There were times when we had to return to a house because the people had invited the bad spirits in again. This would happen when they had been having a bad time. Some of the houses we went to we found the pets would not go near the particular part of the house where there were problems. After a couple of days they would go in the rooms when we had cleared them. This was proof for the people who lived there and we were getting recommendations from them as well. Although it wasn't bothering us any more as we had built up our strength we had to subdue those who were attacking us all the time, in case someone in the open circle tuned in to them. We knew they wouldn't bother anyone else as we were their target but we felt we had to take precautions for the benefit of the sitters. That's why when we were running the circle we never opened up to allow the sitters to tune in and work on us. It became a challenge for some of the old hands to try and give us a communicator and a message. Sometimes if things were quite we would open up a bit to give them a chance, but we couldn't tell them why they were unable to work on us in case we frightened them.

Eventually we came off committee because we were so busy and handed over the open circle to Derek a friend of ours. After a few months we were missing the open circle and someone we knew from another church at Basingstoke asked us if we would start a circle there. We said put it to your committee and if they agree then we would be happy to. It was agreed so we started going to Basingstoke once a week to run an open circle for them. It wasn't long before we became members and then went on the committee there. The building was made of corrugated iron sheets that had seen their best days and were rusting quite badly. The church had no money for repairs and asked me if I would become entertainments manager, they had heard how I had got the income at Camberley up so they could pay the mortgage. I arranged some psychic suppers and special events but the money wasn't coming in fast enough to get the repairs done. I then hired a large hall and booked some top mediums that I knew from around the country and sold all the tickets to other churches and individuals. The night went well to a packed hall and we made about £1200.00p profit, the committee were very pleased and asked if I could arrange another in the near future. I arranged three in all and the result was much the same. Over the time I was entertainments manager I raised about £5000.00p for the church then the president stepped down for personal reasons. The new president persuaded the committee to spend the building fund on revamping the interior. I was disappointed as they really needed to sort out the outside first but I was overruled. We left shortly after that as I was quite happy to raise money for the church but not so they could waste it on whims and such. As we were extremely busy with renovating, building up my business and working for spirit we didn't miss the church but I was asked if I would be willing to sit on the West London Council Committee. I was elected and served on there for a couple of years until I found I couldn't get to the meetings because we were so busy. I stepped down and just concentrated on services, closed circles of which we ran two at home and house clearances. We still had the odd evening when we would sit and talk to Jan's guides as there were a lot of questions still unanswered.

We sat one night to talk to Jan's guides and Richard came through.

"Good evening Richard."

"Good evening."

"We have found when visiting some houses where there are teenagers the people have been told it's because of them that they are having problems why is that?"

"It's not because of the teenagers it's because their emotions are all over the place one minute they are open and the next they are closed. When they are open they inadvertently tune in to what's around them. If it's bad spirits then they will play on their emotions all the more for the fun of it. Up until then they have not been able to get through, but with their emotions all over the place they don't know whether they are coming or going. That's when the bad spirits take advantage of the situation."

"Why is it that mediums think it's the teenagers that are attracting them?"

"In their experience there are always young adolescents in the house where they come across problems."

"They don't go to many houses then if that's all they have come across."

"There are very few people that do what you do, most don't believe in bad spirits and if they do then they think they will get tainted if they come in contact with them."

"Is that why most mediums don't admit to the possibility of two sides, good and bad?"

"Yes much like an ostrich if you don't accept the possibility then it doesn't exist. That is why in most religions it's not talked about"

"So when a medium is asked to help when there are problems around teenagers they say it will stop when their emotions settle down and not to worry about it?"

"You have come across young adults who are having problems because they were not helped when they needed it and the bad spirits have gained a foothold. As you know from your own experiences with this particular problem, it takes longer to convince the young adults that things have been dealt with because they have lived with it for so long and it has become part of their life. It's why there are so many young adults having psychotherapy or being sectioned. Your medical people have not understood what is going on with some of the youngsters in today's world for all their enlightened way of looking at things."

"They have been putting people in institutions for years because they hear voices is that a lack of understanding?

"Not really, a lot of the people they put in institutions are in need of medication as they are ill, the problem is the doctors tar them all with the same brush."

"I suppose if they're not a medium they won't be able to tell those who are schizophrenic and those who are being attacked?"

"That and the way these poor souls have been treated in the past, if the book says to lock them away and fill them with drugs then who are they to argue, that's how it's done."

"I understand a lot of those who are put in institutions are given electric shock treatment, how do they expect to cure someone like that?"

"They know there are electric currents going through the brain and they are trying to shock it back on track."

"What makes them think that will help have they succeeded in the past?"

"They have found people become more subdued after shock treatment."

"Yes so would I be after that kind of therapy anything so they don't do it again. On another subject you know we have a cess pit in the garden is there any way of turning it into a septic tank. When we get a lot of rain it tends to over flow, it doesn't matter whether we've just had it emptied or not it fills up?"

"I believe it was an old well that has been converted into a cess pit wasn't it?"

"Yes I thought as you or maybe Elijah would have had them around in your day and you might be able to tell me how to convert it."

"Elijah says if you put a tee shaped pipe in the top of the wall about three feet down and dig a trench from it across the back lawn, you will need it to be 120feet long in total. Put two shorter trenches in a backwards v about half way along. You will then need to place a large pipe with holes in the sides in the bottom of the trench. Fill the trench to cover the pipe with pea shingle and replace the turfs on top that should solve the problem."

"Ok I will give it a try this weekend thanks for your help we have to go now no doubt you will be watching to make sure I do it correctly good night."

"Good night and god bless."

I got digging the following Saturday having bought the pipe and shingle and by Sunday afternoon I had finished. We would now wait and see whether they were right, it's not that I doubted our guides, after all they have told me in the past has come true, it's just that I wanted that final bit of proof. It took about three weeks before we were going to have the cess pit people visit to empty it. They came every four weeks, when I checked the cess pit is was only half full it poured for about two days and I expected under normal circumstances for it to overflow but it didn't. It never came higher than three feet from the top so I cancelled the cess pit people and we never had to have it emptied again in the following four years that we were there. We had a nice growth of grass all along the top of where the pipe was but other than that we forgot all about it. So we had that final bit of proof, not that I doubted our guides but you would be the same wouldn't you?

Chapter 36

We were visiting a church in north London one day when we came in contact with a couple called John and Pauline who we knew who told us they had started doing psychic surgery. He would go into deep trance and he had a doctor who used to be a surgeon who came through and operated on patients who had come to him. We had heard about it but didn't know a great deal about it apart from it was supposed to be very popular in the Philippines. As they were going to do a demonstration the following week we arranged to go and sit in and observe how they did it.

On the day they set up a healing couch where people could lie down, the first patient was a woman who said she was getting pains to the left side of her abdomen. They settled her down and explained what was going to happen and that she would feel no pain, when the patient was ready John went into trance, this took about ten minutes. They weren't too keen on anyone sitting in but because we had cleared their house and they knew we wouldn't interfere they let us sit at the other end of the hall. We could see John standing behind the couch with his sleeves rolled up just feeling the affected area before he started. Pauline sat on the other side of the couch ready to assist him and to reassure the patient. John turned to a table behind him and when he turned back he pressed down on the area and there appeared to be a little blood. He then started pulling something out of the women and he turned and dropped whatever it was into a dish on the table behind him. He then turned back to the patient and after wiping his hands appeared to rub the area he had been working on then stepped back and came out of trance. In all it took about 30 minutes what with going into and coming out of trance. The lady was helped off the couch and she seemed to be alright as she said thank you and left the room. They did about 5 patients and then John was exhausted so they stopped, they charged £35.00p for each patient. Pauline came over to us and walked us to the door telling us that John needed time to readjust and we left the room. Jan and Pauline had a cup of tea after she had taken one in to John and chatted about how they were getting quite busy going to different churches with their psychic surgery. After we had chatted about how they got into it and Pauline said John had been in trance one day and the doctor had come through and told them they should start doing psychic surgery and he would help them. We noticed how we were escorted from the room without getting the chance to see what John had pulled out of the patients.

During the week we had a chance to talk to Jan's guides so we settled down to ask about it. This is what they said.

"Good evening Richard."
"Good evening."
"We have come across a couple of people we know who have started doing psychic surgery and thought we should like to know more about it."
"What do you want to know?"
"Do they really remove parts of the body that are causing problems?"

"No they just make it look like it."

"Why would they pretend to remove things, the patient is soon going to know it was a lie?"

"The mind is a powerful thing and sometimes if you believe enough, things do go into remission. There is also the psychological effect it can have on the patient."

"But it's still just a big con isn't it."

"Only if you expect the healer to remove something, if you feel better, it is not a con as you say."

"For what they charge I think it is."

"It's no different than regression if you think about it."

"Yes I guess that's true thanks for talking to us good night."

"Good night and god bless."

We chatted about the pros and cons of psychic surgery and compared it to regression and came to the conclusion that regression was about belief and psychic surgery was about health. Although neither of them worked as the patient expected, it was wrong to mess with people's health.

One day I got a call from a lady from the SNU and was asked if I would give an interview about haunted houses on a local television station. They asked me because they knew I did a lot of house clearances. I said I would be happy to and it was arranged with Hertfordshire Television for me to go along. I was a bit nervous as I had never been on television before, but the hostess was very good she chatted to me and made me feel at ease. When the program started she introduced me as the

South of England's leading exorcist. She went on to ask all sorts of questions about what we did and how busy we were. Towards the end she asked if I was a clairvoyant and when I said yes she wanted me to give her a reading. I said no as that was not why I was there and we chatted a bit more then it was over. The lady at the SNU who had asked me to go was pleased with the result so everyone was happy. As a result of the interview the SNU had quite a few inquiries about exorcisms but gradually it died down to normal referrals and life went on.

There was another time when a local paper asked us to go and clear a house where the people were having major problems. When we arrived there was a reporter and a photographer waiting to observe and take pictures while we were working. We refused to have pictures taken and after speaking with the people in the house we had to explain that we could only get rid of the spirits if they wanted us to. The wife was keen to be free of the problems but the husband seemed to enjoy the attention. We sat down and told them that if we cleared the house, they would have to try to forget all about it and get on with their lives. That they would have to stop thinking and looking for spirit as this would invite others back in. The wife was keen for us to sort things out but the husband said he didn't want us to clear the house. When we explained to the wife and the reporter that we couldn't do anything they were surprised and asked why. We told them that all the while the husband wanted the spirits there we could do nothing as we needed the authority of both of them before we could start. As they were not in agreement there was nothing we could do, this of course upset the wife but she couldn't persuade her husband to agree to us clearing the house. When we left the reporter said I don't believe you can do it, I said suit yourself it's not a sideshow find someone else who will play along. I told the wife that if her husband came round to her way of thinking then call me and we would come and sort it out then we left.

Whatever we were doing spiritually we both knew our guides were always going to be there for us. If we got it wrong then it was always going to be our fault. I have seen mediums from the more experienced to the beginners who get so nervous before and when they get on the platform. When I have asked why they are nervous, the more experienced tell me they need to build up energy so that spirit can use it to work with them. You will hear sometimes a medium will say it is an experiment there are no guarantees that spirit will come through. Alll I can say is they have never let me down, when I get up I know if it doesn't work it is going to be my fault and no-one else's.

It doesn't matter how many times a medium has done a service they can always have an off day or not be feeling well. We must never judge others as we don't know how they are feeling or what kind of day they have had. Having said that we must remember that if we allow spirit in they will never let us down, but at the moment we are all human and subject to human frailties.

Of course part of giving a service is to talk about the philosophy of spirit, it's not just clairvoyance, there is an art to speaking as well and any good medium will learn that art. One of the most important things to learn along with your development of clairvoyance is to understand how spirit interacts with us and why. This will form the basis of your philosophy and by talking to your guides and observing life from their point of view you should be able to talk on a subject for at least 10 minutes. There are many that say an address should last 20 minutes but the attention span of most congregations is only about 10 unless you are an exceptional speaker. With what we have learnt from our guides and from our travels to different circles and AFC we have had the opportunity to help a number of mediums develop their skills. They are all working now so I thought I would write down how I would develop a medium. I think the first thing to say is that it is not a gift, you have had to work hard to learn how to do whatever you can do, in spirit. All you are doing now is remembering what you have learnt.

Chapter 37

Meditation is where we will start and when you meditate you are meditating to contact spirit not to have a rest. The object is to get in touch with your guides and when you have quietened your mind you must then work out how you see or hear. Try to remember they don't have ears or eyes in spirit they only have senses. Most people do not hear or see, they may get thoughts or pictures inside their head. You must always be aware of your surroundings during meditation never allow yourself to go too deep. You should be able to open your eyes instantly if required, you are not more advanced if you go deep you are less in control. The first thing to do is recognise what is your thought and what is not, the best way to do this is to practice psychic readings. A psychic reading is a reading that is done on another person who is sitting in front of you. You are reading the spiritual energy that surrounds all of us. You do it all the time. Think about when you first meet someone, for some reason you either like or dislike them, that is you reading their aura. Intuition and body language are all part of what you do when you are doing psychic readings. You are just taking it a step further by tuning in to their aura and telling them how they feel and what they like and what their personality and character are. By saying the first thought that comes into your head you will be learning the difference between your thoughts and your senses. Everything you get for someone will be historical you cannot get information from someone's aura about other people. The future's not what you are trying to predict either just who they are and what they like and dislike and how they feel.

As you get more comfortable with psychic readings you will find you are getting bits of information about things that have happened and maybe even people that they know. This is when spirit is giving you information, it is important that you take notice of how you are receiving this information. Once you recognise how you are communicating you will recognise the difference between your thought and spirits.

Now you are ready to get in touch with your guides one at a time during meditation. The reason you need to get to know your guides is because that's who you will be working with. You are part of a team with them in spirit and you on the earth. You can't work without each other so the better you know them the better you will communicate. During meditation take yourself to a special place. It can be a garden or a building like a church, somewhere where you feel secure, do not sit in open fields in your meditation always have a wall or hedge around you. This is so you can see where you are at all times; do not leave your secure place during your meditation except when you are coming back. Ask for one of your guides to join you. If you don't know any of your guides it doesn't matter they are always with you and one will come forward. Your guide will always come to you slowly they will never just appear or rush in, always watch them approach in whatever way you are aware of them. The first thing you need to be aware of is how you feel about whoever comes forward. They may not be a guide but someone pretending. If you feel warm and comfortable then run with it, if you feel cold or uncomfortable then come back and start again. With practice you will get to know the difference between what is right and what isn't. Your guide will always show him/herself in the exactly same way, they will never wear anything different. If at any time you are unable to see their face ask yourself what they have got to hide. They will always give you the best chance of recognising them and we tend to recognise people by their face or voice so they will comply with what you are used to. You are always in control of your meditation if you don't want something then ask spirit to take it away. Until you know one of your guides well, always ask for the same one. If a different one comes in it will not be a guide unless you have made a mistake with the first one. If that is the case then you will need confirmation from a medium as to which is a guide and which isn't. So come out of your meditation and start again. When you have bonded with your guide you can ask for them to introduce you to another. The one you know will always come in first and then at your request will step back and allow another to take their place.

Here are two examples of meditations you can use if you are running a circle. The first thing to say is if you are able to trance please don't do it in an open circle this is not the time or place. If you should go into trance don't worry we will be watching you and will bring you back safely. If someone does go into trance then gently call their name to bring them back. If you get no response then tell them you are going to gently hold their wrist all the time calling their name. If you still get no response then get some cold water and wet your hands. Then again tell them you are going to gently hold their wrist while calling their name and they will come back.

The circle leader never closes their eyes, they are constantly watching the sitters to make sure they don't have any problems. The circle leader's job is to tune in to each of the sitters during the meditation to see what is happening, and make sure they are where they are supposed to be. It is very easy for an inexperienced sitter to be taken from the place you have taken them to. If that happens then you must remind all the sitters that they are to stay in the place you take them to. A typical meditation goes like this. Picture yourself on a bright sunny day walking along a towpath beside a canal. There is no-one there but you and as you walk the canal is on your right. There are fields to your left and trees along the edge of the towpath. A little way along you can see a bridge going over to the other side. We are going to cross the bridge because on the other side there is a high hedge with a gate in it. As you go over the bridge in the middle it's a bit misty, go through the mist and towards the gate in the hedge. Open the gate and you will find yourself in a garden with a hedge all around the outside and a pathway going round inside the hedge. Along the path at intervals you will see garden benches, find one to sit on and take a look around you. In the middle of the garden is a fountain and there are flower beds scattered around the edges of the pathway surrounded by lawn. As you sit there ask one of your guides to join you, it will not be anyone who you have known on this earth not a relative or a friend who has passed. But a friend from spirit someone you knew before you started your journey through life. Stay on the bench do not get up or leave the garden until I tell you. They will come towards you slowly and sit by your side. Remember how you are aware of spirit this is how you will be aware of your guide. If at any time you don't feel comfortable then ask them to leave, if they don't come back and open your eyes. Talk to your guide, use your mind ask them questions and take note of what they are wearing, I will leave you there for a few minutes to get to know them. Now thank them for coming to join you and make your way back to the gate. Go through the gate and back over the bridge, walk along the towpath until you are back where you started and come back to the circle and open your eyes.

The circle leader should only leave the sitters for about three minutes it's long enough in the beginning for them to get something but not long enough for them to get bored or leave. You must watch all the sitters and tune in to who they have with them, be aware of how they are feeling and stay in control of the meditation. If the spirit that comes to the sitters wants to take them away from where you have taken them then you must make the sitters aware this will not be one of their guides. Everyone's guides will abide by the circle leaders instructions. It is not unusual for a sitter to say I know one of my guides and he/she always takes me to wherever. To this you should reply you are going to meet a new guide who will stay in the meditation with you. Never accept a guide unless you the circle leader can

337

verify them for yourself, it doesn't matter who the sitter is check for yourself. Working as a circle leader is a lot different from sitting in the circle and you will find your guides will feed you information as you go along so you can help the sitters to understand things. It is a whole new experience. The second meditation goes like this:

Close your eyes and imagine it's a bright sunny day and you are walking along a tree lined path towards a country house, as you approach the gates to the house on your right is an old church. Walk over to the church and open the door and you will see rows of pews and at the far end an altar. Around the walls there are tall windows letting in the sunlight. The church is empty apart from you, take a seat and ask your guide to come and join you. It will not be a friend or relative but someone who you knew when you were in spirit before you were born. They will approach you slowly and sit beside you, take note of what they are wearing. Remember how you are aware of spirit you may see them or feel them it doesn't matter how. Just tune in to them and ask your guide some questions about themselves. I will leave you there for a few minutes while you get to know them. Do not leave the church until I tell you, if you feel uncomfortable then come back to the circle and open your eyes. Now we will thank our guides for coming and make our way to the door we came in. Go through the door and back along the path and as you go along you will come back to the circle and open your eyes.

Both these meditations are designed to keep you safe and providing you follow them you shouldn't have any problems. There is always a chance that you will not like one or the other, if so use the other one. Do not play music during these meditations as it will distract from what you are trying to achieve. Your objective is to meet a guide and be able to describe them for future reference. Once you have met a guide ask for the same one in subsequent meditations until you have formed a bond of friendship between you. After the meditation the circle leader should talk you through and ask you to describe what you saw on your way and whilst you were sitting in the garden or the church. You will be surprised at how different people saw the same meditation. It's not all your imagination, your guides will be showing you what you see. They are already with you but you may not be aware of them yet.

Remember how you received your communication when you were giving a psychic reading and ask for a guide to come and join you. Using your communicating skills you will be aware of something different around you like a warm feeling or a feeling of peace and wellbeing. If you don't feel comfortable then open your eyes and try again. Next time you try it may be the same if it is then leave and try again. Keep doing this until you are comfortable with whoever has joined you in your meditation. Sometimes you will see and sometimes you will just know, either way they will always look exactly the same. If they look the same but won't show their face or communicate with you then leave and come out of your meditation. Keep doing this until you are satisfied they are always the same person. Once you have established contact in whatever way you communicate, remember you will not always get all the information they are giving you to start with, as you have to learn to stay tuned in. Because it is new you will find yourself tuning in and out until you are more used to keeping the link. Once you are able to stay tuned in ask questions about them and what they want to be called. The more you get to know the better your link will be and the easier you will find it to recognise them. Don't rush this stage of your development because this is the foundation from which you will build your trust and confidence with yourself and your guide. Your guides are friends who you knew when you were in spirit. You have asked them to look after you whilst you are on your journey through your life on earth. You will not have a guide who was alive less than 200 years ago. This is because like everyone they will want to see all their loved ones safely back to spirit before they do anything else. When you consider they will want to make sure their grandchildren and maybe even great grandchildren are safely back, it can take at least a couple of hundred years for that to happen. Your guides will always be people, never animals or arch angels, they have to be credible and so do you when you are working with spirit. They will never be from mythical places like another planet or even from Atlantis as there is no proof yet that it actually existed.

The next step is to sense your guide with you when you are not in meditation and practice getting information from them with your eyes open. Ask for information about someone sitting in the circle and see if they recognise what you tell them. If they do then you are starting to pass information from spirit which is your objective. Don't rush yourself be satisfied that you have given something that has been understood. Although you can sit and meditate by yourself once you have made contact with your guide and they have been confirmed by a medium it is better to sit in a circle if you can. Now you have gained the ability to communicate, practice and trust your guides. At some stage you will want to know about another guide, don't try this until you are at one with the guide you know. You can then ask them to introduce you to another one. In getting to know your guides always follow the advice given for the first one never deviate from that pathway they will always follow the same rules. If you feel cold or uncomfortable then it will not be your guide but someone trying to mislead you, open your eyes and try again. Your guides will never make you feel uncomfortable but if you allow others in they will let you, and they will make you feel uncomfortable. After all how will you know when it is wrong if you haven't experienced it? I can't emphasise this enough as it is going to be your yardstick for telling whether it is a guide or not.

As you become more accustomed to communication you will find how you receive information will change, it will become more subtle. If you hear then you may find you get more thoughts than words. If you see objectively you may find yourself getting more impressions subjectively. Whatever way you communicate you will find as you progress it will change, be aware of this and watch out for it. If you don't notice the change you will still be trying to communicate in the way you started and you

341

will miss a lot of the information you are being given. You will always progress towards just knowing what you want to say, you will always get a mixture of ways, during your communications as you progress from one type to the next. To see objectively is to see as you would another person, over there. To see subjectively is to see inside your head or mind. People talk about the third eye it's not an eye it is your mind, remember your mind is the spiritual part and the brain is the physical part of you. The mind is also your soul or spirit it is the bit you take with you when you pass.

The next stage is to give your guides the authority they are going to need to keep communicators organised. You do this because when you are getting information you only want to talk to one communicator at a time. If you talk to anyone that shouts out to you then you will get conflicting information which your recipient will not understand. Like when you are describing someone and the recipient will say I understood what you said at first then you seemed to go off track. This is because either you have more than one communicator or you lose focus. An example of losing focus is when you stop listening to spirit because you are talking to the recipient. When your mind goes back or you tune in to spirit again you may very well have tuned in to someone else. Stay focused and maintain your link, you can still talk to the recipient but don't focus on them. You will have certain criteria you will want for you to be able to describe your communicator and who they were and how they might have passed. Write a list of what you would want to know and read it a couple of times a week so that you have it in your mind. This will then go into your aura so that anyone who wishes to communicate to or through you will know what is expected. In other words they will have a list of what you want to know. They will sometimes be excited at the prospect of getting a message across and it will help them to settle down, and help you to pass on the information accurately. The list you have memorised will also give your guides the authority to organise your communicators on your behalf. You will also have to learn when someone in spirit is shouting at you or talking to you when it's not their turn. When that happens you must tell them to wait in line or ignore them until it is their turn, by doing this you will strengthen the authority you give your guides. You don't have to have a conversation with the air to get your point across just send your thoughts out. Talking to spirit out loud does nothing for the credibility of spiritualism it makes it look like play acting.

I know it all sounds difficult and a lot to remember but over the time of your development it will become second nature and you won't have to think about it because it will be there for all to see in spirit. You will need to sit in a closed circle where the lessons will be understood and explained by the circle leader. The circle leader should also be able to tune in to what you are getting and see where you are going wrong and help you to correct it. There is no set time that it takes to develop but any good circle leader will have you give a communicator on your first night. You may not give a message, but someone that is understood by another of the sitters. After that you will have to go through the lessons until you are able to do it without their help.

To help someone to give a communicator the circle leader should ask the sitter to answer questions without thinking. Then fire questions from the list that they would use when talking to a communicator. It is essential the sitter gives the first thought that comes to mind. One of the problems when you first start to communicate is you think and try to rationalise your answer and that is when you get it wrong. It doesn't matter in the beginning if you only get a bit of information as long as it is understood you can build on that. In my experience woman find it easier to get going than men but with a little patience they will succeed also. Don't worry about a message until all the information you are giving is understood. An example of a list is below:

1. Gender
2. Who for
3. Build
4. Height
5. Age
6. Describe face
7. Hair
8. Moustache
9. Glasses
10. Smoker
11. How they dress
12. The way they stand
13. Relationship

14. Character
15. Personality
16. Illness's
17. How they passed quick or slow
18. When they passed
19. Type of work
20. Why they have come
21. Thank them for coming

From this list anyone should be able to give a communicator if they don't think before giving the information they asked for.

Getting to know your guides is the first step to all types of mediumship and should not be ignored. It is with them that you will rely on to work whether it's communicating, healing, trance, psychic art, writing or anything else, it all comes with the help of your guides.

The lessons you get are given by your guides and with the help of the circle leader they are explained to you. You will be given them again and again until you recognise them while you are working in the circle and sort them out. The circle leader doesn't teach you anything they are just there to keep you on track and should answer your questions. The most important part of any circle is when it is finished and you discuss what has happened over a cup of tea. This is when you must ask questions as the circle leader will not know what you don't understand until you ask. There are no silly questions if you don't know always ask. If you are not satisfied with the answer then ask someone else who you think may be able to help you. The reason you sit in circle is so that you can learn from other people's lessons as well as your own, so when you are not working you must be alert and try to tune in to whatever is going on. A circle is held once a week so that you have time to think about what you did and put everything you have learnt into perspective ready for the next sitting. A closed circle has the same sitters sitting in the same place each week. If a member of the circle can't be there then their chair should be left in. The duration of the circle can be anything from one to two hours and must always start and finish on time. This is because you have made an appointment with your guides and it is good practice to be punctual in all that you do in your spiritual work. You should never do private readings on the spur of the moment always make an appointment even if it is for five minutes later, this is so your guides can get things organised. It also reinforces the authority you have given your guides and you will find the reading will always be more successful.

As you progress in your development the circle leader should ask you to get specific communicators like an aunt or a grandparent. This will help you to tune in to individuals and your guides will bring forward the right person when you ask. It will take practice but it will work if you persevere. Always be specific in what you ask in your opening prayer and of your guides. If you are asking for a communicator for someone then ask for someone they know. Until you specify what you want you will get someone for the recipient but they may well be from their great grandparent's era. That is no good to you as if they don't know their family tree then although it's for them they will not be able to recognise the description you give. The same as when you open a circle in prayer, the prayer is a request to your guides for help in your development. When you say the opening prayer ask for assistance in the type of work you are going to be doing in the circle. For instance if you are practicing clairvoyance then ask for communicators that are known to the sitters. If you are sitting for psychic art then ask for your guides to come and help you with your art and to show you the person you are drawing. All circles sit for a specific reason when you open in prayer then ask for help with that particular discipline. Remember a prayer is a request or thank you to your guides as they are the ones who are working with you.

If you are lucky enough to have a trance medium in your circle who can bring their guides through to answer questions make sure you write down your questions first. The guides will only answer to the understanding of the least advanced sitter, so if you want answers to deeper questions then be aware of who is listening to the answers. If you don't get a full answer then rephrase your question until you are satisfied with your answer. If at the end of your questions you can't accept what has been said, then put it to one side for the time being and come back to your question on another occasion with someone else. You do not have to accept the answer that you are given if it doesn't feel comfortable, always question spirit about the answers they give you. They will always give you an explanation if you ask for one.

347

Once you are at one with two or three of your guides and are able to communicate successfully you may wish to try trance or as some would say overshadowing. This is not deep trance but what one would call light trance where the medium is able to hear everything that is said. They will also be able to stop the trance at will by opening their eyes. A light trance medium will sense their guide and allow them to come forward. When they feel secure that it is their guide with them they can allow them to talk. They will speak in the mediums voice but the phraseology will be different. The way to do this is for someone to say good evening when they think the guide is through. The medium will respond likewise, it doesn't matter whether they say it or their guide what matters is that you have started the conversation. The sitter should then ask questions of the guide that the person in trance won't know the answer to. The questions should be spiritual, not messages, for instance, ask something about your own guide that the medium doesn't know. The answers will confirm they are in trance and it is spirit speaking and not the medium speaking. This is important as it gives the medium confidence that the information is not coming from them. Once the medium has gained confidence in their guides it is time for the sitter to learn to recognise the guide when they come through. This is when the senses become invaluable as you will not see the guide any other way unless you see spirit. The sitter should always be in charge of the session although the medium is at liberty to open their eyes at any time if they are unhappy with the proceedings. There will be times when the guide that comes through is an imposter and as soon as you realise you must throw them out. To do this the medium just opens their eyes. Once you have discussed what happened it is important that the medium goes back into trance and gets a proper guide through. It may be wrong two or three times, if it is then stop and try again another time. Before going into trance the medium must establish their connection with their guide, this will help limit mistakes. If it does go wrong look upon it as a lesson don't despair learn from it and move on. It is important that you don't touch or allow anyone else to touch the medium whilst they are in trance as this could unsettle them. Initially the medium will ask for a particular guide to come forward with the agreement of the sitter so that you are both aware of whom you are expecting. Once the sitter can recognise the guide then the medium should ask another guide to come forward. This will give both the medium and the sitter experience in communicating with the mediums guides and how to recognise and talk to them. Spirit will never speak first and if interrupted will wait until you have finished speaking before they answer, so is up to the sitter to welcome the guide when they first come through. You will be expected to welcome them by the name they have given you to use for them.

If you get to this stage in the mediums development you are in a rare position to learn from spirit and get your answers straight from those who know. You must be aware that once the medium has taken the decision to light trance they will never be able to deep trance so think carefully before you proceed with this way of working. Light trance is very good for giving a talk on spiritual philosophy when you are taking services; because the medium will know when their guide is close and they can allow them to inspire them. It is not necessary to go into trance for this as they will be accustomed to allowing their guides thoughts to come through. Light trance is how you would work if you decided to run a rescue circle and all you need to know about any type of mediumship is but a question away. This type of mediumship takes time to develop and needs a constant partnership so that the medium and the sitter are familiar with each other and the guides.

Chapter 38

To run a rescue circle you need a light trance medium who is familiar with their guides and has some experience with imposters, which they should have as they will have had to get rid of them. They should be able to control who is coming through and stop the wrong one. There should be someone who is used to talking to spirit and able to be specific in their questioning. You will always start by asking for protection around the circle in your prayer and do not ask for loved ones, they will not be allowed as it will be dangerous for them. By using your senses you will pick up who has come to your circle from spirit. They will have been allowed in by your guides to help you learn and they will be people who are lost, or bad spirits who are there to try and waste your time. The bad spirits who try to waste your time are an invaluable source of knowledge. Learn how to recognise them and how to deal with them when they come through. It doesn't mean you are getting it wrong it means you are progressing. You will have to learn the difference between those who want help and those who are playing games with you and deal with them accordingly. When you first start to rescue lost souls you will learn to sense who they are and what their story is. This is important as you will need to know about them so that you can ask the right questions. It will help you to sort out the imposters as their story will be different. Trust your instincts if you think they are lying then say so, be confident, if you are wrong and you throw the innocent out your guides will help them to get to the right place. Even if you make a mistake, because you have spoken to the lost souls, they will realise there is a difference in how they feel, because subconsciously they will have felt the weight of the body. This is how they will realise their situation has changed and your guides will then be able to take them to heaven. You will never rescue just one spirit, your guides will always make sure there are others who have similar problems are able to hear what you are saying. When you are working in circle you ask for protection to be put around the circle. If you are going to visit some ones house where they are having problems you will put protection around the house before you visit. This is to stop the bad spirits from leaving before you get there, otherwise you will arrive and find no bad spirits, but once you have left they will come back. When you have cleared the house you will leave the protection around it for as long as the people who live there need it. It will be maintained by their guides who if they don't know how to maintain it will be shown by your guides.

An example of a straight forward rescue would be:

"Hello what's your name?"
"Hello my name is Mary."
"Do you know what has happened to you?"
"I was walking along the pavement when I saw a car coming straight for me then everything went black."
"So what do you think happened to you?"
"I think I was killed by the car."
"Yes you were, are you in pain?"

"Yes my head hurts."

"Ok we will take that away, how's that?"

"That's much better thank you."

(As the pain they are feeling belongs to the body which they no longer have it is a simple thing to take away their pain. By saying it has gone your guides will take away the feelings of discomfort.)

"Where do you go when you die?

"I thought you went to heaven but this doesn't look like it."

"No you have got lost would you like us to take you there?"

"Yes please."

"Ok open your eyes and tell me what you can see."

(By asking them to open their eyes they will automatically open their senses)

"I can see a tunnel with a bright light at the end."

"Yes that light is coming from heaven shall we go towards it?" (At this point you should use your senses or ask the lady if there is anyone else there who needs help.)

"How do you feel now?"

"It's nice and warm and bright."

(This is where you will use your senses to find out who is waiting to meet her)

"What can you see now?"

"I can see my mother and father."

(You should be able to pick them up as well)

"Would you like to be with them?"

"Yes please."

"Go in peace."

"Thank you, good bye."

"Good bye."

Always watch them go to make sure they get there safely, they will only be a few steps away from their loved ones and when you see them embrace you know they are home.

That would be a simple rescue there are no complications the lady knew what had happened to her and where she should be. It was just a simple matter of making her feel comfortable and taking her to heaven.

The complications come when spirit don't know they have died and you mustn't tell them. You have got to help them to realise what has happened to them without saying they are dead. Another complication is if they don't believe in heaven. That's not as difficult as you can tell them they should be in heaven. With practice and the help of your guides you will become used to dealing with the different scenarios. It is a good idea if the trance medium is a woman, to wear waterproof mascara as some of the rescues can be quite heartrending. They will feel the emotions of the spirits they are rescuing. If you can have a male and female trance medium it will make things easier because some will not want to come through one or the other. Sometimes they are uncomfortable talking to a male so if you have another female who can talk them through it will make it easier on the spirit. People pass for all sorts of reasons so be prepared for the unexpected. It is a good idea for all the sitters to tune in to the spirit before the trance medium brings them through. This is so you know you are picking up on the same spirit and you can get an idea of their circumstances before they come through. This makes it easier for whoever is talking to the spirit if they know what has happened to them.

Everyone in the circle should stay tuned in to what is going on and if necessary offer their observations, if they don't agree with the scenario that is being portrayed. In this way you can back up each other and if you get an imposter, it is better if you have confirmation from each other. There will be times when you have bad spirits trying to play games with you. By everyone tuning in you will be able to spot them sooner and deal with them accordingly. If you make a mistake during circle your guides will correct it for you, this is why it is so important to discuss with each other after the circle. If you have doubts then consult your guides and they will put you right.

An example of another slightly more complicated rescue is as follows:

The trance medium will tune in to the individual that you have all described and bring them through.

"Hello what's your name?"
"My name is James"
"How did you get here?"
"I don't know one minute I was wandering around and then I was here."
"Do you know what's happened to you?"

"I don't know."

"What's the last thing you remember?"

"I was in bed when I was woken by a noise."

"Yes then what happened?"

"It was very hot and there was a lot of smoke."

"So what do you think happened?"

"There was a fire."

"What did you do next?"

"I got out of bed and ran down the stairs."

"Did you get outside?"

"There was a loud noise and it all went black."

"What do you think happened?"

"The house fell down."

"If the house fell down and you were in it what do you think happened to you?"

"I must have got trapped."

"Do you remember getting out of the house?"

"Yes I was carried to an ambulance and taken to hospital."

"Where were you when they put you in the ambulance?"

"I was in the stretcher."

"When you got to the hospital what happened then?"

"They put me in bed and I went to sleep."

"Are you in pain?"

"No I feel alright."

"What's the next thing you remember?"

"I was wandering around in the dark."

"So if you were in a fire and the house fell down while you were in it what do you think happened to you?"

"Are you saying I was killed in the fire?"

356

"Don't you think that is likely as the house fell in on you?"

"Yes I suppose so but I am here talking to you. I don't know how I got here but I don't feel dead."

"Well I'm afraid that's what happened to you. But where do you go when you die?"

"You just go to sleep that's all there is."

"If that were true how are you able to speak to me?"

"I don't know maybe you don't just go to sleep."

"No life continues in another way have you heard of heaven?"

"Yes but I thought was for people who believed in god."

"It's for everyone would you like to go there?"

"Will I be allowed to?"

"Yes of course open your eyes and tell me what you can see."

(The idea of asking them to open their eyes is they are actually opening their senses. This is the way spirit sees and they will then be able to see the spirit world.)

"I can see a light it's as though it is at the end of a long tunnel."

"That is the light from heaven and we are going to take you there where you can be with your loved ones."

"Ok will they be waiting for me?"

"Yes are you ready?"

"Well I'm not sure."

"It will be ok let's go and see, how are you feeling now?"

"I feel ok its warmer here."

"Good what do you see now?"

(At this point never ask who they can see it should always be, what can you see.)

357

"I can see lots of people, is this heaven?"
"Do you recognise anyone?"
"Yes I can see my wife."
"That's your wife in the yellow dress isn't it?"
"Yes and I can see my dad."
"You mean the man with the pipe?"
"Yes there are lots of my family here."
"Yes do you want to stay?"
"Yes please."
"Ok god bless go in peace."
"Ok thanks for your help."

Whilst in trance the medium can see everything the lost soul can see, they will see the loved ones and watch them being greeted. Once they are with their loved ones the trance medium will open their eyes.

An example of an imposter is as follows:-

"Good evening what is your name?"
"James"
"How did you get here?"
"I was brought here."
"Who brought you?"
"That man over there."
(You should have tuned in by now and will know if there is a man there and if he is good or bad.)
"What is he wearing?"
"A suit and a hat."
(By now you should have verified whether the man is in fact there and what type of spirit he is. It is very unlikely

that a man in a suit will bring someone to your circle they are mostly brought by guides. When you have tuned in to the man in the suit you will be aware that something doesn't feel right. Trust this instinct and confront the person who is trying to waste your time.)

"Why are you wasting my time you are telling lies your name is not
James and the man standing there is one of your friends?"
"How do you know about the man?"
"Because I can see him what do you want?"
(We should give all spirits the opportunity to go to heaven if they want to.)
"I was just looking to see what you were doing."
"We are helping people who are lost and taking them to heaven."
"I've heard about heaven but I couldn't find it are you sure there is such a place?"
"Yes we have taken many people there do you and your friend, want to go?"
"No we are going to stay here."
"You can't stay here you either go to heaven or we will have to brand you and send you back into the dark."
"Why do you have to brand us we aren't doing any harm?"
"Because when we leave there will be no spirits left in the house we are here to clear it one way or another."
"Well we are staying."
"No you are not you will be branded now and you can be on your way." (This is when you tell the trance medium

to throw them out. They will open their eyes and the bad spirits will have been assisted in their departure by your guides.)

If the trance medium was watching and sensing they would know he wasn't telling the truth. When you have a genuine lost spirit you will, when you take them to heaven be able to see what they see. In this way you can verify who they see. You will also know who is waiting for them. If you can't tune in to who is waiting then you should be suspicious. You will also be feeling doubts about whether it was right or not and you would be right. You must not just listen to what is being said. It is important that you look behind the words and sense the truth.

With practice you will if you work together get it right but you must be prepared to get it wrong that's how you learn.

After you have closed the circle discuss the different scenarios and listen to each other. Although nothing may have been said someone will have a gut instinct that some of them weren't right. You can always talk to the guides of the trance medium to get confirmation and to see where you went wrong. If in doubt always ask your guides they will explain where and if you went wrong so next time you will be more prepared.

There is not much else I can tell you that you won't pick up as you progress, just remember this is another type of healing. There are many healers who work on the living but very few on our side of life who work on those who have passed.

Chapter 39

If you want to sit for transfiguration it is useful if you are a trance medium but not essential. Place a chair in the middle of the room and put two infra-red lights pointed from the sides towards the sitters face. The best effect is to sit in the dark with the two lights on. It will take a few sittings for you to start getting good results but you should get something when you start. The sitter will go into meditation and spirit will build up a face on theirs. If you are a trance medium it helps, if you want to talk to the spirit. You don't have to go into trance just allow their thoughts to be spoken. It can also be done with ordinary lights but most people in the beginning will see better with infra-red. Initially you will get a guide building up on the sitters face but after some practice you may be lucky enough to get relatives or friends coming forward. It will take time as your guides will need to make the conditions amenable to the work they are doing but you should get something fairly quickly. The sitter should sit for about 20 minutes to give your guides time to build a face. You may notice the hair line or style changes and maybe the cheeks become filled out or sunken, depending on the sitters face will depend on the work to be done by your guides. The eyes and ears are a good reference point to see any changes. You must be patient and when any of those observing sees a change, they should speak up it will not disturb the sitter. This will draw the other observers to the change and they will be able to offer confirmation. Give it a few sessions before you try and get a voice link and then talk as you would to someone who has a guide with them in trance.

I still run three circles two development circles for clairvoyance and one rescue circle where I am teaching the sitters to rescue lost souls. We also clear houses and I still do services at the local churches. Knowledge is useless unless you pass it on to others.

What has been written is how I was taught and some of my experiences. Take from it what you will, and put the rest to one side for future reference. Always question and never take the first answer, double check all that you hear and be prepared to answer questions if asked. If you don't know the answer then say so don't pretend find out for yourself.

Autobiography

Author Mike Williamson has been a clairvoyant for thirty years only discovering his gift in his thirties. He has taught many mediums to use their gifts and continues to teach to this day. He and his family live in Surrey and he is still clearing haunted houses of ghosts and poltergeists.

K
e
y
n
o
t
e

Key search words

Ghosts, poltergeists, curses, vendetta, spirit realms, evil spirits, teacher, clairvoyant, paranormal, haunted houses, possession, exorcism

Category   non-fiction

Published: 7/14/2011

ISBN-13: 978-1-4567-8736-3

Printed in Great Britain
by Amazon

33303409R00214